POLITICS IN IBERIA

POLITICS IN IBERIA

The Political Systems of Spain and Portugal

Howard J. Wiarda
University of Massachusetts at Amherst

HarperCollins*CollegePublishers*

Acquisitions Editors: Catherine Woods/Maria Hartwell
Project Editor: Melonie Parnes
Design Supervisor: Mary Archondes
Production Manager/Assistant: Willie Lane/Sunaina Sehwani
Compositor: BookMasters, Inc.
Text and Cover Printer/Binder: Malloy Lithographing, Inc.

Politics in Iberia: The Political Systems of Spain and Portugal
Copyright © 1993 by Howard J. Wiarda

All rights reserved. Printed in the United States of America. No part of this book may be used or reproduced in any manner whatsoever without written permission, except in the case of brief quotations embodied in critical articles and reviews. For information address HarperCollins College Publishers Inc., 10 East 53rd Street, New York, NY 10022.

Library of Congress Cataloging-in-Publication Data

Wiarda, Howard J., date–
    Politics in Iberia : the political systems of Spain and Portugal / Howard J. Wiarda.
      p.   cm.
    Includes bibliographical references and index.
    ISBN 0-673-46432-6
    1. Spain—Politics and government. 2. Spain—Constitutional history. 3. Portugal—Politics and government. 4. Portugal—Constitutional history. I. Title.
JN8111.W5   1992
320.946—dc20   91-45284
                                                                 CIP

92 93 94 95   9 8 7 6 5 4 3 2 1

To a remarkable group of teachers, who first taught me about Iberia, Latin America, and the interrelations between them:

> Irving A. Leonard
> Lyle N. McAlister
> Donald C. Worcester
> Harry Kantor
> and
> Alva Curtis Wilgus.

Brief Contents

Detailed Contents ix
Preface xiii

1 Introduction: Why Study Iberia and Its Place in the World? 1
2 The Long Sweep of Iberian History 16
3 The Franco and Salazar Regimes 43
4 The Transitions to Democracy 70
5 Political Culture in Iberia 90
6 Interest Groups and the Political Process 120
7 Political Parties and the Party System 155
8 Government and the Role of the State 182
9 Public Policy: Domestic and Foreign 208
10 Conclusion 241

Suggested Readings 251
Index 257

Detailed Contents

Preface xiii

1 **Introduction: Why Study Iberia and Its Place in the World?** 1

   Why Study Spain and Portugal? 2
   Spain and Portugal in Comparative Political Development—
      What Place in the World? 4
   Political Development in Iberia: The Uncertain Trumpet 7
   Development: Universal or Particular? 10
   A Recapitulation—And a Look Ahead 12
   Notes 13

2 **The Long Sweep of Iberian History** 16

   Iberian Geography 17
   Early Peoples 19
   The Roman Impact 20
   Moorish Rule 23
   The Reconquest 24
   The Forging of National Identity 26
   The Hapsburgian Model 29
   Iberia in Decline 32
   Civil Conflict in the Nineteenth Century 34
   The Republican Interlude 37
   Invertebrate Spain, Invertebrate Portugal 40
   Notes 42

3 The Franco and Salazar Regimes 43

Early Origins and Coming to Power 44
The Corporatist Revolution 47
Authoritarianism and Repression 55
Opposition Politics 60
Economic and Social Modernization under Authoritarian Auspices 63
Stresses and Tensions within "The System" 65
Notes 69

4 The Transitions to Democracy 70

The Portuguese "Revolution of Flowers" 71
The Spanish Transition 77
Has Iberian Democracy Been Consolidated? 86
Notes 89

5 Political Culture in Iberia 90

Political Culture as an Explanatory Device 91
Historic Political Culture 93
The "Two Spains"; the "Two Portugals" 104
Authoritarianism, Repression, and a Subject Political Culture 106
Social Change and Culture Change 110
A New Spain, a New Portugal? 113
So, Is Democracy Fully Consolidated? 116
Notes 118

6 Interest Groups and the Political Process 120

Basic Social and Economic Data 121
The Social Basis of Politics 124
Family, Clan, and Patronage Interests 126
The Historic Triumvirate of Power: Army, Church, Economic Elites 129
Social Change 136
Limited Pluralism Under Authoritarianism 138
Democracy and the Proliferation of Interest Groups 142

Liberalism, Pluralism, and the Contract State **151**
Notes **153**

7 Political Parties and the Party System **155**

History of the Political Parties **156**
Political Parties under Authoritarianism **157**
The Emergence of a New Party System **160**
The Party Spectrums **162**
Bases of Party Cleavage **172**
Weaknesses of the Political Parties **175**
Other "Parties" within the System **177**
Conclusions **179**
Notes **181**

8 Government and the Role of the State **182**

Historical Patterns **183**
Power and Authority under Franco and Salazar **186**
Post-Franco, Post-Salazar **190**
A Democratic and Bureaucratic State? **200**
Regional Autonomy **203**
State-Society Relations: A New Balance and a New Model? **205**
Notes **207**

9 Public Policy: Domestic and Foreign **208**

Domestic Policy **209**
Foreign Affairs **221**
A Summing Up **238**
Notes **239**

10 Conclusion **241**

Notes **249**

Suggested Readings **251**
Index **257**

Preface

Spain and Portugal have emerged as very important countries, both in their own right and as key nations in American foreign policy; and yet we lack a good, solid, readable book about them that can be used as a textbook by college and university students or to which an interested general reader might turn. For a long time during the authoritarian dictatorships of Francisco Franco in Spain and Antonio Salazar in Portugal, it was difficult to do serious research and writing in either country, and the few good books published then have long been out of print. Since the overthrow of the Salazar/Caetano (Marcello Caetano was Salazar's successor) regime in 1974 and the death of Franco in 1975, there have been numerous detailed scholarly accounts of one aspect or another of the postauthoritarian decompression and transitions to democracy, as well as several journalistic and quite a number of highly partisan accounts—but no balanced, serious, readable overviews of the entire process and the social and political systems of these two countries.

One can think of many reasons for having a good, new book on Spain and Portugal: the endlessly fascinating history, culture, and sociology of Iberia; the longevity, character, and dynamics of the Franco and Salazar regimes; the transitions from authoritarianism to a form of democracy; the use of Spain and Portugal in this regard as models for democratic transitions in Latin America; the controversial Spanish entry into NATO and the recent admission of both countries into the European Community; the economic boom in Spain (although Portugal is also developing), which has made it the recipient recently of more U.S. investment than any other European country; the 1974 "Revolution of Flowers" in Portugal and the coming to power in 1982 of a Socialist government in Spain; and the dynamism of these two societies as well as the considerable and continuing tensions within them regarding their futures and destinies. These and other issues relating to the question of "Why study Spain and Portugal?" are discussed at greater length in Chapter 1.

Obviously very solid reasons exist for doing separate books on both Spain and Portugal. But here both countries are treated within a single volume, often utilizing a common intellectual framework for both. The reasons for the common treatment include: (1) the similarities between these two countries on a variety of cultural, historical, social, and political dimensions; (2) their often parallel development patterns and trajectories; (3) the differences as well as what are complementary between them (useful for comparative analysis); (4) their geographic location together in that westernmost promontory of continental Europe called the Iberian Peninsula; (5) their close identification together in the literature and the popular mind; and (6) the fact that Spain and Portugal, viewed together, have often constituted an alternative development model—an alternative to the paths taken by Britain, France, Germany, Scandinavia, or Eastern Europe—and not always exactly congruent with or the mirror images of the development patterns of these other nations and areas.

Related to this last theme is the suggestion—and the underlying thesis of this book—that Spain and Portugal, even with their recent integration into Europe and into the community of Western, democratic nations, are still unique, still often distinctive. This uniqueness has been ameliorated over the years as politically, culturally, socially, and even morally these formerly aloof and isolated countries have been more closely integrated and homogenized into the larger European and world culture and mores. However much the citizens of Spain and Portugal might wish to forget their distinctiveness and now be considered as truly European, and although some scholars might want to utilize universal categories to analyze Iberia's development processes, the fact remains that on many dimensions Spain and Portugal remain different. Anyone who has ever traveled or lived in Iberia knows *immediately* and often *vividly* that he or she is not just in a less developed version of Germany, Britain, or Scandinavia but in a place where the smells, sounds, behavior, sociology, and politics are not quite like those of the north of Europe. It is toward the analysis and unraveling of this issue of how Iberia is different and where and how it corresponds to global processes of change that this book is dedicated. Hence, although the book provides comprehensive treatment of the history, culture, sociology, economics, and politics of Spain and Portugal, it also wrestles and *struggles* with some larger issues of development and where Iberia fits—or doesn't fit—into these bigger social and political processes.

A few words should be said about the sociology of this issue and the author's approach to it. I began life, intellectually and as a scholar at least, as a student of Latin America. But wherever I studied in the 1960s in my early academic career (Argentina, Brazil, Central America, Chile, the Dominican Republic, Mexico, Paraguay, Peru, Venezuela), I kept discovering—in regimes both of the Left and the Right, in civilian regimes as well as military ones—the same organicist, integralist, top-down, corporatist (in its historic and almost medieval sense), patrimonialist features and institutions. The widespread nature and persistence of such patterns in such diverse Latin American regimes could not merely be coincidental, I reasoned. So in the early 1970s, after having lived and studied Latin America for many years, I determined to get at the origins of these organicist/corporatist patterns by studying the history and development of Spain and Portugal. In a sense, therefore, stemming from my earlier research background, I think of Spain and Portugal as "Latin American" countries, or, better, countries of what the late Kalman H. Silvert called the "Mediterranean Ethos," who have "made it"—albeit still incompletely—into the modern democratic world. Most residents of Spain and Portugal, however, as well as many students of the area whose intellectual beginnings were in Europe rather than Latin America, prefer not to think of their countries as "Latin American" countries that have ultimately made it, but rather as European countries that somehow got left behind or sidetracked (for approximately 13 centuries, since the Moorish invasion of the peninsula in 711 A.D.!) and are now, finally, returning to their proper European fold. Actually both of these perspectives have validity, but to my mind it is precisely the cracks and interstices in each explanation and the fact that Spain and Portugal have ingredients from both interpretations, are both "Latin American" and European, that makes Iberian development so interesting—and so distinctive.

I lived in Portugal from 1972 to 1973 and traveled extensively and did research in Spain. Since then, I have also lived in Spain and have returned to Iberia on an almost yearly basis. The intellectual fruits of these labors and travels include six books and monographs on Iberia and a host of articles and papers.* I feel "at home" in the language and culture of both countries—hence my desire to write a book about them and to sum up what I have learned about the Iberian (and by extension Latin American) development process.

At one level, this is a factual book about Spanish and Portuguese history, culture, sociology, politics, economics, and policymaking. But at another level it is a book that tries to *understand* and *interpret* Iberia: what makes it tick, where and how it is different from other areas and countries, as well as where and how Spain's and Portugal's development processes run parallel to and have come to approximate those of other countries. Hence, the book contains conjecture as well as facts, theoretical models as well as straightforward history, interpretation as well as reportage, and maybe even (some critics will doubtless say) an occasional flight of imagination or fancy. This is a book of synthesis that brings together in coherent, integrated, and hopefully readable form a large body of research and writing that has been done on Spain and Portugal in recent years; but it also contains some original research and ideas that may make it of interest to specialists as well as general readers.

The writing of this book would not have been possible without the help of thousands of persons who have assisted me over the years in my own efforts to study and understand Spain and Portugal. These include scholars, government officials, and many persons in all walks of Spanish and Portuguese life. Foremost among these is Iêda Siqueira Wiarda, a Brazilian-born but U.S.-trained political scientist who also ranges across both Latin American and Iberian cultures and civilizations and over both their Spanish- and their

---

*Howard J. Wiarda, *Corporatism and Development: The Portuguese Experience* (Amherst, Mass.: University of Massachusetts Press, 1977); *Transcending Corporatism? The Portuguese Corporative System and the Revolution of 1974* (Columbia, S.C.: Institute of International Studies, University of South Carolina, 1976); *From Corporatism to Neo-Syndicalism: The State, Organized Labor, and the Changing Industrial Relations System of Southern Europe* (Cambridge, Mass.: Harvard University, Center for European Studies, 1981); *The Iberian–Latin American Connection: Implications for U.S. Policy* (Washington, D.C., and Boulder, Colo.: AEI and Westview Press, 1986); (with Iêda Siqueira Wiarda) *The Transition to Democracy in Spain and Portugal* (Lanham, Md.: University Press of America, 1988); and (with Thomas Bruneau and Howard Penniman) *Portugal at the Polls (Durham, N.C.: Duke University Press*, forthcoming).

Portuguese-speaking parts. She is now the Luso-Brazilian culture specialist at the Library of Congress in Washington, D.C., with responsibility for Spain as well as Portugal. Jonathan Siqueira Wiarda, born in Portugal in 1973 (and still a Portuguese citizen), has been a rock of support to his father; my first book on Iberia was dedicated to him. Lawrence Graham, University of Texas; Michael Kryzanek, Bridgewater State College; William Salisbury, University of South Carolina; and Larman Wilson, American University have read and offered useful comments on the manuscript.

Numerous organizations have also supported this long-term work: Deserving of mention among research institutions are the Center for International Affairs of Harvard University; the American Enterprise Institute for Public Policy Research in Washington, D.C.; the Foreign Policy Research Institute of Philadelphia; and the Department of Political Science of the University of Massachusetts at Amherst. Financial support has come mainly from the Social Science Research Council, the American Philosophical Society, the Rockefeller Foundation, the Mellon Foundation, the National Endowment for the Humanities, the Tinker Foundation, and the Twentieth Century Fund. I am deeply grateful to all these individuals and supportive institutions but—for good or ill—the analysis and interpretations that follow are not their responsibility, but mine alone.

Howard J. Wiarda

POLITICS IN IBERIA

Chapter 1

Introduction

Why Study Iberia and Its Place in the World?

Spain and Portugal are among the least studied and written about countries of Western Europe. We have abundant literature on Great Britain, France, Germany, the Soviet Union, Scandinavia, Italy, and now, increasingly, Eastern Europe, but very little, in English, on the two countries that share the Iberian Peninsula. This situation has begun to change, particularly since the 1974 overthrow of the dictatorship of Antonio Salazar/Marcello Caetano in Portugal and the death the following year of dictator Francisco Franco in Spain; but we still lack a brief, balanced, readable introduction to the politics and society of Iberia that also comments on its history, culture, development, economics, and public policies.

The problem is not just a dearth of literature; it also involves great uncertainty as to how to classify Spain and Portugal. Where do they fit in our scheme of things? How shall we characterize them? What approach or model of interpretation shall we use? Are the nations of Iberia like the Latin American countries—to be studied using a Latin American frame of reference, or are they basically European countries? Is it still true, as it often used to be said pejoratively, that Europe ends at the Pyrenees Mountains separating France from Spain, and that Africa begins there; or has this historic "separateness" (with its racial as well as cultural and political overtones of superiority) from Europe now been erased as Spain and Portugal have become democratic and have joined the European

Common Market and the European Community? Does Iberia still lie, as French statesmen Talleyrand-Perigord (1754–1838) said disparagingly about Greece, "beyond the pale," or has it joined the family of modern, civilized nations? Are Spain and Portugal part of the First World of developed, democratic, capitalist states; or—with their continued poverty, bloated and often inefficient statist structures, and underdevelopment—are they still to be classified with the Third World? We know and talk extensively in our history courses about the "Western tradition," but are Spain and Portugal, with their nearly eight centuries of Moslem rule and powerful authoritarian traditions, really Western? Or are they only partially Western, or perhaps fragments of *some* (Roman, Catholic, Thomistic) Western traditions, but not, at least historically, of the West's capitalist, modernizing, rationalist, pluralist, and democratic tendencies?[1]

These are the larger issues that this book aims to explore. We begin with the question of why we should study Spain and Portugal.

WHY STUDY SPAIN AND PORTUGAL?

Spain and Portugal are increasingly important nations. Both their domestic politics and their international positions have made them the subject of worldwide attention in recent years. Here are some of the reasons for their importance and why we should study these two Iberian nations.

1. The culture, history, and sociology of Spain and Portugal are very colorful, full of contradictions and fascinating themes, divergent oftentimes from the rest of Europe, and able to provide endless opportunities for study and controversy.[2]
2. The long-standing (1930s–70s) regimes of Francisco Franco in Spain and Antonio Salazar in Portugal provide examples of modern, developmentalist corporatism and authoritarianism; for a long time they served as models to many other nations of how to achieve modernization through authoritarian control methods, as distinct from both democracy and socialism.[3]
3. The upheaval in Portugal in 1974–75 seemed for a time to be offering an example of socialist revolution in the Western

and European core area, distinct from most socialist revolutions occurring in the Third World, therefore attracting worldwide attention; but then the revolution faded and the country calmed down.
4. Beginning in the mid-1970s, both Spain and Portugal undertook some remarkable transitions to democracy; these democratic openings were important not just for the two countries involved, but because they began a process of democratization that later spread—with Spain and Portugal as the models—to East Asia, Latin America, and Eastern Europe.[4]
5. Spain and Portugal have long been considered *apart from* Europe; now, through their memberships in NATO (North Atlantic Treaty Organization) and the European Economic Community (EEC), they are becoming *a part of* Europe. But all these new connections have been—and remain—enormously controversial.[5]
6. While much of the world was in economic recession in the 1980s, Spain was booming ahead at miracle, Japan-like growth rates; Portugal lagged behind but was also developing. These economic transformations attracted, and were stimulated by, large-scale foreign investment; economic development in turn gave rise to widespread social change and modernization in both countries, which may also be having the further long-range effect of fundamentally altering Iberian behavior, our image of the area, and these nations' possibilities for a stabler form of democracy.
7. Yet Spain, especially, even with all the recent modernization, still has regional separatist movements, principally the Basques, some of whom have turned to bloody terrorism. There are signs indicating a lack of national integration, and they, along with other factors, may yet point toward renewed instability and fragmentation.
8. Spain and its Canary Islands command the western gateway to the critically strategic Mediterranean Sea; the Portuguese islands (Madeira, the Azores) are also of major strategic value. Both countries are of significant importance to U.S. foreign policy; yet in Europe, Latin America, Africa, and the Middle East, both Spain and Portugal are following a more assertive and independent foreign policy not always in accord with U.S. wishes.

9. Although Spain and Portugal have made some remarkable strides toward democracy in recent years, these two countries are still riven by tensions. There are many elements in both societies that are not particularly democratic, and democracy is still not well institutionalized or consolidated. This means that Spanish and Portuguese politics remain more open-ended, and potentially more volatile, than we might like to believe.[6]

SPAIN AND PORTUGAL IN COMPARATIVE POLITICAL DEVELOPMENT—WHAT PLACE IN THE WORLD?

If we agree with the French that Paris is the center of Europe, Spain and Portugal are a very long ways from the European center. Lisbon, the capital of Portugal, is a good, solid four days' driving time to Paris, and Madrid, the capital of Spain, is at least three long driving days away. In the era before the development of modern highways, of course, Lisbon and Madrid were even more distant.

Spain and Portugal have long been set apart from Europe—not just in a geographic sense, but in a social, cultural, economic, political, and even a moral and psychological sense as well. Because of the long Moorish occupation (711–1492), Iberia was thought to be outside the main European historical currents. Spanish Catholicism was similarly thought to be more absolutist and inquisitorial than Catholicism elsewhere in the world. The rigidities and authoritarianism of the Hapsburg and Bragança monarchies in the sixteenth and seventeenth centuries meant that Spain and Portugal missed out on all the great movements that we associate with the modern age: the Renaissance and the Enlightenment, the Protestant Reformation and the movement toward religious pluralism and toleration, the English revolution leading to limited and representative government, the scientific revolution ushered in with Galileo and Newton, the Industrial Revolution and its accompanying social change.

There followed in Iberia *centuries* of decline, torpor, incompetent leadership, instability, lack of industrialization, conflict leading to strife and (in Spain) civil war, and lack of progress. Then came Franco and Salazar, whose regimes seemed to imply a resurrection of the ancient Hapsburgian model (top-down, authoritarian, corporatist, dictatorial, if not fascist) and a snuffing out of even the limited movement toward democracy that had been made. In all this history, Spain and Portugal were often seen by other Europeans as both distant and different. "Different" in the sense of both not keeping pace with development in the rest of Europe and of their wanting to go their own separate and independent ways, with their own distinct institutions and practices. European attitudes were often condescending and patronizing toward their Iberian neighbors, toward those two countries that lay over the Pyrenees. Because of Iberia's proximity to North Africa, its long Moorish occupation, and the "Mediterranean" appearance of some Spanish and Portuguese, these attitudes were often tainted by racial prejudice.

As Europe often looked down its nose and rejected Spain and Portugal, the Iberians responded defensively by saying they didn't wish to be part of Europe anyway. Franco and Salazar presented their authoritarian/corporatist regimes as an alternative "third way"—neither an open-market economy nor a command one, neither a liberal democracy nor a socialist or communist regime;[7] and they rejected outside interference in their internal affairs. As these (and earlier) Spanish and Portuguese regimes were treated condescendingly and repudiated by Europe, the Iberian reaction was to respond defensively, go increasingly their own way, express even greater pride in their own institutions (however retarded they might be), and state that they didn't want to be part of a Europe that could not accept them as they were.

But now Franco and Salazar are gone and Spain and Portugal have entered a more democratic era. Now they are no longer rejected by Europe, and, in turn, Spain and Portugal want to be considered a part of Europe. This gives rise to an interesting paradox and one of the key clues to understanding Iberia: When Spain and Portugal are rejected by Europe, as was often the case historically and then again during the long Franco and Salazar eras, they tend to get their backs up; emphasize their distinctiveness; reach out to Africa, Latin America, and the Third World; and say they don't really want to be part of Europe. But when Europe embraces them, the Spanish and Portuguese, with their acute sense of rejection and acceptance, are only too happy to be a part of Europe and to be integrated into it.

So the question remains: Where do Spain and Portugal fit in? Because of their long isolation and sense of distinctiveness, as well as the fact that they have not historically conformed to the main European developmental models, Spain and Portugal are seldom included in our usual comparative politics and comparative political development books and courses. Under Franco's and Salazar's authoritarianism, these countries could not really be considered a part of the First World of free and democratic nations. Nor were they part of the Second World of developed Communist countries, although both Spain and Portugal had (and have) strong socialist and communist parties. Nor, with their considerable economic development and European location, could they be thought of as part of the Third World—although when they were rejected by Europe under Franco and Salazar, both countries flirted with "Third Worldism" and a Third World foreign policy. How to classify these regimes and determine where Spain and Portugal fit in the European or global development schemes remained a conundrum.

Now, however, Franco and Salazar have disappeared from the scene, and Spain and Portugal have joined Europe. They have joined Europe not just economically but socially, culturally, politically, and psychologically as well. Spanish and Portuguese young people no longer want to be thought of, as their elders often did, as "different"; they want to be considered *European*. They want European (and American) freedoms, affluence, rock music, jeans, Coke, and all the other accoutrements of our modern, consumer-oriented society. They also want democratic governments like the Europeans. Moreover, it may well be that by this point the Spanish and Portuguese economies are so tied into Europe in terms of trade, banking, tourism, investment, and commerce that the earlier choices of Europe or something else, the First World or something else, are no longer open to them. Iberia now seems to be irrevocably European and First World in these ways, whether we or they are fully cognizant of the irreversibility of the process or not.[8]

And yet, let us for now keep an open mind on these issues. The main questions seem to have been settled, but there remain elements of disquiet. There are just enough doubts and reasons to be skeptical concerning Spain's and Portugal's "making it" to First World levels as to keep the issue interesting. Economically, Spain's per capita income is still only about one-third to one-fourth that of the rest of more affluent Europe, and Portugal's per capita income is only about half of Spain's. Spain and Portugal are now members of the EEC, but they remain its poor stepchildren, and there could be problems ahead. Politically, Spain and Portugal are currently democracies, but in both countries there are some decidedly un- and even antidemocratic elements: the social and economic base for democracy (especially in Portugal) is still weak, many Spanish and Portuguese are "success democrats"—supporting democracy as long as the economy is booming but perhaps prepared to abandon it for something else if prosperity were undermined, and in both countries democracy is still young and not so well institutionalized as we would like, or that would enable us to feel entirely comfortable and satisfied about Iberian democratic prospects.

These comments should not lead one to conclude that Spanish and Portuguese democracy is in trouble and about to be overthrown tomorrow—or even the next day. But they should serve to flash some warning lights. The problem is that we so much *want* Iberian democracy to succeed—after all these centuries of turmoil and lack of democracy—that we risk allowing wishful thinking about the area to get in the way of needed, hardheaded analysis. In fact, it is "all those centuries" without democracy that should serve as the first cautionary sign. To be sure, this author also wishes Spanish and Portuguese democracy to succeed, but he knows from Iberian history as well as from some present undercurrents that the process and institutions of democracy may be more tenuous and uncertain than they appear. At the least, we should reserve judgment until completing the book, for this is a critical theme to which we return again and again.

Now let us add some further notes of complication to an already complicated picture.

POLITICAL DEVELOPMENT IN IBERIA: THE UNCERTAIN TRUMPET

Eastern Europe and Southern Europe (including Spain and Portugal) are alike in various ways: both represent the less developed parts of Europe, both exist on the peripheries of Europe, both were sidetracked for many decades by exotic (and ineffective) political philosophies, both have rather complex relations with the European (and First World) core, and both exhibit considerable and continuing uncertainty, even national nervousness, about their future.[9]

Spain and Portugal were long isolated and apart from the world's greatest economic and political mainstreams, but even while Franco and Salazar were still alive, this began to change. Both countries, beginning in the 1950s, determined to break out of their historic isolation, both opted for a strategy of industrialization and more rapid economic development and took the necessary policy steps to begin that process, and both were successful in achieving growth—although Spain, with far more resources, larger internal markets, an already more developed infrastructure, and greater proximity to Europe, was more successful in achieving its goals than poorer Portugal.[10]

As Spain and Portugal developed and built up their economies, they also began in the 1960s to modernize social programs. New public programs, although still often rudimentary, were introduced in the areas of health care, education, housing, electrification, and social welfare. In both countries the long-moribund corporatist agencies, created during the heyday of corporatism in the 1930s (more on this in Chapter 3), were now revived as social security agencies. As Spain and Portugal (especially the former) achieved considerable success in the economic and social fields, they became models of development for many like-minded authoritarians from all over the world. Hundreds and maybe thousands of military leaders and civilians from right-wing and dictatorial regimes in diverse continents flocked to Madrid to see how the Spanish had done it. How had they been able to achieve far-reaching economic and social modernization without producing what the authoritarians knew from experience and the literature on development to be the usual concomitants of socioeconomic change: increased participation, popular or mass mobilization, and ultimately the hated (to the authoritarians) liberalization and democratization. The Spanish and Portuguese, in turn, already outcasts in Europe, were only too eager to show off their institutions to admiring foreigners. In countries as diverse as Argentina, Brazil, Chile, Iran, the Philippines, South Korea, and Taiwan there were efforts to emulate the Spanish "model."[11]

But note that this Spanish model—when Spain finally emerged as a model for anything—was an authoritarian model, not a democratic one. It was an authoritarian-corporatist model designed to achieve socioeconomic modernization but at the same time to hold political development and democratization in check, even to repress those who got out of line. The fact that it was only two decades ago that Spain and Portugal were still widely viewed as models of authoritarian-corporatist development—perhaps permanently cast in that mold, and not as liberal, pluralist, or democratic societies—should give pause as we assess Iberia's present democratic possibilities.

Now, however, Spain and Portugal have embarked on a more democratic course. But here, too, a series of anomalies enter that should give us further pause. For the questions are: Even though Spain and Portugal are now democratic, do they mean the same thing by democracy as Americans do? Do they have the same priorities? How badly do they want democracy? The answers are not always reassuring.

Though Spaniards tend overwhelmingly to favor representative democracy,[12] when they are polled as to what exactly they mean by those terms, some curious answers emerge. Some say democracy means "patronage," a favor for a favor: "I'll vote for you if you give me something in return." A majority favor a strong or statist regime, not a *laissez-faire* one, thus rejecting the economic liberalism on which political liberalism often rests. "Representation" is often construed to mean group or corporatist representation, not individual representation, a concept remarkably continuous with the Franco/Salazar system and offering immense difficulties to a human rights policy based on *individual* human rights. Democracy may also have populist meanings, or be associated with authoritative and effective government regardless of that government's means of achieving power—not all that different from the system and ideology of quasi-Fascist Juan Perón in Argentina. The Portuguese also favor democracy in the abstract, but when asked to name the best government they have had in the last 30 years, a majority say that of Salazar/Caetano![13]

Democracy has therefore been established in Iberia, but its meanings and priorities are often different than what most Americans mean by the term. Democracy may give way to "strong government," especially in unstable times or under emergency conditions. Moreover, in Spain and Portugal democracy's roots are often Thomistic or, in secular form, Rousseauian, not Lockean.[14] The Iberian conception of even democracy is thus often organic, integral, corporatist, and top-down, not Jeffersonian or Madisonian. Government historically has been viewed not as the result of a popular compact (and therefore limited) but as natural, powerful, and unified. Rulers must know and personify the "general will" (Rousseau's term) but need not always or necessarily reflect the "will of all" (majority vote). These can obviously be dangerous concepts: Under some conditions such organicist and top-down ideas can work well, and democracy may be preserved (as in de Gaulle's France), but under other conditions the Rousseauian concepts can often lead—and have led—to totalitarianism. So, if Spain and Portugal are now being touted as models of "democracy," we had better be very clear what exactly they or we have in mind by that term.

The situation is even more complicated because actually, at present, Spain and Portugal represent overlaps of the older Rousseauian and the newer liberal forms of democracy. Both kinds of democracy are present—often in confused, overlapping, hybrid ways—in both of the Iberian political systems. In fact, one of the main goals in this book will be to sort out exactly where and how Spain and Portugal conform to the modern American or European forms of liberal democracy and where they still conform to the more traditional, patronage-governed, top-down, integralist, and corporatist Rousseauian forms.

Hence, we have two main anomalies with which to grapple in this book. First, when Spain and Portugal initially became models admired and imitated in some quarters abroad, the model emulated was that of a corporatist-authoritarian (Franco and Salazar) state, not a liberal-democratic one. The second anomaly is that when Spain and Portugal finally became democracies, they did so under a special form of democracy—or at least a mixed system—that showed many continuities with their organicist-corporatist pasts. These are troubling themes that we will have to analyze carefully.

DEVELOPMENT: UNIVERSAL OR PARTICULAR?

In much of the 1960s political development literature,[15] social, economic, and political modernization were assumed to be harmonious and to go hand in hand. That is, it was thought that economic growth gave rise to social change and increased mobilization and pluralization, which in turn begot democratization. That, after all, was the dominant Western European/United States model, from which so much of the development literature arose.

But that, of course, was not the pattern in Iberia. Economic and social change occurred, but the main "political development" was to make the authoritarian Franco and Salazar regimes more modern and efficient, not to lead necessarily to democratization. Indeed, much of the literature on Spain and Portugal in the early 1970s tended to portray those two countries as examples of successful *authoritarian* modernization.[16] Modernization in Iberia did not lead inevitably to democracy, as the early development literature posited, but, seemingly, only to more entrenched authoritarianism.

But now Spain and Portugal are also democratic. Does that mean the literature on development was correct all along? That is, as compared with the 1950s, Spain and Portugal are now much more literate, more urban, more middle class, with far more communications media, more developed, and more affluent. These are precisely the elements of social and economic modernization that are supposed to lead to democracy. So, were S. M. Lipset, W. W. Rostow, and the early development school correct from the beginning? Wrong in the short term (the Franco and Salazar eras), but correct when viewed in longer terms? Certainly, with democracy breaking out all over, and not just in Spain and Portugal, the Lipset-Rostow school of thought looks far better from the vantage point of the 1990s than it did from the vantage point of the 1970s, when authoritarian regimes were ensconced in power in a large number of nations.[17]

These are complex issues; they require careful thought, not pat formulas. It is not necessarily true that there is very much that is inevitable, automatic, or universal about the development process. There is no necessary causative relationship between socioeconomic modernization and political development, although there *are* often strong correlations between the two. Nor do all nations go through the same sequences and processes of growth. We may now be in a context of seemingly almost global movement toward greater pluralism and democracy, but even those features may take different forms in different nations. Increasingly, we have become impressed, in one study after another, by the persistence of traditional forms, institutions, and ways of doing things that, instead of being overwhelmed and eliminated as modernization proceeded, as the early development literature suggested, have demonstrated often remarkable durability, staying power, and capacity to accommodate. Rather than a sudden lurch from one developmentalist stage to another, or the definitive discarding of the traditional as modernization went forward, most societies—Japan, India, and many others—have shown a considerable overlap and crazy-quilt pattern, where traditional and modern are blended in a variety of complex ways.[18] The one seldom finally and irrevocably replaces the other; rather the process is almost always slower, more evolutionary, with various fusions and hodge-podges of old and new.

Hence, while modernization proceeds and change goes forward, persistence of traditional practices and continuity with the past (even if the names and precise institutional arrangements vary) are also powerful forces shaping society. This is no less so in Spain and Portugal than in other countries. The changes since Franco and Salazar may be both more *and* less dramatic than we would prefer to think.

A RECAPITULATION—AND A LOOK AHEAD

Spain and Portugal have developed rapidly in the last several decades, but they still lag considerably behind the advanced industrial democracies of Western Europe, Japan, and North America. Spain and Portugal have also undergone a quite remarkable transition from authoritarianism to democracy, but that process is also still incomplete, uncertain, and unconsolidated.

Hence, we ask a series of questions, which also provide the main themes of the book.

1. Just how firmly established is democracy in Spain and Portugal? Is it permanent or only temporary, another crest in the periodic waves of authoritarianism and liberalization that have washed over Iberia, or does it have a stronger societal base now than previously when class and political divisions tore these countries apart?
2. Are Spain and Portugal now definitively in the camp of the First World of modern, capitalist democracies? Have they passed the point where revolutionary socialism and communism ("diseases of the transition," Rostow called them) might still be attractive? Is their development now irreversible, or might they still fall back into the ranks of the Third World as poor and miserable nations?
3. With whom are Spain and Portugal presently to be compared? Are they now fully and completely *European* countries, with all the sophistication, affluence, middle-classness,

democracy, advanced welfare programs, consumerism, and so on that the term implies and to which most Spaniards clearly aspire—even though they occupy the lower ends on the European scale? Or are they still only advanced *Latin American* countries, with the potential for instability, fragmentation, and radical reversals of direction which *that* term implies?

4. Related is the question of what development model Spain and Portugal have to offer their own populations and the rest of the world. Have they become, since Franco's death and Salazar's demise, just "ordinary nations," struggling and coping to varying degrees, but with little that is unique or special? Or is there still something "different" about Iberia (as Franco and many others proudly stated and the tourist posters proclaimed), something distinctive and unique, an Iberian model of development as distinct from those of other nations? If so, what is it? And can this be made to blend with its new-found Europeanness, or does it mean Spain and Portugal will always diverge from the European pattern somewhat? And if they do so diverge, does that make them once again more like Latin America; and have we therefore come full circle? Or is there a truly unique, indigenous Iberian development process that can also be democratic, and that can be achieved by the Iberians?[19]

These are the questions (hypotheses, if one prefers) with which the book begins. We return to them at various points in the analysis and once again in the conclusion, where we try to arrive at definitive answers.

NOTES

1. On these themes see Louis Hartz (ed.), *The Founding of New Societies* (New York: Harcourt, Brace, Jovanovich, 1964), especially the introduction and Richard Morse's chapter on Iberia and Latin America.
2. A very readable account is John Crow, *Spain: The Root and the Flower* (Berkeley, Calif.: University of California Press, 3rd ed., 1985); a less colorful but historically more accurate rendering is Stanley Payne, *A History of Spain and Portugal* (Madison, Wis.: University of Wisconsin Press, 1973).

3. Howard J. Wiarda, *Corporatism and Development: The Portuguese Experience* (Amherst, Mass.: University of Massachusetts Press, 1977); and Wiarda (ed.), *The Iberian–Latin American Connection* (Washington, D.C., and Boulder, Colo.: American Enterprise Institute for Public Policy Research and Westview Press, 1986).
4. Guillermo O'Donnell, Philippe C. Schmitter, and Laurence Whitehead (eds)., *Transitions from Authoritarian Rule* (Baltimore, Md.: Johns Hopkins University Press, 1986); and Enrique A. Baloyra (ed.), *Comparing New Democracies: Transition and Consolidation in Mediterranean Europe and the Southern Core* (Boulder, Colo.: Westview Press, 1987).
5. On these complex and ambivalent feelings between Iberia and Europe, see Howard J. Wiarda, *Does Europe Still Stop at the Pyrenees or Does Latin America Begin There? Iberia, Latin America, and the Second Enlargement of the European Community* (Washington, D.C.: American Enterprise Institute for Public Policy Research, Occasional Papers Series No. 2, 1981).
6. These uncertainties are discussed in greater detail in the author's previous book (with Iêda Siqueira Wiarda), *The Transition to Democracy in Spain and Portugal* (Washington, D.C.: University Press of America for the American Enterprise Institute for Public Policy Research, 1989).
7. These themes are elaborated in Chapter 3.
8. Erik Baklanoff makes this persuasive argument in his chapter, "Spain's Emergence as a Middle Industrial Power: The Basis and Structure of Spanish–Latin American Economic Relations," in Wiarda (ed.), *The Iberian–Latin American Connection* (Washington, D.C., and Boulder, Colo.: American Enterprise Institute for Public Policy Research and Westview Press, 1986).
9. Giovanni Arrighi (ed.), *Semiperipheral Development: The Politics of Southern Europe in the Twentieth Century* (Beverly Hills, Calif.: Sage Publications, 1985).
10. Charles W. Anderson, *The Political Economy of Modern Spain* (Madison, Wis.: University of Wisconsin Press, 1970); and Erik Baklanoff, *The Economic Transformation of Spain and Portugal* (New York: Praeger, 1978).
11. The theme is discussed at greater length in the author's chapter, "Interpreting Iberian–Latin American Interrelations: Paradigm Consensus and Conflict" in Wiarda (ed.), *The Iberian–Latin American Connection* (Washington, D.C., and Boulder, Colo.: American Enterprise Institute for Public Policy Research and Westview Press, 1986). See also Frederick B. Pike, *Hispanismo 1898–1936: Spanish Liberals and Conservatives and Their Relations with Spanish America* (Notre Dame, Ind.: Notre Dame University Press, 1971).

12. An excellent study is Richard Gunther, Giacomo Sani, and Goldi Shabad, *Spain after Franco: The Making of a Competitive Party System* (Berkeley, Calif.: University of California Press, 1986); the poll data presented here also derives from United States Information Agency (USIA) surveys carried out in Spain and made available to the author.
13. Thomas Bruneau and Mario Bacalhão, *Os Portugueses e a Política* (Lisbon: Meseta, 1978).
14. See the discussion in Richard M. Morse, *El espejo de Prospero: un estudio de la dialéctica del Nuevo Mundo* (Mexico: Síglo Veintiuno, 1982); and Howard J. Wiarda, *The Democratic Revolution in Latin America* (New York: Holmes and Meier, A Twentieth Century Fund Book, 1990).
15. Especially, W. W. Rostow, *The Stages of Economic Growth* (Cambridge: Cambridge University Press, 1960); S. M. Lipset, *Political Man: The Social Basis of Politics* (Garden City, N.Y.: Doubleday, 1960); and Gabriel A. Almond and James S. Coleman (eds.), *The Politics of the Developing Areas* (Princeton, N.J.: Princeton University Press, 1960); as well as a whole genre of other literature.
16. Philippe C. Schmitter, "Still the Century of Corporatism?" *The Review of Politics*, 36 (January 1974): 85–131.
17. The argument is set forth in the conclusion in Howard J. Wiarda (ed.), *New Directions in Comparative Politics* (Boulder, Colo.: Westview Press, 2nd ed., 1991).
18. Thomas O. Wilkinson, *The Urbanization of Japanese Labor* (Amherst, Mass.: University of Massachusetts Press, 1965); Lloyd Rudolph and Suzanne Rudolph, *The Modernity of Tradition* (Chicago, Ill.: University of Chicago Press, 1967); Reinhard Bendix, "Tradition and Modernity Reconsidered," *Comparative Studies in Society and History*, 9 (April 1967): 292–346; A. H. Somjee, *Parallels and Actuals of Political Development* (London: Macmillan, 1986); and Howard J. Wiarda, *Ethnocentrism in Foreign Policy: Can We Understand the Third World?* (Washington, D.C.: American Enterprise Institute for Public Policy and Research, 1967).
19. Earlier efforts by the author to wrestle with this same theme include "Interpreting Iberian–Latin American Interrelations: Paradigm Consensus and Conflict" in Wiarda (ed.), *The Iberian–Latin American Connection* (Washington, D.C., and Boulder, Colo.: American Enterprise Institute for Public Policy Research and Westview Press, 1986); and *Politics and Social Change in Latin America: Is the Tradition Still Distinct?* (Boulder, Colo.: Westview Press, 3rd ed., 1992).

Chapter 2

The Long Sweep of Iberian History

Spain and Portugal are old nations—far older than the United States or most countries of Western Europe. The recorded history of the Iberian Peninsula goes back nearly 3000 years. Iberian *civilization* and *political culture* began to take definitive shape around 2000 years ago, when Rome conquered the peninsula and put its indelible stamp upon it.

The weight of all this history hangs heavily over Iberia. It is a legacy, sometimes a burden, that Spain and Portugal must bear and that they cannot escape—nor are they consistently sure they want to. The heavy hand of History still guides and shapes Iberian politics in significant ways that we in the United States, with our less-than-400-year history, the absence of a feudal or medieval tradition, and our frequent lack of interest in the historical past as a shaping influence on the present, have a difficult time comprehending.

This chapter traces that long sweep of Iberian history, from ancient times to the twentieth century, in order to try to understand the main, underlying currents that shape and condition present-day society and politics. The presentation is necessarily brief and interpretive rather than detailed and chronological. Our aim is to try to *understand* Spain and Portugal, not to present every obscure name and date of their histories. We begin, however, with a brief survey of the geography of Iberia, for that has also been a conditioning factor in the development—or lack thereof—of Spain and Portugal.

IBERIAN GEOGRAPHY

Spain and Portugal are conditioned by, if not determined products of, their geography. Here are some of the most important features of that geography.

First, Iberia is remote from the rest of Europe, a peninsula separated by distance and impassable mountains from the heartland of central Europe. Iberia is the westernmost promontory of the European continent, jutting out southerly and westerly toward Africa and the Atlantic, and not well tied to or integrated into the rest of Europe.

Second, as a peninsula facing in different directions, Iberia was long confused as to its destiny. Historically, the peninsula was divided into three main (and many smaller) parts, all with different orientations and themselves quite different sociologically, economically, and politically. (See Figure 2.1.) Aragon, initially (and in many respects still today) the most developed part of the peninsula, faced east, toward the Mediterranean (then the center of the world's main civilizations) and toward the main centers of European trade and culture, with which it was closely connected. Lusitania (modern-day Portugal) faced south and west, toward Africa, the Atlantic islands, and Brazil; it was never sure if its destiny was in Europe or elsewhere. Meanwhile Castile, the heartland of the peninsula, was confused about its destiny and deeply divided internally, sometimes facing east and north toward the Mediterranean and Europe, and sometimes facing south and west toward Latin America and the Third World. Yet it was confused, chaotic Castile that would eventually dominate the peninsula. Part of Spain's difficulties and eventual decline as a nation could be attributed to this confusion—Mediterranean or the Atlantic, North or South, Europe or the Third World—as to its geographic destiny.

A third geographic feature is Iberia's topography. Looked at cross-sectionally, the peninsula appears to be a truncated pyramid, with mountainous escarpments rising quickly from the sea and then a vast tableland that is high and mountainous. (See Figure 2.2.) The amount of fertile agricultural land is very small, limited largely to the coastlands and some valleys, which means Iberia (unlike France, England, and Germany) was never able to develop the agricultural surpluses on which later economic growth could be based. The central plateau is itself interrupted by successive ridges

18 CHAPTER 2 THE LONG SWEEP OF IBERIAN HISTORY

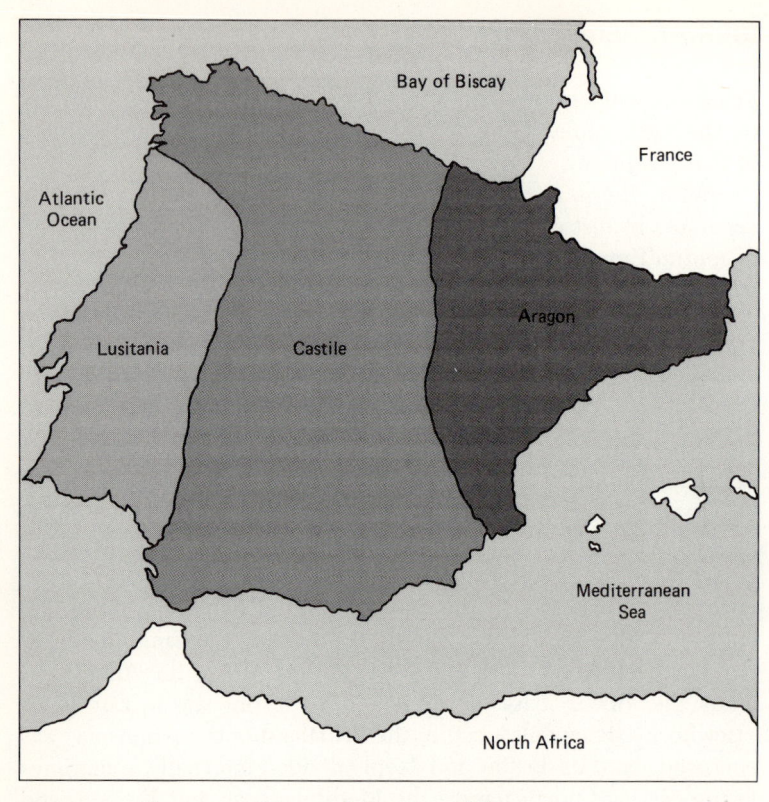

Figure 2.1. Three main historical divisions of Iberia.

of mountain dividing Iberia into smaller regional units (*patrias chicas* or "small countries"), making movement within the peninsula very difficult historically and retarding unity.

Iberia is thus cut into multiple compartments, each with its own customs, traditions, forms of speech, and proud self-awareness. Just as the Pyrenees cut Iberia off from Europe, so the coastal escarpments cut the peninsula off from the sea and the internal mountain ranges cut the Iberians off from each other. In addition, because of the mountains and the sharp drops from the tableland of the *Meseta* to the sea, the river system is navigable generally only for short distances and, unlike North America with its vast internal river and lake system, has not served as an instrument of internal trade, transportation, and national integration.

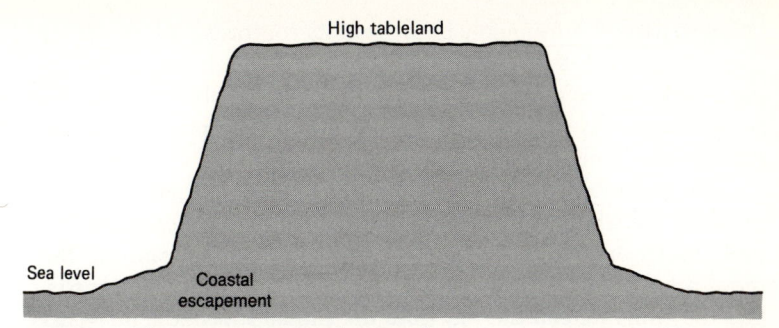

Figure 2.2. Iberia as a truncated pyramid.

Moreover, Iberia is not rich in resources, or the resources are of the wrong kind. Spain and Portugal were originally agricultural, but the rocky topography, while appropriate for grazing, is hardly conducive to more intensive farming. Nor is the mountainous terrain of Iberia, in contrast to the American Midwest, amenable to modern, mechanized agriculture. Iberia really has a weak base for agriculture, and the situation is not much better for industry and manufacturing. The peninsula has some natural resources (tin, coal, copper, gold, silver) but not those important for industrial processes (petroleum, for example) and not in juxtaposition (iron ore and coal for the smelting of steel).

Iberia is a large territory, about the size of France, Germany or Great Britain; but it is the most geographically broken up and has nowhere near the resources—agricultural or mineral—that these other countries have; therefore, Iberia's development was destined to lag behind.

EARLY PEOPLES

Spain has sometimes perceived of and presented itself as a "pure race," different from other nations and identifiable as a distinct people. But this is a social myth, for in fact the Iberian nations are a mixture of many ethnic influences.

The origins of the first Iberians are unknown, a matter of pure speculation. It is thought that many came from France, central Europe, and Italy, but some also came from North Africa across the Mediterranean or the Strait of Gibraltar. The term "Iberia" (meaning "river") is itself a word derived from North Africa, the peninsula being so named presumably because of its contrasts with the desert areas from which these inhabitants came. Some scholars argue that the North African origins of some of the original inhabitants of Iberia account for its clannish, familial, almost "tribal" politics, but that may be stretching the known information too far.

The Basques, who live in Spain's northwest mountain area, like to claim that they were the original people in the peninsula, but their background is not entirely clear, with some surmising that they came from the Euro-Asian heartland and others suggesting that they migrated all the way from the Indian subcontinent. Whatever the actual situation, it is the case that northern Spain (along with southern France) has some of the earliest, prehistoric cave paintings (at Altamira) to be found anywhere in Western Europe.

The Celts were an Indo-Germanic element that settled in the peninsula in the sixth century B.C. They were similar to the Celts who migrated west and settled in Ireland.

In the same century the Greeks settled on the eastern shores of Iberia. They named the peninsula Hesperia, "land of the setting sun."

The Tartesians (from Tarsus in Asia Minor) settled along the banks of the Guadalquivir River. They had also found their way to Iberia in the centuries before Christ.

The Phoenicians, who were from the eastern Mediterranean, from an area that is now Syria, were traders and merchants who came in contact with the Tartesians. Looking for precious metals, they founded Cadiz in the south of Spain as a trading center. The Phoenicians exploited the mines in that area and also founded the city of Málaga.

The Carthaginians were called in to help the Phoenicians in their struggles against the Tartesians. Carthage was also a trading and cultural center on the North African coast.

Thus, from the beginning Iberia was settled by diverse peoples, of North African, Semitic, Indo-European, and doubtlessly other origins. All these groups left their impact, but none so indelibly and permanently as the Romans who settled there next.

THE ROMAN IMPACT

Roman military legions began to enter Iberia as an offshoot of the Punic Wars in the third century B.C., in part to defeat Hannibal and the Carthaginians who had also attacked Rome. But it took Rome nearly 200 years, until 19 B.C., to subdue the fierce Iberians—and even then some pockets of resistance remained in the north of the peninsula. However, for the next 400 years a *Pax Romana* prevailed throughout the peninsula, and in that context of peace and stability Iberia progressed rapidly. Many Roman retired soldiers settled in Spain, acquired land, married the natives, and Romanized the peninsula. Iberia was the most Romanized of the Roman provinces; some say it became more Roman than Rome itself.

The Roman influence was deep and long lasting, and it touched all aspects of Iberian life. The Romans built roads and aqueducts, and thus brought unity and a level of urban civilization to the peninsula that it had lacked before. They increased trade, agriculture, and production. Roman law served as a further unifying force. A common language, with regional variations, evolved out of the Roman Latin, serving as an additional element of peninsular integration. Rome brought its architecture to what it called "Hispania" as well. Later, Christianity spread to Iberia under Roman auspices, a very important development that added one further element of unity and that would continue to shape peninsular life all the way to the present. Hispania became not only more Roman but also more Christian than Rome itself—often more intense, more absolutist, and more intolerant.

The social and political influences of Rome on Iberia are most important for our purposes. To begin, Roman rule imposed a class structure on the peninsula for the first time, replacing the chaotic tribalism that had gone before—a class structure that was reinforced by racial and ethnic criteria. The Romans formed a beginning aristocratic class, which was also lighter-skinned, at the top; the lower classes were not only poorer but also darker. Moreover, Rome emphasized group, class, and corporate (army, religion, elites) rights and obligations over individual rights, a concept that would later prove at variance with the emphasis on individual rights in the Anglo-American tradition and that would give rise to numerous conflicts over human rights violations.

The political institutions that Rome brought to the Iberian peninsula were not the republican precepts of Cicero but, rather, the alternative authoritarian, imperial, and autocratic tradition. Power was highly centralized and top-down, with the chain of command running from the emperor in Rome to his governor-general in the provinces to the local notable or landowner. The structure was military as well as political, with the two reinforcing each other and leaving little opportunity for grass roots, democratic, or participatory rule. Rome, after all, was an empire, and this is how it ruled its far-flung lands—not through democratic participation but by top-down, authoritarian command. It is interesting that when Spain and Portugal in the fifteenth and sixteenth centuries acquired their own global empires, the model they used was the same central, autocratic structure of the Roman *imperium*. Hence, neither Iberia nor Latin America, the Philippines, Angola, Mozambique, or other countries governed by the Spanish and Portuguese empires would receive any training in self-government or democratic procedures.

In the early fifth century A.D., as the Roman empire itself came under barbarian attack and began to break up, three different German tribes—the Suevi, the Alani, and the Vandals (whose brutality gave rise to the term "vandalism")—entered the peninsula, destroying the Roman accomplishments and power structure. Another German tribe, the Visigoths, swept into the peninsula a few years later, conquering the other German tribes as well as the remnants of Roman rule. The Visigothic domination lasted approximately two centuries, but it had only one important lasting impact for our consideration. The Visigoths, who had previously conquered much of Italy, had already been Christianized by the time they entered Iberia. Their lasting contribution was to establish the Church and the state as one entity, mutually reinforcing each other. The Visigothic king was simultaneously head of the Church—a lasting tradition reflected in the pope's later granting to the Spanish king the right of royal patronage to appoint clerics. The predominance of a rigid, orthodox Christianity grounded in a crystallized doctrine, and with the civil and religious authority fused, constituted the Visigoths' main lasting contribution.

The Visigoths lacked the organization power that Rome had, however, so the many-faceted Roman influence had a more lasting impact on Iberia than did the Visigothic. In fact, it was the very disorganized and violent nature of the Germanic invasions and rule that caused the Iberians to look back on the Roman period with admiration and to elevate the Roman system into their model for later national organization and empire. Meanwhile, the lack of a strong central organization and strife among the Visigothic factions paved the way for a new invasion, that of the Moors.

MOORISH RULE

Within a century of Muhammad's death in 632 A.D., the wildfire of the Islamic faith had enveloped virtually all of the eastern and southern Mediterranean. In 711, invited by one of the feuding Visigothic factions, the Berbers of North Africa, otherwise known as the Moors, crossed the Strait of Gibraltar into Spain. They defeated the main Visigothic force and soon overran most of the peninsula, except for some impassable mountain regions in the north. Moorish rule persisted until 1492 (the same year as Columbus's voyage to America), when the last of the Moors were expelled from southern Spain.

Despite the over seven centuries of occupation, Moorish influence in Iberia was less penetrating and less indelible than the long time frame would suggest, and it was not nearly as significant in its permanent effects as the briefer (by one century) Roman occupation. Moorish rule remained primarily North Africa–oriented, and hence the Moors left the Iberians pretty much alone. They supplanted the Visigoths as overlords, but they did not fundamentally alter the structure of Iberian society.

Though Islam was elsewhere a proselytizing religion, in Iberia the Moors were tolerant—they didn't force conversion—and hence the Iberians continued to practice their Catholicism without interference. Moreover, although the Moors had overrun virtually the entire peninsula, they remained concentrated in the south (Seville, Cartagena, Granada, Córdoba); the Moorish presence north of present-day Madrid was quite thin. In addition, the Moors almost constantly feuded among themselves, another factor enabling the Iberians to largely carry on their own lives as before. Finally, although the center of crusading Islam was then in Damascus, only a nominal connection existed between that capital and Iberia; and the peninsula continued mainly under self-rule. All these conditions made the Moorish influence in Iberia less penetrating, less deep-rooted, and less permanent than one would expect it to be.

Although the Moorish presence was limited in its long-range effects, the Moors did succeed in making Spain for a time the most enlightened kingdom in Europe. While the rest of Europe experienced the Dark Ages, Spain under the Moors flourished and became a center of intellectual life. The philosophy and thought of ancient Greece, largely lost in Europe during this period, was reintroduced into Spain by the Moors via North Africa; only much later would the richness of Greek thought be revived in the rest of Europe. Moorish architecture, construction, and book design were similarly spectacular. At this time Spain had the largest and most sophisticated cities in Europe. The Arab philosopher Averroës and the Jewish scholar Maimonides, to name only two of many, flourished in Spain during this period; intellectual life was not only surprisingly tolerant but also vigorous and robust. Under Moorish control the economy similarly flourished, with merchants and traders from many lands. Iberia was the one bright spot in an otherwise quite dismal period in European history.

Moorish rule in Iberia was not deep-seated, but it did leave its influence. Centuries later, the architecture, gardens, and accomplishments of the Moors in the south of Spain are still impressive. It is thought also that the Moors introduced polygamy and a secondary role for women into Iberia, although these charges may well be exaggerated. It may also be that the Moorish conquest had something to do with militarism in Iberia, with the creation of a separate warrior caste, and with a certain culture of violence—although these assertions have yet to be proved. Finally, it may be that the Moors introduced separatism, tribalism, and disintegrative, centrifugal forces into Iberia—decentralizing forces that would forever clash with the centralizing, concentrating, centripetal institutions introduced by the Romans. The conflicts between these opposed tendencies would repeatedly tear Iberia apart all the way to the present.

THE RECONQUEST

Along with Roman rule, the centuries-long Reconquest of the peninsula from the Moors is generally thought of as one of the major determining periods in Iberian history. Spanish historian Américo Castro has called the Reconquest the "loom on which the history of Spain was warped."[1] No other European country went through a similar experience; the Reconquest is one of those major influences that helps make Iberia distinctive.

The Iberian uprising against the Moors began in Covadonga in 722 A.D., a legendary town in the rugged Cantabrian mountains in the north of Spain. The battle raged off and on for centuries. It ebbed and flowed; there was no firm line marking the frontier between the competing armies and peoples. Generally, however, the Reconquest proceeded from the north of the peninsula toward the south, as the Iberians slowly pushed the Moors toward the Strait of Gibraltar. The Reconquest culminated in the final defeat of the Moors in 1492; this conquering effort then carried over to the New World in the Americas, which was discovered the very same year.

The impact of the Reconquest was enormous on Iberia's future development. The Reconquest was not just a nationalistic uprising of Iberians against their Moorish overlords; it was a religious crusade (Christian versus Moslem) as well. The Reconquest helped make Spanish Catholicism more absolutist than elsewhere in Europe, made it more intolerant, and gave rise to the Inquisition, that institution established to ensure the purity of Spanish Catholicism and to weed out other influences. The Reconquest also gave rise to the attitude of "get rich quick by military action," which was also carried over to Latin America. Agriculture, therefore, languished in the north of Spain because it was easier to become wealthy by military exploits than by farming. The Reconquest similarly gave rise to heroic and even xenophobic individualism, *machismo*, and militarism—traits that continue to plague Iberia and its former colonies to this day.

Institutionally, the Reconquest was also critically important. Both the Church and the military were greatly strengthened during the Reconquest, becoming the major institutional pillars of the emerging Spanish and Portuguese regimes. The constant fighting forced the Iberians to build walled enclave cities, drained the countryside of people and agricultural production, and gave rise to the phenomenon of preindustrial urbanization. In addition, there was not just one Spanish army fighting the Moors but many, in different parts of the peninsula, producing and reinforcing intense regionalism. The form of Iberian feudalism was also related to the Reconquest, for as the rampaging armies conquered new territories, the military leaders received not only rights to the lands they had conquered but also the right to the labor of the persons living on those lands.

Iberian feudalism was thus more militaristic and tied to conquest than it was elsewhere in Europe. The feudal lord was not only the military leader in his territory but often its political authority, religious voice, and social and economic elite as well. The system of rule was authoritarian, hierarchical, militaristic, and top-down—all characteristics that would remain dominant in Spain, Portugal, and their colonies for many centuries.

THE FORGING OF NATIONAL IDENTITY

A separate kingdom of Portugal began to emerge in the late Middle Ages, as early as the eleventh and twelfth centuries. The main forces encouraging the formation of this new nation were a separate dialect of the vernacular Latin, the unity of the province under a hereditary monarchy, mountain ranges that kept Lusitania (the Roman name for Portugal) isolated from the rest of Iberia, the freeing of this area from the Moors earlier than in Spain, and a spirit of self-reliance and distinctiveness forged by fighting off both the Vikings and neighboring Spanish provinces. Lusitania went its own way beginning in 1096. It consolidated its separation from next-door León in 1143. The last of the Moors were driven out by 1249, thus giving Portugal the approximate borders that it has today. And by 1385 complete independence from neighboring Castile had been achieved.

Spain's unification, encompassing a far larger territory, took much longer. The first kingdoms (now provinces) to emerge, after having been liberated from the Moors, were all in the north: Asturias, León, Galicia, Navarre, Aragon, Catalonia. Next came Castile, Valencia, Extremadura; and then, as the Moors were more and more isolated, the southern provinces. Some of these provinces coalesced into larger kingdoms (Castile, Aragon), but for a long time (and continuing even today) Spain was more sharply riven by regional discord and lack of unity than was Portugal.

Our main concern in this section, however, is the institutions (including their lasting impact) that Spain and Portugal used to forge national unity. The differences between Iberia and the northern European countries are, once again, striking.

We are talking about the period from approximately the twelfth through the fifteenth centuries. During this formative period Portugal and the Spanish kingdoms were gradually consolidated. They were consolidated under centralizing, royal authority that used absolutist techniques to cement control. Resisting these centralizing tendencies were the nobles as well as the functional corporations:

the clergy, the military orders (Templars, Hospitalers, Calatrava, Alcantara, and others) that emerged from the Reconquest, the towns and regions with their charters of independence, sometimes the universities, and in Spain a very important economic interest of sheepherders called the *mesta*. All these groups were governed by organic laws spelling out their rights and obligations in relation to royal authority. In the early (disorganized and nonconsolidated) part of this period, "society" (the corporations) was dominant and largely autonomous, but in the later part, the state began to emerge as dominant and society and its corporate units were subordinated.

Society, by which in Iberia we mean its corporate sectors, was represented through the *cortes* or parliament, which in León and Aragon preceded the British parliament and the hallowed Magna Carta of 1215. But the Iberian *corteses* never developed the independent lawmaking, tax-assessing, and monarchy-limiting powers of the British parliament. Nor did the *corteses* ever develop into separate, coequal branches of government. They were occasionally consulted by the monarch, but they had no independent authority. The *corteses* were more or less representative of society's corporate interests (hence the long history of corporatism in Iberia—see Chapter 3), but they never developed the concepts of geographic and individual representation or rights as did their British counterpart. In fact, neither the *corteses* nor the courts ever developed into effective checks on absolute power; and over time the monarchs called them into session less and less often, and then only to ratify their decrees. Eventually the *corteses* and the corporate agencies they represented were entirely submerged under the rising power of absolute despotism and centralized state authority.

The powerful compelling logic of Thomistic (from St. Thomas Aquinas) Catholicism carried to Iberia during this period gave a reinforced Christian blessing and legitimacy to this emerging hierarchical and absolutist order. The rediscovery of Aristotle about this same time gave added legitimacy to the Thomistic conception of society as consisting of God-given hierarchical estates and to natural inequalities among people. Similarly, the rediscovery of Roman law provided further rationalization for a top-down, absolutist, highly centralized, even imperial political structure. None of these trends and features would be conducive to the growth or emergence of democracy and representative institutions in Spain and Portugal.

In the absence of genuine democracy, Iberia developed its own meanings of such terms as "participation," "representation," and "popular sovereignty." Participation meant involvement in national affairs through officially sanctioned institutions that were controlled and limited by the state. Representation was carried out through corporate or functional bodies similarly structured, if not created, by the central government. Popular sovereignty was not in the form of one-person, one-vote but through the ceding of power to the absolute state in return for charity, patronage, and benefits. None of these could be considered democratic precepts.

The main arena of national political life consisted of the struggle of the emerging, absolutist central state to expand and consolidate its power, versus the efforts of society's corporate units (towns, universities, military orders, economic interests) to maintain some degree of contractually derived independence from it. Under the best of the Spanish and Portuguese kings (Alfonso X the Wise or João II), the central state and the societal corporations were viewed as existing in joint harmony, mutually reinforcing, with rights and obligations accorded to each. Or else, the central state would take on a paternalistic role, doling out positions, patronage, and favors in return for loyalty and service.

But all too often the trend was toward centralized absolutism and away from these patronage and contractual obligations. During the early years the corporations often had the upper hand, but in the fourteenth and fifteenth centuries it was the central state that proved dominant, ignoring or riding roughshod over local and corporate *fueros*, or rights. The struggle by the local or corporate units to restore their autonomy and resurrect what they called a contractual state of *mutual* rights and obligations was frustrated for centuries under the yoke of royal absolutism. But that is what largely defined the political struggle in Iberia and gave it its characteristic features.

For a long time "democracy" in Spain and Portugal meant the restoration of these historic group rights, not what the Anglo-American countries mean by "democracy." Now that historic struggle has been superseded by a more modern conception of democracy, but alongside (or sometimes below the surface of) the democracy debates there still lurks that more ancient struggle between the central state and its component corporate groups.

THE HAPSBURGIAN MODEL

By the fifteenth century Iberia was divided into three main kingdoms: Portugal in the west under a cohesive national monarchy; Aragon in the east, cultured and relatively prosperous, oriented toward France and under centralized authority; and Castile in the middle, encompassing the heartland of the peninsula, chaotic, disorganized, run by the nobles and fighting orders, with little respect for the monarchy.

Isabella (later called *la Católica*) was the heir to the throne of Castile, and it was suggested that she marry a Portuguese prince in order to unify the two kingdoms. But instead she married Ferdinand of Aragon, a clever and resourceful monarch who served as the scheming, manipulative model of Machiavelli's *Prince*. The marriage of Isabella and Ferdinand brought unity to the Spanish kingdoms, but it was an artificial unity imposed upon a country still dominated by regional loyalties. It also involved Spain in a century-long war with France (and others) that nearly destroyed Spain.

The marriage contract said that Ferdinand was supreme in Aragon, Isabella was supreme in Castile, and that their heirs would preside over a unified kingdom. Isabella then set out to bring unity and centralization to chaotic Castile. Her methods are instructive because they tell us a great deal about how Spain would be run under its "Hapsburgian Model."

Isabella was tough, disciplined, and clever but also bigoted and fanatic. She used the Santa Hermandad (Holy Brotherhood), a traveling kangaroo court with arbitrary rules, to weed out all dissenters, Moors, Jews, and other "undesirables." She awarded high-sounding titles to the feuding nobles, drew them out of their castles and into her own court, and then destroyed their castles and their power. She eliminated the military orders similarly by awarding them titles and making them only honorary organizations. The independent, self-governing cities were also a problem from her point of view: She sent out her own representatives (*corregidores*) with royal authority to reorganize and destroy the local town councils. In addition, she reduced and largely eliminated the power of the *cortes*, where the seeds of Spanish democracy had once been planted, and erected advisory councils in their place, giving rise to a large central bureaucracy that eventually bled Spain dry. The Inquisition was used further by Isabella to get rid of dissenters and unify Spain under Catholic orthodoxy. In these ways the possibilities for Spanish democracy and pluralism were snuffed out; the country was unified under a rigid, absolutist, top-down, and authoritarian system that was one of the main ingredients in the Hapsburgian Model.

Of Ferdinand and Isabella's five children, only one, Juana (*la loca*—"the crazy one"), who was married to an Austrian Hapsburg, produced any surviving heirs who would inherit the now unified kingdom. The heir, Charles, was born in Belgium, knew no Spanish, came to the Spanish throne in 1517 while still a teenager, and brought with him Flemish advisors who also knew no Spanish but took all the choice government positions. Charles was never well liked by the Spanish people. But then in 1519, the emperor Maximilian I of the Holy Roman Empire, which was centered in Austria (and, as the French philosopher Voltaire quipped, was neither Holy, nor Roman, nor an Empire), died; and Charles was elected emperor, simultaneously ruling as Charles I of Spain and Charles V of the Holy Roman Empire.

From this time on, preoccupied with larger European affairs and determined to snuff out the Protestant heresy, Charles was seldom in Spain and he ignored Spain's problems; but he used Spanish military power as well as the gold and silver from Latin America to fight a steady stream of religious and dynastic wars in Europe. After his abdication in 1555 to 1556, he was succeeded by his son Philip II, who ruled until 1598 and continued and expanded his father's and greatgrandparents' (Ferdinand and Isabella's) centralizing, warmongering, and authoritarian policies. Thus, for the entire, formative period from 1479 until the end of the sixteenth century, Spain had only three very powerful rulers: Ferdinand and Isabella, Charles I(V), and Philip II.

This was a positive period in many respects. Iberia roared but it never quite took off. Spain (and Portugal) conquered vast global territories in Africa, Asia, and Latin America and became the world's most powerful imperial nations. Their armies and bureaucracies were the largest and most rationalized in Western Europe. Their monarchs were smart and efficient. Vast wealth was flowing in from their empires—although we now know it flowed right out again for arms and armies and hardly benefitted Spain and Portugal. Plus in literature and the arts, this was the *Siglo de Oro*, the "century of gold"—a period of vast cultural flowering when Spain and Portugal vaulted to the forefront of Europe. But even while these significant, even world-shaking developments were taking place, the seeds of Spain's and Portugal's decline were also planted.

The Spanish and Portuguese associated their prestige and elevated position with the sociopolitical structure put in place by Ferdinand and Isabella and the first Hapsburgs. Because this structure was so important in shaping Iberian institutions, and became the model to which Spain and Portugal looked in their later centuries of decline, and was actually resurrected in the regimes of Franco and Salazar, it behooves us to know what this "Hapsburgian Model" was.

Politically, the Hapsburgian Model was hierarchical, top-down, authoritarian, and centralized, running roughshod over and submerging the historic group rights and regional autonomy of Iberia. Socially, the model was similarly hierarchical, two-class, and rigidly stratified, with "God-given" rights and privileges. Economically the model was statist, feudal, and mercantilist, a milk-cow economy that drained the resources of Iberia and Latin America but put little emphasis on productivity. Religiously, the Hapsburgian Model was also absolutist, based on a particularly virile and intolerant Catholic orthodoxy, rigid and unyielding. And educationally and intellectually, the model was based on scholasticism, on revealed truths and rote memorization, on deductive, nonscientific methods. Interestingly, this same Hapsburgian Model is what Spain and Portugal carried with them in their colonization of Africa, the Philippines, and Latin America.

The Hapsburgian Model was essentially a feudal and medieval construct that Spain and Portugal sought to hang on to even while other countries were beginning to modernize. Consider the contrasts of this model with the more dynamic, modernizing tendencies in the Netherlands and England. Politically these last two countries were already moving toward limited and representative government while Iberia remained locked in an absolutist pattern. Socially, the northern countries were moving toward pluralist, multi-class societies. Economically they were dynamic and capitalistic, freeing themselves from the fetters of the kind of feudalism and mercantilism that remained cemented in place in Iberia. Religiously they were becoming pluralist and tolerant. And educationally and intellectually, the Renaissance, the scientific revolution, and the Enlightenment had a profound effect in England and the Netherlands but almost no effect in Iberia. These differences define the historical contrasts between the medieval and the modern worlds. Spain and Portugal remained locked in the former, which explains why they were destined to lag behind while the nations of northern Europe forged ahead.

IBERIA IN DECLINE

The top-down Hapsburgian Model could work well as long as there were efficient, hardworking, effective monarchs, as Spain had in the persons of Charles I and Philip II. But after Philip II, the monarchy also went into decline under a series of weak, ineffective, and ultimately imbecilic kings. Without strong leadership at the top, the Hapsburgian Model could not function effectively and was ill-suited to the needs of a modern or modernizing political system. But because the Spanish and Portuguese identified the Hapsburgian Model with their great exploits, conquests, and triumphs of the sixteenth century—the "golden century"—they subsequently sought to strengthen and resurrect that model rather than, as in the more modernizing parts of Europe, evolving toward a new and more effective system of development.

Actually, there were multiple causes for Spain's and Portugal's decline from the early seventeenth century on. These included:

1. Their empires were too spread out, too large, too unwieldy to be effectively ruled from the center. Beginning with the revolt in the Netherlands against Spanish rule in the 1570s, the vast Spanish and Portuguese empires began to unravel.
2. Spain and Portugal, seeking to defend Catholic hegemony in Europe and to reverse the Protestant Reformation, squandered their resources and those of their colonies in a series of wasteful and ultimately futile religious wars.
3. The vast wealth of the two empires was drained out of Spain and Portugal for weapons and soldiers; it was not used to foster local industry and production. Similarly, the Spanish tax system fell heaviest on the shoulders of its most productive elements—farmers, craftsmen, artisans—and drove them into bankruptcy; but it did not touch unproductive or wastefully used land or the expanding but also unproductive nobility.

4. The social class structure became hardened, unbending; it provided few escalators, few opportunities for advancement.
5. To raise funds for their many foreign wars, the Hapsburgs began the practice of selling public offices. This gave rise to a gigantic public bureaucracy, dominated by sinecures, that was woefully inefficient. The issue of a patronage-dominated, nonmeritorious bureaucracy remains a problem today.
6. Spain and Portugal experienced a severe population decline. Many of their ablest people went to the New World; many were killed in the virtually nonstop wars of the time; many others flocked into monasteries both out of religious conviction and as a way of escaping being impressed into the army. As the countryside was drained of ablebodied people, agriculture went into a decline and industry languished.
7. Popular rule was increasingly subordinated to Hapsburgian absolutism. The monarchy became even more absolutist as its kings exhibited less and less competence. All the local rights, the local *corteses*, and the vestiges of representative rule were snuffed out, subordinated to royal absolutism, strict centralization, and rule by royal councils.
8. The monarchy resorted to spectacles (as well as the Inquisition) to keep Renaissance and Enlightenment ideas out of Iberia. This was the baroque period in Iberia—elaborate details but no real basic simplicity of ideas—resulting in the isolation of Iberia from the main cultural and intellectual currents of Europe.
9. Spain and Portugal had driven out and persecuted many of their most productive and enlightened persons: Jews, Moors, Protestants. The Hapsburgs put a curtain around Iberia (from 1580 to 1640 the two countries were united under a single rule) to keep European ideas out and used persecution to snuff out local nonconformists, thus curtailing what, since the Moors, had been a flourishing intellectual life.
10. Meanwhile the royal family degenerated as a result of disease and inbreeding. It produced a series of sickly and mentally retarded monarchs in the seventeenth century,

reaching its nadir in the person of Charles II who was moronic, infantile, and infertile.

The Hapsburg monarchy thus died out in 1700. Spain had at that moment reached the lowest point in its history. There were four claimants to the throne, all of them representing foreign families whose interests were chiefly dynastic rather than concern for the good of the peninsula. The winner of this competition was the royal family of France, the Bourbons.

Bourbon rule in the eighteenth century brought a needed shot in the arm to Spain. The Bourbons were modern-oriented, progressive, European-looking. A succession of able, effective, Bourbon monarchs introduced many reforms to the peninsula. They introduced street lighting, improved roads, began a mail service, built public buildings, drained swampy areas, brought in European styles of dress and behavior, reforested the denuded mountainsides, and built canals and backwaters. The Bourbons also stimulated intellectual life, introduced reforms in the method of taxation, put restrictions on the Church, and expelled the Jesuits. In Portugal in a parallel fashion, the eighteenth century minister Pombal introduced many of the same enlightened and rational reforms.

These changes were often welcomed outside Iberia, by some elements within Spain and Portugal, and by admirers today. But several points should be remembered. First, the Bourbons kept in place—and expanded—the bloated, mercantilist bureaucracy and economic system inherited from the Hapsburgs; no changes or reforms were introduced in this area. Second, the means by which the Bourbons carried out their reforms was through a central state system that was even more absolutist than that of the Hapsburgs and that continued to allow no room for democratic participation. Third, the reforms introduced, particularly those directed against the Church or that involved changes in traditional dress and lifestyles, were strongly resented and resisted by the Spanish masses, who were often even more conservative than their leaders.

CIVIL CONFLICT IN THE NINETEENTH CENTURY

Although the Hapsburgian (now modified by the Bourbons) Model remained dominant, by the late eighteenth century a split had developed in the Iberian soul, and in Iberian society. On the one side was traditional Iberia: conservative, Catholic, authoritarian, and absolutist. The social base of traditional Iberia was in the monarchy, the nobility, the military, and the countryside—both among landowners and their equally conservative peasants.

On the other side was a more rationalist and modern Iberia: progressive-looking, shaped by the Enlightenment, oriented toward Europe. The social base of this "other Iberia" was in the cities and among intellectuals, the new commercial elements, and an emerging middle class. Henceforth there would no longer be just one model, the Hapsburgian Model, of society and governance but a second, more liberal model growing alongside of it. These two models were poles apart, giving rise to the phenomenon of two societies and ways of life uneasily coexisting within the nation: two Spains and two Portugals. Much of nineteenth century Iberian history could be discussed in terms of the clash between these two quite different conceptions and ways of life. Because of these perpetual conflicts and the conditions of endemic civil war all through the nineteenth century and on into the twentieth, Spain and Portugal largely missed out on the great developmental engines of economic growth and industrialization that enabled other European countries during this period to forge ahead.

With the outbreak of the French Revolution in 1789, the Spanish Bourbons had been immediately concerned with the fate of their French cousins. A Spanish army rushed pell-mell into France to rescue Louis XVI, but it was driven back. Later, the fervor of the French Revolution carried its armies across Iberia to occupy both Spain and Portugal, and Napoleon put his brother Joseph on the Spanish throne. Like Bourbon rule in the eighteenth century, Napoleonic rule was enlightened and modernizing in some ways, but it was strongly resisted by the conservative and nationalistic Spanish masses who eventually succeeded in driving the French occupation forces out. Scenes from these struggles were immortalized in the paintings and sketches of the great Spanish artist Francisco Goya.

Debate now centered on the constitution—the first in Spanish history—of 1812. This was a rather mild document, based on the scholastic tradition but liberal in orientation. The constitution was Thomistic and Rousseauean in origins, not Lockean as in the Anglo-American tradition. It provided for a limited monarchy, said that sovereignty rests ultimately with the people, and incorporated some of the classic nineteenth century freedoms. But even this restrained constitution was too much for the newer Bourbons and Spanish traditionalists, who during the following years not only repudiated the constitution but restored the Inquisition, brought back the Jesuits, and nullified most of the earlier Bourbon reforms. This conflict between a crystallized and hardened tradition and the new, emerging liberalism characterized much of the Iberian nineteenth century history and led to repeated civil wars.

Eventually the Spanish crown came around to accepting the notion of a constitutional, and therefore limited (like the British), monarchy; but for most of the nineteenth century that remained unacceptable to the traditionalists who were almost constantly in revolt. These revolts took the form of what were called the Carlist Wars, named after the conservative pretender to the throne, Don Carlos. Meanwhile, the countryside was characterized by extreme disorder, the abandonment of agriculture, and the comings and goings of numerous regional *caudillos*, or "men on horseback." Power was scattered, fragmented, localized; the countries of Spain and Portugal remained chaotic, disorganized, and without the networks of associational life (well described in the United States by French statesman Alexis de Tocqueville) necessary to hold society and polity together. With all the confusion and political upheaval, Spain and Portugal lagged behind the rest of Europe economically as well.

By the last quarter of the nineteenth century and on into the early twentieth century, some order had emerged out of the prevailing chaos. A new royal family was installed in Spain, and the country began to settle down. The form of government remained monarchical but it was limited by constitutional precepts. The Carlist revolts petered out. Spain even began, belatedly, the process of economic growth and industrialization. But because it began so late, Spain's workers were even more impoverished than their European counterparts, and they turned to more radical ideologies: anarchism, syndicalism, and communism. At the marriage of King Alfonso XIII in 1906, the anarchists threw bombs at the wedding party! That's how bitter, nasty, and eventually violent Spain's class relations had become.

Portugal's history in the nineteenth century was less violent than that of Spain. But it was similarly disorganized, chaotic, and marked by the absence of much progress. The Bragança monarchy remained in power, but as in Spain it was now a limited monarchy, and political authority had drained away and become decentralized. Local political chiefs, who were also usually the local landowners or of notable families, dominated political life. They rotated (*rotativismo*) in and out of national office as ministers or cabinet officials, taking advantage of the opportunities for patronage, spoils, and family favoritism that the occupancy of high positions afforded. The system remained paternalistic, family- and clan-oriented, and patronage-dominated, giving rise to many of the traits that continued to characterize Portuguese politics on into the twentieth century. The lack of national organization (*falta de civilização*) also retarded Portugal's, as well as Spain's, economic development.

THE REPUBLICAN INTERLUDE

But Portugal, like Spain, had also begun to change. A larger middle class grew up in the cities and a nascent trade union movement began. The power of the Catholic church, the monarchy, and the old noble or oligarchic families began to wane. The military officer corps came increasingly from the middle sectors and was divided on social and political issues. Republican sentiment began to build.

Exhausted and bankrupt, the Portuguese monarchy collapsed and went into exile in 1910. Leading the opposition were the middle class, Republican intellectuals, the emerging working class, and even some factions of the army. The Portuguese First Republic lasted for 16 years, until 1926. The Portuguese were inexperienced in republican, democratic rule, and the republic was very chaotic. Ministers and governments came and went on an average of every few months; by the actual count of one historian there were more bombs thrown in Lisbon during this period than in any other European country.[2]

The same patronage- and family-oriented politics that characterized the period of the monarchy now characterized the republic. Only the names and some of the beneficiaries changed. Rival politicians and clans continued to "rotate" in and out of office, giving all the factions a turn at the great public watering trough: the national treasury. By the 1920s the economy was in deep trouble, and a fraudulent bank note scheme caused both scandal and hyperinflation. In 1926, fed up with the political and economic mess, the army stepped into power, paving the way for the dictatorship of Salazar.

The Spanish experience with republicanism during this period was no less chaotic and even more tragic. In 1923, following World War I, the monarch Alfonso XIII, faced with growing social and economic disorder, had turned to the army under General Primo de Rivera to maintain order and to help him govern. Primo assumed dictatorial powers, curtailing the limited freedoms the Spanish had by now come to enjoy. Primo was not a cruel dictator, but he did rule in an authoritarian manner (the Hapsburgian Model restored) and became increasingly unpopular. In 1929, faced with political opposition as well as the damage caused in Spain by the world market crash of that year, Primo was forced to resign.

The monarchy hung on for two more years. In 1931, assuming he would win, the king called for a plebiscite on the question of monarchy versus republicanism. But the king badly underestimated the degree of republican sentiment; meanwhile the world economic depression had deepened. When the vote showed a preference for republicanism, the king sailed peacefully into exile.

The Spanish Republic began under fairly moderate (liberal and Socialist) leadership. However, it adopted a new constitution that antagonized the Church. Its liberalism and orientation toward socialism alarmed the traditional sectors, who began to arm themselves. Society began to fragment and polarize. The Carlist civil wars of the nineteenth century were about to be reenacted in their final, bloodiest, and most violent form, compounded now by real class and ideological conflict.

Liberals and Socialists were the dominant elements in the republic during its first two years, facing strong opposition from the Right. During the next two years power passed back to the conservative elements, but they could not govern effectively either. Meanwhile, the economy remained in the depths of depression. The political parties were severely factionalized; none of them had sufficient power or following to govern as a majority. Violence began to spread as each of the major parties established its own militia—private armies that were well armed and wreaked havoc on the opposition. One day it would be conservative leaders who were gunned down, the next it would be Socialists who were assassinated. The army, watching the spreading chaos and alarmed by the strength of the Left as well as all the guns in the hands of irregular civilian groups, grew restless.

The political pendulum began to swing wildly. In 1935–36, it swung way back to the Left. The Left at this time consisted no longer of moderate liberals and Republicans but was dominated by Socialists, Communists, and Anarchists. In many respects the Socialists were even more extreme than the Communists, calling for the overthrow of capitalism and the establishment of a dictatorship of the proletariat. Chaos and violence spread. The left-wing parties now formed a radical, Popular Front government. Fearing the establishment of a Bolshevik regime, the Spanish army, important parts of which were located in the Spanish enclaves (Ceuta, Morocco) in North Africa, issued a *pronunciamiento* against the republic and invaded the peninsula. The Republican government responded by opening the arsenals in the major cities and giving guns to the workers and to the Popular Front political parties. With these acts, full-scale civil war began.

The Spanish civil war raged from 1936 to 1939. It was one of the bloodiest and most vicious civil wars of all times. No quarter was asked—or given. On both sides there were scenes of mind-numbing violence and brutality. Republican forces raped and murdered nuns, while the army sometimes wiped out whole villages. The stakes were high and the ideological passions were fervent. The war seemed to epitomize the history of the time, pitting "fascism" against "communism," and thus was larger and more important than just the Spanish theater. It attracted worldwide attention, with intellectuals, writers, and activists of all kinds flocking to Spain to write about the conflict, join it, or both. The Spanish civil war gave rise to some of the great literature (Hemingway, Orwell, Dos Passos, Malraux) of the twentieth century.

The Spanish civil war, being waged as the dark clouds of World War II loomed ominously, also attracted the attention of the world's powers. The Soviet Union for a time gave assistance to the Republican forces—though it gradually dawned on leftist intellectuals like Orwell who had joined the Republican forces that what the Soviets were interested in was power, not democracy and republicanism.[3] At the same time, Fascist Italy and Nazi Germany gave military assistance to the Spanish army and used Spain to experiment with the techniques they would employ during World War II. With superior organization and firepower, the Spanish army slowly turned the tide of the battle. The Republican forces were confined to the main cities of Barcelona and Madrid. Eventually these two cities surrendered as well. In 1939 Francisco Franco and the army stood atop a devastated, bleeding, and sorely fractured Spain.

The Spanish civil war was a wrenching, bloody, passionate conflict. It tore Spain apart and polarized the nation. It was the culmination of the conflict between the "two Spains" that had begun to emerge in the eighteenth century. It produced Franco and the snuffing out of democracy and republicanism in Spain for the next 40 years. There was horror and massive destruction. But it also produced a lasting positive effect. When Spain did finally return to democracy in the 1970s, it did so cautiously and prudently, hoping to prevent what was on every Spaniard's mind: the avoidance at all costs of a repetition of the 1930s' conditions that produced such a destructive civil war.

INVERTEBRATE SPAIN, INVERTEBRATE PORTUGAL

In the 1920s and 1930s, both Spain and Portugal faced severe, almost unresolvable problems. First, there was the agrarian problem: neglected and unmechanized agriculture, severe rural poverty, farmers leaving the countryside, large estates that didn't produce enough food alongside millions of peasants who owned no land. Second was the labor problem: backward industry, low wages, an illiterate and unskilled labor force, a radicalized trade union movement. Third was the social problem: mushrooming populations, extreme poverty, high illiteracy, inadequate or nonexistent health care, poor housing, few social services, welfare that was no longer adequately provided by the Church but that the state had not yet taken over. The economy was a fourth problem: backward, statist, largely nonindustrial, and premodern.

A fifth problem was the Church: conservative to the point of being reactionary, controlling education and restricting intellectual life, wealthy but with little responsibility, still absolutist and antirepublican. The army was a sixth and parallel problem: a separate state within a state, highly reactionary, a powerful vested interest and not subordinate to civilian authority. Seventh was other political institutions—parties, interest groups, public bureaucrats—which lacked effective organization or were very thin in terms of leadership and serious programs. After all, neither Spain nor Portugal had

ever had any training or experience in democratic self-governm
Eighth was the disintegration of the Spanish empire (Portugal also lost Brazil; its African empire would fall apart later), which began in the early nineteenth century in Latin America and was completed in 1898 when Spain lost Cuba, Puerto Rico, and the Philippines to the upstart United States—a terrible blow to Spanish pride and its psyche. Finally there was the regional problem: Provinces that, despite Hapsburgian centralization, had never been fully integrated into the Spanish nation, resented the control emanating from Madrid, and still wished to go their own separate ways.

These and other tensions had been building for decades, maybe even centuries, in Spain and Portugal.[4] In addition, the kind of delayed, uneven, disorganized, even retarded development that Spain and Portugal had experienced gave rise to severe social dislocations and to political fragmentation and unraveling. The social fabric of these nations began to come apart; the political system came unglued. The Hapsburgian Model, that system that had so powerfully and for so long shaped Iberian development, seemed no longer adequate; but liberalism and republicanism had not worked well in the two nations either.

In the mid-1930s, at the height of this disintegrative period, the Spanish philosopher José Ortega y Gasset wrote a famous little book called *Invertebrate Spain*.[5] By this image he had in mind the backbone of his country, separated into distinct vertebrae, bending and breaking with no connecting tissue between them. That was Spain and Portugal: deeply divided lands, fractured, fragmented, and polarized; with no underlying consensus or legitimacy; with little that tied them together; lacking the cement and the associational life (communities, neighborhoods, intermediate groups of all sorts) that bind people into a true nation. Instead Spain and Portugal consisted of revolving satellites that, with the unleashing of modernization's early forces, were flying in separate and increasingly centrifugal orbits, with no attachment to a central core.

It was this problem, really a series of problems, that the Franco and Salazar regimes sought to address. Rejecting both communism and liberalism, they sought to fashion a new philosophy and framework of national organization, which they called corporatism, as a way out of the malaise, as a way of solving their nations' manifold problems. They also argued that corporatism was uniquely Spanish and uniquely Portuguese, that they had therefore found their own nationalistic "third way," that corporatism was not only the twentieth century's other great "ism" (besides liberalism and communism) but that it represented the wave of the future. Therefore, Franco and Salazar were not just reactionary throwbacks to the past, as they are often portrayed; they were also nationalists and reformers who thought they had a new handle on, a new formula for, national development.

In this quest they ultimately failed. Both Franco and Salazar came to rely on dictatorial rule and an authoritarian state system that was not very progressive but represented an updated, modern, twentieth century version of the Hapsburgian Model—at a time when both countries and their societies had sufficiently changed and modernized that they needed not old-fashioned rule but a dynamic formula for accommodating new realities. However, despite the failure, the experiment itself was an interesting one—and very controversial. It helps explain why Spain and Portugal later repudiated corporatism wholeheartedly and why they went subsequently toward liberalism. But whether this most recent turning of the wheel will enable them to solve their long-term problems and search for legitimacy is a question that is still not fully answered. It is a question to which we return later in this book.

NOTES

1. Américo Castro, *The Structure of Spanish History* (Princeton, N.J.: Princeton University Press, 1954).
2. Douglas Wheeler, *Republican Portugal: A Political History, 1910–1926* (Madison, Wis.: University of Wisconsin Press, 1978).
3. George Orwell, *Homage to Catalonia* (New York: Harcourt, Brace, 1952).
4. Among the better books on this background are Gerald Brennan, *The Spanish Labyrinth* (New York: Cambridge University Press, 1943); and Edward Malefakis, *Agrarian Reform and Peasant Revolution in Spain: Origins of the Civil War* (New Haven, Conn.: Yale University Press, 1970).
5. José Ortega y Gasset, *Invertebrate Spain* (New York: Norton, 1937).

Chapter 3

The Franco and Salazar Regimes

*F*rancisco Franco ruled Spain from 1939 until his death in 1975, a period of 36 years. Antonio de Oliveira Salazar ruled Portugal from 1928 (when he was appointed finance minister; he became prime minister in 1932) until his incapacitation in a fall in 1968, a total of 40 years. Thereafter Salazar's regime continued for six more years under the leadership of his protegé Marcello Caetano, until it was overthrown in the Portuguese "Revolution of Flowers" of 1974.

The regimes of Franco and Salazar were two of the longest lived regimes in the world in the twentieth—or any other—century. In longevity, they matched the earlier rule of Ferdinand and Isabella, Charles I, and Philip II. In their authoritarianism and top-down structures, they were also very much like these earlier "Hapsburgian" systems.

Franco and Salazar were not just long-lived authoritarians, however. Nor will we understand the significance of their regimes if we just dismiss them as "dictators" or, worse, "Fascists"—although neither of these two labels are entirely inaccurate. In fact, the Franco and Salazar regimes were much more complex and much more important than the labels suggest. First, both men were very clever, very skillful politicians who enjoyed strong support in many sectors in their nations, especially in their early years; they did not rule by blood and force alone. Second, both were adherents of corporatism as an ideology and form of national sociopolitical organization, and

43

tried to elevate corporatism to a "third way," a position alternative to liberalism and communism and one that they argued was uniquely attuned to Iberian realities.

Third, both Franco and Salazar presided over and helped usher in a period of unprecedented economic growth in their countries, the model for which was admired and often emulated abroad. Fourth, economic development gave rise, in turn, to accelerated social change (urbanization, a growing middle class, new workers' movements) that eventually produced new political demands as well. Following the overthrow of the Salazar/Caetano regime and the death of Franco, these pent-up aspirations bloomed forth, and both Portugal and Spain underwent heartening transitions to democracy. But in both countries—and that is the fifth reason for their importance—there remained considerable admiration for the social peace and economic development that Franco and Salazar ushered in, for the model of authority and order that they provided, and for the corporative idea of an integrated, organic social order with labor, business, and government all cooperating for the common good. To the extent that these ideas and the institutions supporting them remain in place today, we will need to question how much has really changed since Franco and Salazar, how secure the democratic order is in Spain and Portugal, as well as the degree to which authoritarianism and corporatism remain as continuous features of the political systems.

EARLY ORIGINS AND COMING TO POWER

Antonio de Oliveira Salazar was the son of small-town shopkeepers in the north of Portugal. Like the area from which he came, Salazar was austere, hardworking, and very Catholic. A brilliant student, he quickly attracted the attention of the local priests who provided his early education and sent him on to the University of Coimbra. He at first studied for the priesthood, but eventually he became a university professor, a specialist in economics. Economics in Portugal in those days was very traditional, pre-Keynesian, and a branch of law.

As a young professional, Salazar was witness to the chaos and corruption of the Portuguese First Republic. As a lover of order and hierarchy, he despaired of the chaotic pluralism that was Portuguese democracy. Meanwhile, he was caught up in a variety of Catholic political movements that similarly stressed the organic, integral, corporatist unity of society. He was also influenced by Benito Mussolini's coming to power in Italy in 1922 and by certain ideas (although not totalitarianism or genocide) of the Italian Fascist creed. The question was which would dominate in the young Salazar: the softer, more pluralist, corporatism of association of the Catholic social movement, or the harder, more monolithic system of authoritarian-corporatism that Mussolini's state system represented? The answer in Salazar's case: quite a bit of both.

Salazar was at one point called to Lisbon by the republic to serve in a public capacity, but he so despised the incompetence and the political logrolling of the republic that he quickly hurried back to Coimbra. He remained active on behalf of Catholic conservative positions, and he supported the military takeover that overthrew the republic in 1926. The military regime was opposed to liberalism, as Salazar was, and got rid of the parties of the old republic. But other than a vague desire for order and discipline, the military had no real program of its own. That is precisely what Salazar and his fellow corporatists could provide.

In 1928, two years after it had taken power, the military regime called Salazar to be finance minister and to correct the sorry state of the economy after years of Republican mismanagement. Salazar worked hard, balanced the books, put the economic house back in order, and even managed to eke out a little surplus. Impressed by his performance with the economy, the military in 1932 asked Salazar to become prime minister. Salazar spent the next year consolidating his power base and then moved to restructure Portugal along corporatist lines. In a short period of time he ushered in some fundamental, even revolutionary changes. Quite a number of commentators have compared Salazar's rash of legislation in the early 1930s to the first 100 days of Roosevelt's New Deal in the United States. From this time until the end of the regime in the 1970s, it was Salazar who effectively ruled Portugal, and no longer the armed forces who had called him to power. The armed forces, of course, remained a major influence in the country and, as we shall see, the ultimate support upholding the Salazar and, later, Marcello Caetano regime. But it was Salazar who effectively governed—this was a one-man and a civilian regime, not a junta or a military dictatorship.

Francisco Franco's early career was very different from that of Salazar, but the two ran parallel at various points; and once in power the similarities in styles and systems of rule were quite remarkable.[1] Franco's career was up the military ladder; his father had also been a military officer. The Franco family came from Galicia, the province in the far northwest corner of Spain which is very much like northern Portugal. It is similarly austere, poor, and very Catholic. It clings to the traditional values of order and hierarchy and has little use for the liberalism, egalitarianism, and "advanced" ideologies of the large urban centers.

Salazar had been "discovered" by the priests and worked his way up through a university career; Franco "made it" in Spanish politics and society through the armed forces. These two, the university and the army, were among the only social escalators available, in the Spain and Portugal of those days, as avenues of upward mobility for able, ambitious members of the lower middle class. And, whereas Salazar excelled in his university studies, the similarly energetic and hardworking Franco was outstanding in his military career. He graduated first in his class from the military academy. As a young officer he earned numerous awards and commendations. He was the youngest officer ever in Spain's history to achieve the rank of general and the youngest general in Europe since Napoleon. Like Salazar, his accomplishments at an early age attracted the attention of mentors and admirers who helped guide his career and push it forward.

Thus, both Franco and Salazar came from the lower middle class. Both were very bright, able, and ambitious. Blocked because of their class origins from entry into the social, economic, and political elite, Franco and Salazar had to turn to other outlets and avenues to satisfy their energies and ambitions. One rose to power through a university career, the other through the army; but what is striking is how closely parallel their ambitions and careers ran. In the hierarchical, nonegalitarian society that was Spain and Portugal at that time, it was highly unusual for members of their social class to reach the highest pinnacles of their respective systems. They accomplished this by intelligence, discipline, persistence, ability, and hard work. Although we may not like some of their policies, the accomplishments of Franco and Salazar in transcending their origins and rising to the top of such class-conscious and highly stratified societies as Spain and Portugal were nothing short of remarkable. In fact, one could say that both ushered in a social revolution in their countries, bringing in the middle class and considerations of merit and achievement above all else, replacing the elite-dominated societies that had gone before.

As a Spanish military officer, Franco had watched with apprehension as the republic came to power in 1931. Thereafter his worst fears were confirmed as the republic gradually degenerated into chaos and bloodshed. His suspicions of civilian politicians and of divisive party politics only deepened as he witnessed the tumult and vote trading of the republic. The leftist Popular Front, the formation of the armed party militias, and the dispensing of guns to workers and peasants (thus breaking the army's historic monopoly on weapons, a matter of major institutional concern to the military who feared that the 1917 Bolshevik Revolution was about to be repeated) all added to his concerns.

Along with most of the army, Franco was stationed in Spanish North Africa when the 1936 civil war began. He was not yet then the highest-ranking general in the army, but his abilities were known and admired by his fellow officers. Franco played a major role in the war in squeezing and eventually crushing the Republican forces. Meanwhile, some of the more senior generals were killed in the conflict, died of natural causes, or retired. By the end of the civil war in 1939 Franco was not only the highest-ranking general, but his forces were overwhelmingly victorious in the conflict and he was *de facto* the effective ruler of Spain.

THE CORPORATIST REVOLUTION

In the 1920s and 1930s—the period between the two world wars and encompassing the Great Depression as well as political breakdowns in numerous European societies—corporatism was a very popular idea.[2] Corporatism was offered as a "third way," between liberalism and Marxist socialism; its popularity was enhanced as liberalism and capitalism apparently broke down in the 1930s and because to most of the Spanish and Portuguese people, Soviet-style socialism was unacceptable. A major brand of corporatism grew out of Catholic social teachings of the late-nineteenth and early-twentieth centuries, as the Church sought to formulate a positive ideology to recapture its flock in an increasingly secularized world and to replace the negativism associated with the Church's political position since the upheavals of the French Revolution. But corporatism took secular forms as well as Catholic ones. Similarly, although corporatism was most firmly established in the Latin and Mediterranean countries of southern Europe (Greece, Italy, Spain, Portugal, Austria for a time, even France and Belgium albeit partially), it was also present in various forms in the Protestant countries of northern Europe.

There are two main definitions of "corporatism"; both of them deserve our attention for purposes of this book. The first definition suggests that corporatism is an ideology (like Marxism or liberalism), a way of life, a general pattern of political cognition. Corporatism in this sense connotes the political world view of the Aristotelian-Thomistic synthesis (hierarchy, authority, discipline, an integrated and well-ordered polity), now updated and modernized to deal with the newer contingencies reflecting an industrialized and more socially differentiated world. Corporatism is based on organicist and integralist principles: It pictures society as an organic whole with all its functional parts interrelated. A corporative regime is made up of the polity's *corporative* units; that is, entities recognized in law as having juridical personality, constituted by one or more persons, and having duly prescribed rights and obligations. In Spain and Portugal the main *corporations* were the family, the community, the neighborhood association or parish, the Church, the armed forces, organized labor, the university, and so on. Typically, supreme authority in a corporatist regime is centered in a governing body, made up of representatives of these key corporations, exercising authority over labor relations, banking, and other arenas of public life. Corporative regimes of this sort have been most prevalent in Catholic, Mediterranean Europe and in Latin America.

The second definition sees corporatism as a general model of the political system with no particular cultural, religious, or regional base. Corporatism, in this sense, is a particular way of structuring state-society relations that is hierarchical, disciplined, monopolistic, and state-centered. Corporatism, in this view, is a model (like pluralism or totalitarianism) that is part of the taxonomy of political regimes. Corporatism, as defined in this way, may exist in the advanced industrial nations as well as the developing ones, in Protestant countries along with Catholic ones. Corporatism, in this sense, typically seeks to integrate labor, business, and government in a functioning, well-ordered, harmonious, and technocratic regime.

The confusion comes from the fact that Spain and Portugal embodied both of these definitions of corporatism, although in different forms and with significant changes over time.

Portugal, at least initially, was closest to the ideological, the Aristotelian-Thomistic synthesis, definition of corporatism. Salazar, a university professor, was more of a corporatist ideologue than Franco ever was; there is no doubt that Salazar really *believed* in corporatism. He believed that both liberalism and Marxism were unacceptable—the first because it produced social unraveling (witness Portugal during the 1910–26 republic, which were Salazar's formative years), the latter because of Stalin's bloody and anti-Christian excesses. He thought that corporatism represented the wave of the future. In keeping with the Catholic precepts then current, Salazar wanted to bring capital and labor together in harmony rather than having them in perpetual class conflict (the Marxist view). He wanted Portugal to be restructured in terms of its "natural" corporative units (the family, the parish, the neighborhood, and so on), rather than through institutions imported from abroad (British-style parliamentary government, U.S.-style interest group pluralism, European-style class conflict) which had proved to be not very workable in the Portuguese context.

Salazar, therefore, set out to restructure Portugal along corporative lines. Recall that he had a formula for changing Portugal—the corporative one—that the military regime, which had overthrown the republic and brought Salazar to power, lacked. The military had already abrogated the Republican constitution, abolished the political parties, and put the trade unions under wraps, so part of Salazar's task—the abolition of the liberal regime—was already accomplished. There followed a flurry of new legislation establishing the corporative system.

In 1933, a new constitution, drafted by Salazar and his brilliant young protegé Marcello Caetano, who would in 1968 succeed Salazar as prime minister, proclaimed Portugal a republican *and* a corporate state. The parliament was weakened, the executive (Salazar himself) was strengthened, and a functionally organized Council of State (with representatives from each of the major corporate units in society) was established as a high-level advisory body. The parliament itself was bicameral, with one house organized on the familiar basis of party/geographic representation and the other corporately organized with representation based on society's functional or corporate units (Church representatives, armed forces representatives, wine growers representatives, and so on).

Along with the constitution, a new labor statute was promulgated in 1933, proclaiming the corporatist philosophy of harmony in labor relations, prohibiting both worker strikes and owner lockouts, and guaranteeing labor and capital an equal voice in government and industrial relations. That same year a subsecretarial of state of corporations and social welfare was created, which was later elevated to the status of a full ministry.

Replacing the liberal and pluralist charter of associability of 1891, a host of decree laws was issued in 1933, which reorganized the national interest group system. Trade unions had to be reorganized as *sindicatos,* with the government playing a strong role in their organization, choosing their leaders, and exercising control over them. Employers' organizations were reorganized as *gremios* (guilds) of industry and *gremios* of agriculture. "Fishermens' Houses" (*Casas dos Pescadores*) were organized for Portuguese fisher folk, and community "Peoples' Houses" (*Casas do Povo*) were created for small-town persons and peasants. The capstones of this system were supposed to be the corporations—one for each industry (fishing, wineries, wheat, and so on)—in which labor and capital were again to be equally and functionally represented. But the formation of the corporations was postponed indefinitely; they were not created until the late 1950s, by which time corporatism was already discredited and the nature of the Portuguese regime had changed.

The reasons for delay in creating the corporations, the *cupulos* of the corporative system, had first to do with crises and then later with uncertainties about the future direction of the regime. The first crisis in the early-to-mid 1930s was the world economic depression and the regime's fear that extensive restructuring at this stage might just make the Portuguese economic situation worse. Next, in the mid-to-late 1930s came the civil war in next-door Spain; and since Portugal is always affected by what happens in its larger neighbor, it watched the unfolding events closely. Then came World War II—another crisis that postponed still longer the implementation of Portugal's corporatist system.

Meanwhile, some decided biases had begun to appear in the corporatist system. First, the Salazar regime was much harsher in the treatment of trade unions left over from the earlier republican and pluralist period than it was of employers. It suppressed strikes, broke up unions, and jailed their leaders. Second, the regime bought the argument presented by the country's leading and privileged economic groups that tampering with the economy in a period of depression and crisis would make matters for the national economy even worse. Hence, the regime reorganized the workers in government-controlled *sindicatos*, but it largely left bankers, business people, and commercial interests to carry on as before and did not force them into the *gremios*. Third, the restrictive laws governing interest group activity that were part of the corporatist plan and that presumably made capital and labor coequal were much more strictly enforced against workers' organizations than against employers. Finally, although there was much talk in Portugal initially of a free, open "corporatism of association," in fact right from the beginning the Salazar regime was a top-down, dictatorial "corporatism of the state." These features, plus the admiration that Salazar had for Mussolini's Italy and his hostility toward liberal democracy, led many to call the regime "Fascist."

World War II and the defeat of the Axis powers led to a general discrediting of all such corporatist experiments. And Portugal, which had made such a heavy commitment to a corporatist system of social and political organization, did not know what to do. Unlike the Axis powers, it had not been defeated in the war (Portugal stayed neutral) and its regime had not been overthrown, but its ideology and system were discredited. Salazar did not want to go toward the despised liberalism and pluralism of the United States and Britain, but he was also reluctant in these circumstances to go forward with implementing corporatism. So, for a long period in the 1940s and 1950s the regime stagnated, uncertain of its future directions, not knowing which ways to go. Meanwhile, the Portuguese economy—similarly stagnant, heavily state controlled, and without much foreign assistance—failed to keep pace with the impressive postwar economic gains beginning to be generated in the rest of Europe. The Portuguese people remained exceedingly poor, without economic opportunities or social programs; many of them began thinking with their feet during this period and left Portugal for the greener pastures of the United States and Western Europe.

The corporative system struggled on, now mainly as a system of wage, price, and political controls; but few people inside or outside of Portugal took it seriously anymore as the ideology of the future. Later on, two things happened. First the reorganized Corporations Ministry, in the absence of very many other things for it to do, was gradually converted in the 1960s and early 1970s into a social welfare ministry, administering the many social programs (health, unemployment, welfare, and so on) that Portugal belatedly began to enact. In this way the Portuguese corporative system finally found a role, but one that was not very much different—albeit far behind—from the welfare ministries of other modern nations. Second, Portuguese corporatism shifted away from the ideological form that it had taken in the early 1930s (when corporatism as an ideology did, in fact, seem likely to be the wave of the future) and moved toward a form that meant the close integration of business, labor, and the state. The regime remained authoritarian in many ways, but it did open up somewhat, and eventually its form of corporatism became not all that much different from the limited types of government-labor-capital joint partnerships (often called "corporatism") found in France, Belgium, or other countries.

Franco was never so committed to the corporatist ideology as Salazar had been. Salazar, after all, had been a seminarian, a university professor, a member of the Portuguese Christian-Democratic movement, and an ideologue. But Franco, a military person, was more practical, less doctrinaire. He undoubtedly supported many of the same elemental values as Salazar did: order, hierarchy, Catholicism, discipline, social peace. But he had not been brought up in the corporatist movement as Salazar was, and he was not as committed to it. For Franco, corporatism was a matter of expediency, not principle; a way of filling organizational space; a means of organizing national society when all other means seemed bankrupt or exhausted.

Salazar had been invited by the Portuguese military to come to power and put his ideas into practice, but Franco had come to power as the triumphant general in a bloody civil war following the unraveling of the Spanish republic. In 1939, Franco found himself rather like the Portuguese generals in 1926: triumphant in a military movement but lacking a formula for governing, other than the vague ideas of order and hierarchy. Hence, he turned to the Spanish Falangist movement, a right-wing quasiFascist group, and other advisors to provide the political model and organization that Franco himself lacked. The Falange advocated a corporatist restructuring of society, but it was much closer to the Italian form of fascism than was Salazar, whose roots were Christian-Democratic and who in the mid-1930s had snuffed out the small Portuguese Fascist movement.[3]

The Falange thus provided the corporatist political model and the intellectual arguments for it that Franco lacked. In the early years of the Franco regime, the Falange was undoubtedly influential, leading many to label the regime itself "Fascist." But Franco never gave the Falange—or any other group—too much power. Instead, he kept most of the power concentrated in his own hands. Unlike the Portuguese generals who appointed Salazar and then saw their own power wane as Salazar enhanced his, Franco kept the reins of power in his own hands. He used the Falange, and it certainly had influence; but power always was concentrated with Franco himself. Eventually, when the Falange's usefulness to Franco had declined, he shunted it aside and, with it, a good part of the corporatist system and ideology.

Under Franco, Spain had an authoritarian government that was at least partly corporatist. Unlike Portugal, it had no formal constitution, but instead it had a series of charters, laws, and statements of national principle laid down over the years and considered the fundamental laws of the nation, constitutionally binding. Spain had a chief of state (Franco), a council of ministers (cabinet), and a Cortes (parliament). The Cortes was a consultative body—not an independent legislative one—where representation was corporative by functions, including municipalities, syndicates (labor organizations), professional associations, and the Falange (later renamed the National Movement). Spain, like Portugal, also had a high-level advisory body, the Council of State, similarly organized on a corporative basis, but it performed few important functions and, like the Cortes, never developed as an independent body.

Spain had a Ministry of Syndicates, comparable to Portugal's Ministry of Corporations. Its role was to oversee the country's national Syndical Organization, which was the only officially recognized and, therefore, the only legal bargaining agent between labor and management. All employees and employers were obliged to belong to the syndicate appropriate to their field of economic activity. Thirty national syndicates were eventually created. The syndicates were corporatist agencies in that labor and management were supposedly equally represented; also, the syndicates (like Portugal's "corporations") were vertical, industrywide organizations very much unlike trade unions and craft guilds. They included in their vertical structure all steps in the productive process, from growers (in the case of the wine syndicate, for example) to harvesters, to producers, bottlers, distributors, sales outlets, and so on. Each syndicate, in turn, was divided into various subgroups, including allied associations, guilds, community organizations, and brotherhoods of varying size and importance.

Since Franco had less commitment to corporatism as an ideology than did Salazar, the authoritarian or control mechanisms of the corporative system were more pronounced in Spain right from the beginning. The corporative structure was used to control the labor movement (as well as employers, but far less tightly); to keep its leadership under state control; to fill the organizational space that otherwise would have been occupied by radical Communist, Anarchist, or Socialist unions; to prevent strikes; and to keep Spain from unraveling as had occurred in the 1930s. As in Portugal these negative and control functions took precedence over the original, more constructive, nation-building functions that the early corporatists had envisioned. Rather than serving as especially Spanish and Portuguese institutions, as a means of filling the historic void in these two nations' associational life, and as a uniquely Iberian model of development, the corporative system instead became an agency of top-down, authoritarian control, subordinate to the state or to one-man dictatorship.

Eventually the Spanish corporative system shifted functions, as had the Portuguese. Its importance was downgraded. The Ministry of Syndicates became more like the labor and social welfare ministries of other countries. It still kept close tabs on labor activity, but it also instituted new social programs in the areas of health, education, work-related injuries, unemployment, pensions, and so on. The corporatism philosophy of the 1930s was increasingly ignored except by a few die-hard ideologues. Meanwhile the system opened up somewhat, not toward the still-despised liberalism but to allow slightly greater independence to the trade unions and even a pragmatic willingness to deal with the mushrooming, often underground workers' commissions that had grown up as alternatives to the official syndicate structure.

AUTHORITARIANISM AND REPRESSION

The Spanish and Portuguese regimes of Franco and Salazar have been described with various adjectives, not all of which are very useful. They have been described as military dictatorships, but in fact Salazar was a civilian and Franco ruled not as the head of a military junta but as a one-man regime that manipulated the armed forces as well as other Spanish institutions. They have been called "clerical" or "theocratic" dictatorships; but in reality both men also manipulated the Church and never let it interfere with their own decision making. Nor is the "Fascist" label very useful: There were no genocide policies, no dreams of world conquest, no aggressive and all-encompassing ideology, and no messianic leader seeking to mobilize huge throngs (both Franco and Salazar were poor public speakers). Nor was there dominance by a Fascist party; the secret police were sometimes brutal but most often inefficient and not very technologically proficient like the German SS; and although there was in Spain and Portugal in the 1930s some admiration for the Italian and German systems, there was also ambivalence as well as differences with them, and Franco and Salazar always kept their distance and their own independent counsel.

A good start in describing the Franco and Salazar regimes is Juan Linz's distinction between authoritarianism and totalitarianism.[4] These were obviously not liberal and democratic regimes (although by the 1960s and 1970s they did become more open and somewhat more pluralist), but they were not fully totalitarian either. What, then, do we mean when we describe them as authoritarian?

Authoritarian regimes are political regimes with limited political pluralism, without elaborate and guiding ideology (but with distinctive mentalities), without intensive or extensive political mobilization, and in which a leader or a small group exercises power within formally ill-defined limits but actually quite predictable ones.

Authoritarianism, thus, does not allow unfettered pluralism as in the anarchic American interest group sense, nor does it entirely suppress all intermediary associations as under totalitarianism. Rather, it allows seven or eight main functional groups (military, church, economic elites, labor, students, farmers, bureaucrats, professionals) to operate but also watches and controls their activities. Second, in contrast to totalitarianism, authoritarianism has no all-encompassing ideology like fascism and communism, but it does have "mentalities": order, discipline, hierarchy, Catholicism. Third, unlike totalitarianism, authoritarianism seeks not to mobilize the entire population for some cause but to keep people uninvolved, apathetic, unmobilized. Fourth, authoritarian regimes are not governed by a totalitarian party as under fascism and communism, nor do they have messianic, rabble-rousing leaders. Instead, power is exercised by a leader or small group with few formally defined limits on his authority but where social, economic, and political underdevelopment imposes restraints on his exercising total power.

The corporative system, by which Franco and Salazar ruled their countries, had a particularly interesting set of controls. The corporative system may have been fashioned by regime intellectuals as an alternative, nationalistic ideology and system of coequal social justice, but it turned out, in practice, to be a method to control the trade unions and keep the masses in their place. However, the corporative system was not the only means of control. To understand Spanish and Portuguese authoritarianism better, we need to focus on these other instruments of domination.

First, there was the personal system of one-man rule. Both Franco and Salazar were strong, forceful, domineering personalities. It is sometimes said that Salazar was merely a front for the Church, that Franco was a figurehead leader and that the army or *Opus Dei* (a secretive Catholic organization) really ran Spain. But closer investigation has revealed that it was indeed Franco and Salazar who ran Spain and Portugal. It was *they* who made all the important decisions; they were not fronts for anyone. These other groups were influential to be sure, but the ultimate power really rested with Franco and Salazar.[5]

Second, under authoritarian rule, certain favored families, class groups, cliques, and individuals remained influential and exercised considerable power. Patronage was an important facilitator of government favors, contracts, and largesse. Hence, several of these *grupos* (extended families, encompassing political relations as well as the closer family kinds), who had large stakes in the economy and often held important political or governmental positions (often simultaneously), were critical centers of power in Spain and Portugal. They manned Franco's and Salazar's cabinets, gave the regime economic advice (which usually favored themselves), and served the regime in numerous ways.

A third important influence was the party. These were not totalitarian parties, but both Franco and Salazar maintained a party apparatus that they used as further instruments of control. In Spain this was the Falange or National Movement; in Portugal it was the União Nacional (National Union), later rebaptized as the Aliança Nacional Popular (National Popular Alliance). The two parties also served as patronage organizations, dispensing favors and jobs in return for loyalty and service. They served to keep the faithful in line, as brokerage agencies between the state and the citizenry, and as guardians of regime ideology—what there was of one. Because the elections that Franco and Salazar held were ratificatory devices designed to return their supporters to power, these two "parties" should not be thought of as programmatic or electoral agencies; rather, they were large machines that served the regime in various ways but were never at the real center of power or decision making.

A fourth instrument of control was the armed forces and secret police. The armed forces were the ultimate arbiters of political authority in Spain and Portugal. Both regimes depended on the goodwill of the armed forces. As a military person, Franco generally had good relations with his military; so did Salazar for the most part, though in Portugal there were some tense periods in civil-military relations and several failed coup attempts launched by dissident military factions. In both countries the armed forces jealously guarded their perquisites and specially privileged place in society, though it would be inaccurate to say that these were full-fledged military dictatorships. The armed forces had their special responsibilities and spheres of influence (peace and stability, national security, internal order, and so on), and these went considerably beyond the American sense of the proper role and functions of the armed forces. Nevertheless, it was Franco and Salazar, as strongmen, who ruled these countries, not the armed forces.

Both Spain and Portugal had secret police organizations and networks of informers. The secret police were especially active in the early years while these two regimes were consolidating their hold on power. In Portugal the police were used to harass and repress the opposition trade unions and political parties, and to jail and exile opposition politicians. In Spain, in the aftermath of the civil war, the police or *guardia* were especially brutal, and thousands of Republican loyalists were exiled or killed. But after the

1940s the secret police were less active and less brutal. They kept tabs on the population, to be sure, but the controls were often relaxed and inefficient. Most of the population went about their lives having no contact at all with the secret police. By this time both the Franco and Salazar regimes were firmly in power, and they had neither the need nor the desire—unlike Hitler—to use widespread brainwashing, terror, or torture techniques. On the other hand, if one were politically active on the side of the opposition, then one could expect to be watched, sometimes harassed, jailed, or sent into exile. The result was that few people were politically active: These authoritarian regimes ruled by apathy, not mass mobilization.

The Catholic church was another instrument, the fifth, in this panoply of controls. Both Portugal and Spain are Catholic countries, historically, and within Catholic political and religious thought there has long been a strong emphasis on order, authority, and hierarchy. Franco and Salazar used these Catholic values as means to cement their hold on power. They also worked out close, mutually supporting arrangements with the Church. But these were not "clerico-Fascist" regimes, as some have alleged, nor was the Church in control of either country. Rather, Franco and Salazar used the Church much like they used the armed forces: as mutually supporting props to their regimes. But as with the armed forces, it was Franco and Salazar who actually ruled, and not the Church.

Censorship provided a sixth instrument of control. For a long time opposition newspapers, radio broadcasts, and expressions of dissent were banned—although fliers and manifestoes often circulated clandestinely. Negative or hostile comments from abroad were similarly countered and kept from circulating. Later the two regimes began to allow some opposition newspapers to circulate, but they were often censored. They were not allowed to attack openly the armed forces or the regime, although they often did so indirectly; that is, they would talk at length about elections and democracy in France or Germany when everyone knew the real subject was the *lack* of elections and democracy in Portugal and Spain. By the 1970s the censorship was even more relaxed; it did not function very effectively, and in both countries freer expression was allowed. This is not to say that Portugal under Salazar and Spain under Franco had become models of free speech and a free press; but it is to say that if one were careful and recognized the limits beyond which a prudent person ought not to go, one could say and do a lot in both of these countries without getting into trouble. There were bounds that could not be exceeded (for example, Communist party activities and proselytizing), but within the parameters of the system, shrewd writers and editors were constantly testing the outer limits and could get away with saying and doing a great deal.

A final instrument of control was the huge state administrative structure in Spain and Portugal. Under Franco and Salazar, the size of the state structure increased significantly until the state generated upwards of 25 to 30 percent of the gross national product. This was compared with the approximately 15 percent in the *laissez-faire* United States. The power of the state, of state regulations, of state control, was everywhere. The state became the largest employer by far; it also set wages, prices, and production quotas in major industries; it owned or dominated major sectors of the economy. In this way, over the nearly 40-year histories of the Franco and Salazar regimes, Portugal and Spain became bureaucratic states, administrative states, systems of state (and distinct from individual) capitalism. The state not only closely regulated the economy, but it used that power as an instrument of political control as well. After all, it is not very likely that one will rebel against the agency or government paying one's wages, especially if there are thousands of others waiting to take one's place; and in the Spanish and Portuguese cases, the state came to employ maybe 30 percent of the gainfully employed work force.

If we put together all these various instruments of control—army, party, secret police, one-man rule, censorship, a strong state—the whole structure of authoritarianism in Spain and Portugal was considerably more powerful than the sum of its parts. The regimes of Franco and Salazar dominated most (but not all—that would make them fully totalitarian, which they were not) areas of Spanish and Portuguese national life. However, there were a lot of cracks and gray areas in these systems through which people could function and in which some limited politics and even opposition could take place. Moreover, as these regimes matured, felt less threatened, and also as Spanish and Portuguese society changed and became more pluralistic, the range of freedoms and opportunities for political activity expanded. By the late 1960s and early 1970s, the areas of political space had opened up considerably.

OPPOSITION POLITICS

The early Franco and Salazar regimes had dealt harshly with the opposition. Under Salazar and the army, the older Republican political parties had been abolished, the trade unions had been broken up and reorganized under the corporative system, and many opposition political figures had been forced into exile or into early retirement. The Franco government had been harsher still in its early years, right after the civil war, when thousands of Republicans were killed, jailed, or exiled. Whole colonies of Spanish Republicans relocated to France, England, Mexico, and other countries where they often lived for many years and even decades and where their children grew to adulthood without ever setting foot in their native country. Jobs in foreign countries were often hard to find, and the lives of those in the exile communities were frequently difficult.

Government repression was chiefly aimed at the Left: the Communists especially and the Socialists. The leadership of the Spanish and Portuguese Communist parties spent many long years in jail or in exile, chiefly in Moscow and Prague. But the repression (somewhat milder) was also directed against independent Marxists, Social-Democrats, and even Christian-Democrats, who were often branded as "Communists" even though they were not. Many of these were also forced into exile for varying periods of time, or else they stayed in their native countries, eschewed politics, and remained silent.

The bulk of the repression was employed against the Left, but the Right was not spared either. This fact is often surprising to some because they assume that, since Franco and Salazar headed generally conservative and right-wing regimes, they would be sympathetic to the Right. That is true up to a point, but recall that Franco and Salazar were also skilled politicians who liked power and wanted to stay in power. They therefore took action against threatening right-wing movements as well as against those of the Left. For example, in Portugal there was in the early 1930s a real Fascist or Integralist movement (Salazar was not himself a Fascist) headed by Rolão Preto. The Salazar regime took strong action against the Integralists, broke up the organization, and forced Preto into early political retirement. In Spain, Franco used the right-wing Falangist movement and incorporated some of its ideology, but he never allowed the real Fascists within the Falange to dominate his regime, and he eventually shunted the entire organization toward marginality. The Falange was not persecuted; it was simply shoved into obscurity.

These conditions of a repressive regime dealing harshly with its political opposition persisted through the 1940s, the 1950s, and the early 1960s. But eventually, as Salazar and Franco became more confident of their hold on power, some of the controls began to be relaxed. Meanwhile, the opposition itself became more emboldened. Some of its members came back to Spain and Portugal; and abroad, sensing that the end of the old regimes might be near, the exiled groups began to step up their activities.

At this stage we need to distinguish between five different opposition orientations. In practice, there were many more minigroups or *grupitos*. Both Spain and Portugal have old adages that say: "When two Spaniards [or Portuguese] come together, there is a political party; when they part there are two more." This analysis of opposition groups is important, because these groups formed the nuclei of the political parties and pluralism that would develop after Franco and Salazar.

The exiles may be divided into two major subgroups (and many small minigroups). The Communists were mainly in exile in the Soviet Union and Eastern Europe, although some were in Paris and other places; they would later form the main, old-line, Moscow-oriented Communist parties of Spain and Portugal after Franco died and the Salazar/Caetano regime was overthrown. The non-Communist (Socialist and Social-Democratic) opposition was concentrated in Paris and London, with some exile communities also located in Switzerland, Scandinavia, Holland, the United States, and Latin America. Some of these non-Communist oppositionists, in their old age, reconciled themselves with the regimes in power in Madrid and Lisbon and found their way back to their homelands. But many others stayed in exile until the bitter end, and then came back to Spain and Portugal in the mid-1970s to help establish the Socialist and Social-Democratic movements that subsequently emerged as major, even governing, political parties.

Within Spain and Portugal, three other broad groupings demand our attention. The first of these consisted of opposition figures *within* the ruling regimes. This may sound odd to some because we think of the Franco and Salazar regimes as authoritarian and even "Fascist," but in fact both regimes were considerably more porous and pluralistic by the late 1960s and early 1970s than their popular image sometimes suggests. By this point, *within* the regime, one often found Christian-Democrats, Liberals, Social-Democrats, even Socialists and an occasional Communist. If one were a Communist working within the regime, one naturally kept one's mouth shut. But among the non-Communist oppositionists working within the state, it was sometimes possible to influence public policy. The numerous Liberals and Social-Democrats in these regimes also tried, with some successes and some failures, to push the government in more liberal and stronger pluralist directions. These factions within the Franco and Salazar regimes also helped form the nuclei of the democratic political parties organized in the mid-1970s with the demise of authoritarianism.

A second category of oppositionists within the country formed economic and political study groups. These were often Socialists and Social-Democrats, younger than their exiled counterparts and often employed by private institutions such as book publishing and universities. Since opposition political parties were banned in Spain and Portugal, these persons organized "study groups" instead. They held semisecret meetings, wrote papers, and functioned as political party executive committees in everything except their names. They, too, formed the nuclei of the mass-based movements that would organize after Franco and Salazar.

A third category was the underground. Usually dominated by Communists and Socialists, this group was particularly strong among the trade unions. They formed clandestine "workers' commissions" in the factories and workplaces that often rivaled and challenged the official corporative *sindicatos*. Frequently these workers' commissions were persecuted by the police. But as they grew in strength, the government, wishing to keep the economy booming and hence desiring labor peace, began to deal with them on a more realistic level. They bargained with them (even though their organizations were illegal), permitted some strikes to occur (even though strikes were also illegal), and recognized them *de facto* (even though doing so represented a repudiation of their own corporative structure). This process was sporadic and irregular, but it did reflect the newer, more open climate in Spain of the late 1960s and early 1970s. These groups, too, formed the nuclei of the labor confederations and political movements of the post-Franco and post-Salazar period.

ECONOMIC AND SOCIAL MODERNIZATION UNDER AUTHORITARIAN AUSPICES

Portugal had emerged from the difficult years of World War II, and Spain from its civil war of the 1930s and then World War II, as very poor countries. Portugal had a per capita income at the end of World War II of less than $200 per year; Spain's figures were slightly higher but not by much. Both countries were mired in poverty and illiteracy. During the war years there were shortages of everything because of the German U-boat blockade of the European continent; starvation, malnutrition, and malnutrition-related diseases were prevalent. Because of their neutrality, or "nonbelligerency," in the war, the two Iberian countries were not occupied by German armies and therefore avoided the destruction suffered by Holland, Belgium, and France. Nevertheless, the economic condition of these poorer, southwest European countries was worse than these others because their base was so low. Spain and Portugal in 1945 were closer to what we now call the Third World than to the community of advanced industrial nations.

These conditions of extreme poverty in Spain and Portugal persisted during the 1940s, as Western Europe itself still lay devastated and in rubble from the war years, and on into the 1950s. Then two things happened: Spain and Portugal started to benefit from the general European recovery that began and took off during the 1950s, and both countries took major steps to reform and modernize their outmoded economies.

Portugal in the 1950s was still a largely traditional, unmechanized, agricultural, nonindustrial, inefficient economy. The south of the country was dominated by large estates and peasants whose tenancy arrangements were basically feudal; the north consisted of tiny plots of land where yeoman farmers eked out a meager existence. There was some industry in and around Lisbon, but over 80 percent of the population was rural and illiterate.

In 1953, Salazar enacted his first five-year plan to help modernize the economy; in 1958, came a second five-year plan. These plans were not particularly innovative or world-shaking, but they did open up the country to foreign capital. They gradually did away with the worst features of the earlier autarkic, or self-sufficient, economic system and provided a shot in the arm for manufacturing and industry. These steps, plus the European (and global) recovery of the 1950s, helped Portugal begin to grow economically. Per capita income had doubled by 1961, and by the time of the revolution in 1974 it had doubled again. Most Portuguese had never had it so good—economically at least—as they did in the last years of Salazar/Caetano, which is why many Portuguese look back to that era with nostalgia.

The Spanish economic takeoff was even more dramatic. Spain, of course, started from a richer base, had many more resources than Portugal, and had an internal market about five times as large. Nevertheless the government's action was also dramatic. A major turning point came in 1957. Franco got rid of a number of his older economic advisors and brought into his cabinet a group of growth-oriented technocrats, quite a number of whom were associated with the Catholic lay organization *Opus Dei*. These technocrats helped Franco end the older autarkic economic policies and introduce more rational planning. The economy was streamlined, made less bureaucratic and mercantilistic, and opened up to foreign investment.[6]

The results were spectacular. Foreign capital began to pour in. New factories shot up on the outskirts of Madrid, and eventually in other cities and provincial capitals as well. Manufacturing and industry increased dramatically. Wealth and prosperity began to grow, a more skilled labor force was trained, literacy increased, and the appearance and characteristics of being a Third World country began to subside: People ate better, looked better, dressed better, and so on. During the 1960s and on into the 1970s, economic growth was at the rate of 7, 8, or 9 percent per year. Spain's per capita income doubled in one decade—and then doubled again. The growth rates were so impressive that economists began referring to them as "the Spanish miracle." Among the world's nations in the 1960s, only Japan grew faster than Spain.

The economic growth generated in both Spain and Portugal enabled the regimes in power to expand social programs that had long lagged behind other countries. In addition to the literacy efforts, education in general was greatly expanded, new social security programs were introduced, medical care was improved, and social welfare was expanded. The new social programs were still limited, were not as advanced as those of Scandinavia or other European countries, and often benefitted some groups more than others. Still, the improvements were significant. For a time, as was indicated earlier, Spain and Portugal became models to other developing countries of how to achieve rapid economic growth and social modernization without producing political change or destabilization.

The rapid economic growth experienced by Spain and Portugal also produced vast social changes. The rate of urbanization jumped dramatically as Spaniards and Portuguese left their rural communities in favor of the jobs and opportunities available in the cities. Industry boomed, but the rural areas were left depopulated. The family structure changed as women joined the work force for the first time, which led in Madrid and Lisbon to a much-lamented (among the bourgeois families) maid shortage. The class structure also was altered fundamentally: New commercial and industrial elites grew up alongside the older landed elites, the middle class grew in size and became the dominant class, the trade unions or *sindicatos* saw a large increase in their membership, a *lumpen* proletariat grew up in the cities, and rural peasants and farmers were often uprooted and sometimes politically mobilized. The cumulative effect of all these changes added up to a major class transformation in both Spain and Portugal.

Eventually these enormous economic and social changes would produce political transformations as well. That is, Spaniards and Portuguese would come to seek political changes toward greater freedom and democracy to go along with the vast changes (and greater freedoms) in the social and economic spheres. But during the 1960s the political changes were still held in check. Impressive economic growth had occurred and vast social changes were underway, and yet the Franco and Salazar regimes seemed as firmly entrenched in power as ever. That is what had made them so attractive to other authoritarians, who also wanted socioeconomic growth but not the liberalizing political concomitants that usually accompany such changes. However, although Spain and Portugal seemed calm on the surface and their long-standing authoritarian regimes solidly in control, tensions beneath the surface were already building that would produce quite dramatic changes in the 1970s and on to the present.

STRESSES AND TENSIONS WITHIN "THE SYSTEM"

By the late 1960s and early 1970s, cracks were beginning to appear in the Spanish and Portuguese regimes. Strains were building up, tensions were increasing, conflict lay just below the surface. These tensions were generational, cultural, psychological, social, and political. Eventually they would result in the undermining of the Franco and Salazar regimes. One could even say that the political openings and transitions to democracy in both countries began while their old dictators were still alive.

There were *two* generational strains in both regimes. Franco and Salazar, as well as the people they had around them in their governments, were both old—in their seventies—and increasingly infirm and out of touch. The first generational split, therefore, was between these older leaders (commonly referred to as dinosaurs) and a younger, middle-aged generation of persons in their forties who were far less ideological, who hardly remembered the civil war and intense conflicts of the 1920s and 1930s, who were trained as technocrats and administrators, who wanted to get on with developing and modernizing their countries, and—most important—who wanted to inherit all those cabinet and executive positions still held by the elders.

A second generational split came with young people. They didn't remember the ideological quarrels of the past *at all,* nor did they care. They wanted Coca Cola, rock music, blue jeans, and freedom. They were attuned to European styles and wanted to live like other European or American young people. Often nonpolitical, this generation wanted little to do with the partisan squabbles of their parents and grandparents. They wanted to be free to do "their thing," which often ran contrary to traditional Iberian mores.

Culturally, vast changes were also underway—as already hinted at in the previous paragraph. Through movies, television, and travel, what Lucian Pye once called the "world culture"—freedom, Coke, and so on—began to have its impact on Spain and Portugal. Long isolated from the cultural, social, and political mainstream of Europe, Spain and Portugal now began to be more influenced by outside forces. The freedom that Europeans enjoyed, their lifestyles, their social behavior, the more independent role of women, the greater independence of young people—all these began to have an impact on Iberia. Because of the censorship, for example, many modern movies could not be shown in Spain; but travel agencies in Madrid organized tours for thousands of Spaniards every weekend to take buses across the border to Perpignon in France to watch the latest movies to their hearts' content. Spain also became in the 1960s a major tourist center, attracting millions of visitors each year, and the sight of all those Scandinavians, Germans, and others cavorting nudely and seminudely on its beaches also had a major influence. These are just two of the many ways in which the culture and mores of Spain and Portugal began to change.

For decades Spain and Portugal had prided themselves on being "different" from the rest of Europe. But increasingly the Spanish and Portuguese no longer wished to be different; they wanted to be just like the rest of Europe. For a time this desire to be like their European neighbors was confined to social and cultural spheres, but eventually it became political as well. Being like the rest of Europe in that sense meant being democratic, and eventually that desire would lead to a supplanting of the Franco and Salazar regimes and the establishment of democracy.

Socially, vast changes were also underway. With the industrialization of Spain, new economic elites were clamoring for more efficient governmental decision making and a takeover of the positions long monopolized by the *francistas*. In both countries a large middle class had grown up that no longer fit the old "sleepy," rural, conservative, two-class (elite and peasant) image, and that began to demand political power commensurate with its rising economic and social influence. This new middle class, younger than the persons serving in the Franco and Salazar governments, also desired European political freedoms and democracies, and no longer wanted to have to explain to foreign visitors or their counterparts abroad why they were "different." Urbanization and the rise of a sizable industrial working class also changed the face of Spain and Portugal, leading to vast new working class neighborhoods, increased unionization, real class conflict, and increased impatience to change the system.

The political changes underway, as already implied in earlier comments, were also significant. On the negative side, the Franco and Salazar regimes were increasingly seen as not just old but old-fashioned, out of touch, sclerotic. Their leaders were viewed as doddering, enfeebled old men. Often their lieutenants ruled as if the leaders were already no longer there—as indeed they sometimes were not! In other words, the cultural, social, and now political changes that would lead to democracy had begun even while these two *ancianos* ("ancients") were still alive.

In both regimes the political structures of the past were being bypassed or supplanted. The corporative structures introduced in the 1930s and 1940s were increasingly ignored, or used for such other purposes as the administration of social welfare. Other than some old corporatist ideologues, almost no one whom the author interviewed in Spain and Portugal in the early 1970s could define "corporatism," what it was supposed to do, or why it was introduced in the first place. The censorship still operated, but it was often ignored or unenforced; the secret police were still present, but they were more a nuisance than a real danger. Strikes were still illegal, but "work stoppages" were often carried out that amounted to the same thing, and the government was obliged often to bargain with the unions. In short, all the institutions of the past were still in place, but increasingly either they were not working, not enforced, or they were bypassed by the groups they were designed to control.

Franco was sick and by the mid-1970s was in his eighties. Power was already passing to others who ran the country on a day-to-day basis, although Franco still exercised general oversight. Franco laid plans to perpetuate his regime beyond his passing, but those were dashed when his faithful ally and political heir, Admiral Luis Carrero Blanco, was blown sky-high by a Basque terrorist bomb. Franco also had a plan to restore the Spanish monarchy and to continue his kind of rule that way; but as we see in the next chapter, the monarch he selected, Juan Carlos, surprised everyone, especially the die-hard Franco supporters, by ushering in democracy rather than perpetuating authoritarianism.

In Portugal there were also some special conditions. Salazar was incapacitated in 1968 when his deck chair collapsed and he hit his head; he was succeeded by his former student and longtime ally Marcello Caetano. Caetano wanted to liberalize the regime, but he was hemmed in by the old guard who wanted to retain strict authoritarianism. In addition, Caetano was indecisive, not a strong leader, and he waffled on major policy decisions. First he gave the trade unions more freedom, and then he clamped down again; he brought some liberals into his cabinet, but then he dismissed them; he began reforms but always left them incomplete. Caetano's indecisiveness gave rise to many jokes in Portugal; among them: "You can always tell Caetano's car in traffic because it signals left but turns right."

The other major, distinctive factor in Portugal was its African wars. Since the early 1960s Portugal had been fighting, at the same time, three debilitating, costly wars in Africa in an effort to hang on to its colonial empire. The wars dragged on for years in Angola, Mozambique, and Guinea-Bissau. They sapped Portuguese manpower as well as its already thin economic resources. The wars became exceedingly unpopular in Portugal, just as the long Vietnam war did in the United States, and eventually their unpopularity was transferred to the government. Even the Portuguese armed forces divided over the war, and when those discontents were also transferred into the political arena, the regime quickly collapsed in the spring of 1974.

NOTES

1. The better biographies include J. Fusi, *Franco: A Biography* (New York: Harper & Row, 1988); Stanley Payne, *The Franco Regime, 1936–75* (Madison, Wis.: University of Wisconsin Press, 1988); Hugh Kay, *Salazar and Modern Portugal* (London: Eyrie and Spottiswoode, 1970).
2. See Howard J. Wiarda, *Corporatism and Development: The Portuguese Experience* (Amherst, Mass.: University of Massachusetts Press, 1977).
3. João Medina, *Salazar e os Fascistas* (Lisbon: Livraría Bertrand, 1978).
4. Juan Linz, "An Authoritarian Regime: Spain," in Erik Allardt and Yrjö Littunen (eds.), *Cleavages, Ideologies, and Party Systems* (Helsinki: The Westermarck Society, 1964).
5. Kenneth Medhurst, *Government in Spain* (Oxford: Pegamon Press, 1973); Richard Gunther, *Public Policy in a No-Party State* (Berkeley, Calif.: University of California Press, 1980).
6. The changes are well described in Charles W. Anderson, *The Political Economy of Modern Spain: Policy-Making in an Authoritarian System* (Madison, Wis.: University of Wisconsin Press, 1970).

Chapter
4

The Transitions to Democracy

The Franco and Salazar/Caetano regimes were so long-lived that many analysts had come to think of them as forever. Indeed, a whole body of literature had sprung up focused on the presumed permanence of the authoritarianism and corporatism of the two Iberian nations.[1] Not only theorists but also political elites and practitioners from all over the world had journeyed to Iberia to see how Franco and Salazar had done it—that is, how they had achieved socioeconomic modernization for their nations without, seemingly, giving rise to the "dreaded" liberalism and pluralism.

But in the mid-1970s, both of these longtime regimes collapsed. It was not just that Franco and Salazar died after a period in office averaging for the two nearly 40 years, but that their whole *systems* and *regimes* collapsed as well. Actually, as we saw in the previous chapter, socially and culturally the postauthoritarian transition in these two countries had really begun while Franco and Salazar were still alive. But in the mid-1970s, with the death of Franco and the overthrow of the Portuguese regime, that process was greatly accelerated.

Thereafter, both countries—not without considerable uncertainty and trauma—embarked on a quite remarkable transition to democracy. This transition fundamentally altered the political landscape of Iberia, and we shall, naturally, be concerned with assessing and analyzing just how deep and permanent these changes will be. But the importance of the Spanish and Portuguese transitions to democracy went beyond those two countries. Along with the transition to democracy in Greece, which was occurring during the same time period, the transitions in Spain and Portugal served as models and inspirations for a whole wave of democratic openings that began in the late 1970s in Latin America, then continued in East Asia, in Eastern Europe, and maybe even in the Soviet Union. Although viewed earlier as models of authoritarianism, Spain and Portugal are now seen as models of democratization. Hence, whether Spain and Portugal succeed in their quest for democracy will be important most obviously to those two countries, but the issue also carries global implications.

THE PORTUGUESE "REVOLUTION OF FLOWERS"

The Portuguese revolution began about 19 months before the death of Franco. We, therefore, will look at the Portuguese transition to democracy first.

Portugal in the early 1970s was facing some difficult problems. Salazar had died, but Salazar's authoritarian system lived on under the leadership of Marcello Caetano. Caetano had liberalized the regime somewhat, provided some greater freedoms; but the pace of change was too slow for many Portuguese who were impatient with the old system and wanted to move forward: toward Europe and toward freedom.[2] The economy had been performing quite well, but the growth was uneven and there were periods of slumps. The sharp rise in oil prices in 1973 hurt Portugal badly because it must import *all* of its petroleum. There were many other social, economic, and political tensions. The regime might have survived these problems, however, if it were not for the African wars.

The wars on three fronts in Africa—Angola, Mozambique, Guinea-Bissau—had now been going on for over a decade—longer than the Vietnam conflict for the United States.[3] Moreover Portugal was a small and still a poor country. Yet, it was fighting wars in three countries at once that it could not afford; the wars were draining upwards of 50 percent of the national budget. In the early years of the rebellions, the Portuguese forces had done well, isolating the African guerrillas, keeping the conflict from spreading, and retaining control of the most important parts of their African territories. But later the guerrillas got better training, chiefly from the Soviet Union, as well as sophisticated weapons such as surface-to-air missiles (SAMS), which enabled them to shoot down Portuguese aircraft. During the early 1970s the body bags containing slain young Portuguese soldiers began arriving back in Lisbon on an everyday basis. Portugal is an intimate and close-knit society in which seemingly everyone knows everyone else or is interrelated; those body bags coming home day after day and year after year were devastating to the Portuguese and fueled the fires of popular discontent.

Prime Minister Caetano had a plan to grant greater autonomy to the African colonies and thus to end the wars there, but his being tapped as Salazar's successor had been conditional upon his continuing the struggle and hanging onto the African territories. In a series of interviews with this author,[4] Caetano said he wanted to get out of Africa, but that if he moved too quickly the hard-line Salazar loyalists would have him ousted by the next day. The actual situation was that during certain periods Caetano *did* have enough power to move against the old *Salazaristas* and also to reach a resolution of the African conflicts, but he temporized and failed to use these opportunities.

The war was felt heaviest within the Portuguese military, for it did the brunt of the fighting and dying. One of the myths generated by the Portuguese revolution, perpetrated by those young officers who staged it and found in many academic analyses, is that they had learned to admire the African guerrillas, admired their socialism, and wished to establish that same socialism in continental Portugal. That is an Alice in Wonderland view; the authors of this interpretation must have eaten several of Alice's cupcakes. Actually, the young officers despised the African guerrillas, shared the then-common racial stereotypes about Africans, disliked having their lives and careers disrupted for long periods by several stints in Africa, and above all did not want to be maimed or killed in Africa and shipped back in one of those body bags. There were several occasions in 1972–73 when the troops on the docks in Lisbon, ready to sail to Africa, refused to go. Adding fuel to these fires were the resentments kindled by the fact that the government, desperate for officers, was giving commissions to young university graduates who had only a hasty training course that gave them rank equal to that of the military school graduates who had put in *years* of training. These are all personal, professional, and institutional considerations; the interviews by this author and others conducted from 1972 to 1975 with Portuguese military officers found *none* of the "idealistic" and ideological motivations later emphasized by some other authors.[5] We conclude the idealistic and ideological motivations ("imitating the socialism of the African guerrillas") were myths, post hoc rationalizations offered by the Portuguese armed forces to rationalize and justify actions carried out for baser purposes (saving their personal and professional skins)—myths that were then used to romanticize the Portuguese revolution and perpetrated by journalists and scholars who should have known better or been more skeptical.

By 1973-74 there were several plans, plots, and conspiracies within the armed forces. These military maneuverings overlapped with the activities of various civilian groups, who also wanted change. The Portuguese revolution was not just a military movement, therefore; it involved complex interrelations between various military factions and their counterpart civilian groups. Some of the plots revolved around senior military officials—such as General António de Spínola, a colorful commander who saw himself as a possible successor to Prime Minister Caetano. The publication of Spínola's book in early 1974, *Portugal e o Futuro* (*Portugal and the Future*),[6] in which he offered a way to pull out of Africa in direct contradiction to official government policy, set off a wave of discussions, plots, and counterplots. Other senior officers, and their civilian colleagues, were similarly jockeying for position. Meanwhile the junior officers were also plotting, not only against the government but also often against their senior officers, whose positions they wished to inherit. The government learned about one small conspiracy launched in early 1974 and was able to put it down, but the larger discontents remained, and they soon blossomed full-blown to the surface.

The movement to overthrow the Caetano regime began on the morning of April 24, 1974, with the playing of the song "Grandola" over the radio.[7] That song was a signal to all the conspirators that the coup was on. The old regime fell quickly—which was surprising given our image of it as tough and authoritarian. Within two days the secret police, the official party, the corporative system, the censorship—all the controls—were in disarray or abolished. Caetano and other high officials were exiled. These changes occurred peacefully; the liberated and enthusiastic crowds put flowers in the barrels of the soldiers' guns, hence the designation "Revolution of Flowers." Spínola led the revolution in its first days, but soon he was replaced as well.

Several things happened concurrently. First, the senior leadership of the revolution—such as Spínola, who came to function more as a figurehead than as a real power figure—was replaced by more junior persons within the armed forces. The main group was the Armed Forces Movement (MFA), made up chiefly of junior officers, who wanted and soon discovered that they liked power, that they also desired the high-level positions held by the senior officers, and further that they liked the attention and glory they were receiving at home and abroad for overthrowing the old "Fascist" regime.

Second, the revolution spread to the streets. The Portuguese revolution had begun at the top levels of military and civilian life: a change among the leadership, a rotation of elites (familiar in Portuguese history); but it also unleashed a host of popular frustrations and discontents and soon spread to the lower levels of society. Employees rebelled against employers, government workers against office managers, clerical staff against directors, students against teachers, communicants against the Church, peasants against landowners, faculty against administrators, children against parents, hospital maintenance staffs against doctors, and so on. All the old ties and hierarchies of rank, place, and position kept intact in Portugal for so long were challenged and undermined. In short, what had begun as a fairly simple *coup d'état* launched by the army now became a genuinely popular revolution that spilled over into the streets—which the younger officers in the MFA now sought to guide and direct. Portugal, in other words, experienced two revolutions in 1974–75: one a not untypical barracks revolt with limited goals, with its usual personal and political rivalries and complications, and the other a genuine grass roots revolution at lower levels that showed signs of getting completely out of hand.

A third activity under way was the attempt by various parties and political movements to capture this revolution. A host of left-wing activists—Trotskyites, Maoists, Marxists, Communists—descended on Portugal from Europe and the United States. The Portuguese Socialist and Communist parties, now returning from exile and allowed to function above ground, as well as numerous smaller groups, tried to infiltrate and influence the MFA, to capture the heretofore largely spontaneous street movements, and to control or seize political power.

The movements, demonstrations, and battles among competing groups raged all through the spring and summer of 1974. The MFA was trying to run the country, but it lacked the skills and experience to do so. The question was: Who controlled or would dominate the MFA? It was surely the Left, but did that mean Socialists, Communists, or independent Marxists? No one knew for sure, but there was a lot of political activity, maneuvering for power, and efforts at power grabs. The economy, meanwhile, was thrown into chaos, living standards began to decline, and the impressive economic growth of the previous years was reduced. The Portuguese now moved to grant independence to their African colonies, but that also resulted in the return of several hundred thousand Portuguese from the territories, adding immeasurably to the unemployment problem. At the same time a fourth element was added to the simmering Portuguese brew: the involvement in these tumultuous events of a variety of foreign actors—the U.S. embassy, the CIA, the German Social Democratic and Christian Democratic parties, the British Labor party, the Dutch, the Scandinavians, and others. The Portuguese revolution was no longer just a domestic concern; it became an international issue as well.

Portugal continued to lurch along for at least another year. In the fall of 1974, the country seemed to be inexorably moving to the Left, and there were dark rumors of Communist power grabs and antidemocratic movements. Then in March 1975, General Spínola tried to rally what he called his "silent majority" and attempted to stage a counter-coup to return Portugal to a centrist position; but that effort was frustrated by the MFA and the Communist party. In April 1975, on the first anniversary of the revolution, elections were held that were won by the Socialists; but the MFA and the far Left said that they might not respect the results of the election and took steps to consolidate their own rule and to nullify the poll results. Then in November 1975, the Communist party and its allies attempted their own power grab, seeking to gain full control of what to this point had been a still diverse, often confused, and chaotic revolution. But this effort was also put down by more moderate elements within the MFA.

After this last radical gasp, the Portuguese revolution began to settle down. The Communist party had sought to grab power and was humiliated and embarrassed in public. The MFA, while still playing a leading role, began a gradual retreat to the barracks. Within its ranks the moderates took power from the radicals. People went back to work after the heady street demonstrations of the past year and a half. The Socialist party—which in those days represented the Center of the Portuguese political spectrum—formed a government in 1976 under its longtime leader Mario Soares and was actually able to govern more or less effectively, even though it still had to bargain almost constantly with the MFA, the other parties, and the foreign influences in order to get things done. Gradually the country calmed down and the economy began returning to normal. Democracy was finally established in Portugal after it had been powerfully challenged by both the Right and the far Left.

Portugal is, after all, not that radical a country; it is, in fact, quite conservative in many respects. And the history after 1976 was that of a gradual movement back to the Center and away from the extremes. The Socialist party governed from 1976 to 1978. However, the Socialists gradually lost popular support, and from the summer of 1978 until January 1980, a series of three, short-lived, nonpolitical governments were in power. By this time conservative sentiment was already reasserting itself, and Portugal began to swing back toward the Center.

The main beneficiary of this centrist swing was the Social Democratic party (PSD) under the flamboyant and charismatic Francisco Sá Carneiro. Sá Carneiro organized a coalition with other center and rightist groups, including Christian Democrats and Monarchists, and called it the *Alianza Democrática* (Democratic Alliance—AD). In elections held in late 1979, AD garnered 45 percent of the vote; Sá Carneiro was inaugurated as prime minister in January 1980. But the AD's hopes of winning an absolute majority in the next elections were dashed when Sá Carneiro was killed in a plane crash in December 1980. He was succeeded as prime minister by newspaper editor Francisco Pinto Balsemão who ruled until his government collapsed in December 1982.

The mid-1980s were again chaotic for Portugal, but not so chaotic as the mid-1970s. Balsemão had lost popularity and was not an effective leader or administrator; he lost the confidence of the president, Ramalho Eanes, and was asked to step aside. For a short time Socialist Mario Soares came back as prime minister in an unstable coalition arrangement that included the PSD, but many observers thought that Eanes now wanted the position. He backed away from the prime ministership, however, and in 1985 the PSD returned to power albeit once again in a minority, coalition government.

New elections were scheduled for 1987. The winner once more was the Social Democratic party, now headed by Aníbal Cavaco Silva. An engineer and a technocrat whose austere demeanor and policies reminded many Portuguese of Salazar, Cavaco Silva's party this time, without any alliance partners and without the necessity of a coalition, won an absolute majority—the first time any party had done so since the overthrow of the old regime. Finally, political stability seemed to be returning to the country.

The Social Democrats governed democratically and with full respect for civil liberties. But they also began to repeal some of the radical legislation of the mid-1970s, to open up the economy, and to restore some of the publicly owned enterprises to the private sector. Because of these policies, as well as help from the European Economic Community (EEC, which Portugal joined in 1986) and major investments from the United States, Portugal began to boom. The economy took off, the *retornados* (those who returned from Africa) found jobs, and unemployment was greatly reduced. New wealth was generated—some of it even trickled down—vast construction projects were under way, and the middle class began to grow. With these successes, the PSD won again in 1991 with another absolute majority.

The question we must ask is whether all these changes have been sufficient to overcome Portugal's historic divisions and whether democracy has now been fully consolidated in the country.

THE SPANISH TRANSITION

The Spanish transition to democracy was far calmer, less frenetic, and more institutionalized than the Portuguese.[8] It was evolutionary rather than revolutionary. It ushered in a *reforma* (reform) as contrasted with the Portuguese *ruptura* (rupture). But the Spanish transition was no less significant for taking this gradual route.

In fact, the course of the Portuguese revolution, occurring a year and a half before Franco's death, was *very* closely followed in next-door Spain and had a strong effect there. To the extent the Portuguese revolution was peaceful and achieved democracy, the Spanish admired it and thought of it as something their own country should do. But to the extent the Portuguese revolution produced disorder, chaos, and economic breakdown (frequently the case), or opened the door to a Communist *putsch*, the Spanish shied away from its example. In short, depending on the circumstances, the Portuguese example could and did have both positive and negative ramifications in Spain.

Although we often treat the Spanish and Portuguese openings to democracy in tandem because they occurred around the same time, the differences between these two countries' transitions are as striking as their similarities. Here are some of the major differences:

1. Although Caetano in Portugal was effectively head of the government at the time of the revolution in Portugal and fighting to hang onto power, Franco in Spain was already by the early 1970s, quasi "in retirement." Hence, the Portuguese change was abrupt and precipitous while the Spanish one could occur gradually.
2. The Spanish economy, with a per capita output *twice* that of Portugal, provided a more solid and more comfortable base for the transition to democracy.
3. Similarly, Spanish society was more literate, more urban, more middle class, more sophisticated, already more European-minded. Sociologically, Spain had in fact begun its transition to democracy even while Franco was still alive. To a far greater extent than Portugal, Spain's values were European values (including democracy) even though the Franco era had not yet ended.
4. Spain had before it the example of the 1930s civil war; the bloody, wrenching, fratricidal nature of the conflict made Spaniards determined not to repeat that upheaval again. Portugal had no such experience.
5. Spain had a monarch who provided crucial stability and continuity in the transition; Portugal had no such institution.
6. The Portuguese revolution was initiated and led by the armed forces (principally the MFA); in Spain the transition was led by civilians, and the military remained largely nonpolitical.
7. The Portuguese revolution was a polarizing movement in which the center was ground down and almost disappeared for a time; in Spain it was the political center that guided the transition and never lost control of it to the extremes.

8. The Portuguese revolution was highly conflictual, whereas in Spain "social pacts" negotiated between labor, employers, and the state served to reduce greatly the potential for conflict and violence.

These are the major differences between the Portuguese and Spanish transitions to democracy. Now let us flesh out the story by telling it in narrative form.

Franco had ruled Spain since 1939, even earlier if one counts his role as General of the Nationalist Forces during the civil war. But by the early 1970s he was in his eighties, infirm, and afflicted with numerous medical problems. Hence, Franco had progressively turned over more and more responsibilities to his subordinates and to a prime minister, who ran the country on an everyday basis. Franco still had ultimate control and it was he who made the big decisions affecting the future of the nation. But routine matters were now increasingly handled at lower levels. The post-Franco transition, in short, had begun even while Franco was still alive.

During this same period Spain had become increasingly oriented toward Europe. Its trade, commerce, and tourism were now chiefly with the European Economic community. So, increasingly, were its social mores, thinking (including political ideas), and culture. Because of the association in the European mind of Franco with fascism, Spain could not yet formally be a part of the European community, but in all other ways Spain was becoming a European country. It wanted to think like Europe, to be considered a part of Europe, to behave like Europe, and to be integrated into Europe—politically and psychologically as well as economically. The Franco regime continued to emphasize Spain's uniqueness, its distinctiveness from Europe; but fewer and fewer Spaniards thought that way anymore. Although the process was still incomplete, Spain was a part of Europe long before the formal ratifications of the accords making it an EEC member. Franco was the main anachronism standing in the way; Spanish culture and society were already well on their way to being European.

A personal anecdote may be illustrative of these themes. When this author first did research work in Spain in the early 1970s, he had just come from several years of research and writing on Latin America. He had recently published an article suggesting that Spain, Portugal, and Latin America be treated politically and sociologically as part of a common, distinct, Iberic-Latin culture area, with numerous similar features.[9] That article provoked a storm of controversy in Spain, not all of it intellectual. In fact, Spain did not want to be grouped together with Latin America, which it thought of as part of the Third World. Spain no longer wanted to think of itself as "distinctive" or "unique"—that was considered part of Franco's propaganda. Instead, Spain preferred already at that time to be thought of as "European," not "Latin American." The author's article was controversial not just on scholarly grounds but because it rode heavily over these sensitive political, cultural, nationalistic, and psychological issues.

Franco, however, had begun to take steps to continue and institutionalize his rule. His goal was to provide for a smooth transition with continuity—such as what Portugal experienced in 1968 when Caetano took over from Salazar and the *system* continued, not a sharp break which Portugal had in 1974. Franco, therefore, established the position of prime minister, while he himself continued as head of state and *de facto* head of government. He installed his friend Admiral Luís Carrero Blanco in the office. After Carrero was assassinated by Basque terrorists, the position was filled by Carlos Arías Navarro. But Arías did not have Franco's confidence in the same way that Carrero did, nor had he as strong and dominating a personality. Yet Arías would be the person who would help preside over the post-Franco transition.

The other main institutional innovation was the restoration of the monarchy. Recall that the monarchy of Alfonso XIII in Spain had been abolished in 1931 upon the establishment of the republic. Later, after the civil war, Franco had talked about restoring the monarchy, but for a long time he had not actually gotten around to doing so. Franco had not wanted to share power with a monarch; in addition, the main claimant to the throne, Alfonso's son Don Juan, was a liberal who had lived abroad for many years and was critical of the Franco system. So instead Franco turned to Don Juan's young son, Juan Carlos, brought him back to Spain, gave him a solid military education, trained him in Franco's own values, and eventually restored the monarchy. A lot of jokes circulated in Spain at this time about Juan Carlos's alleged thickheadedness, and because everyone expected his rule would be short, they believed he would be known as *Juan el breve* ("Juan the Brief"). But, as it turned out, Juan Carlos surprised a lot of people with his acumen, steely determination, and sound political judgment.

Franco died in November 1975 of the accumulated medical problems with which he was afflicted. The two basic political institutions in the country were now the prime minister, Carlos Arías Navarro, and the young monarch Juan Carlos. The two did not see eye to eye. Arías was a Francoist whose idea of reform was to proceed *very* slowly. He was like Caetano in Portugal, who wanted to reform the Salazar system but not very much. The king wanted to go faster. A month after Franco died Arías and Juan Carlos agreed on a limited amnesty for certain political prisoners, but the king had wanted a broader amnesty. In the first several months they disagreed on a variety of other issues affecting the pace of change. Spanish public opinion now clearly wanted to move toward greater pluralism and democracy; the question was whether this would be by a gradual *reforma*, which the king favored, or by a precipitous *ruptura*, which would result in a Portugal-like upheaval. The king was known to feel that by proceeding too slowly the prime minister was inadvertently strengthening the arguments of the radicals who favored *ruptura*.

In the summer of 1976, eight months after Franco's death, the king moved to replace Arías as prime minister. He appointed Adolfo Suárez, a young and handsome man, but a political unknown. Suárez, as an official of the only authorized political party The Movement, had grown up in the Franco system and accommodated himself to it; he had never been in opposition, let alone in exile. Nevertheless, he was known to favor pluralism, liberalization, and democratization. He was also a generation and a half younger than Arías and symbolized the new generations and the new thinking in Spain, which were definitely non-Francoist. In addition, he was a friend of the king and had worked closely with him.

Now the pace of change accelerated. At this stage the main issues were no longer maintaining fealty to the Right (the Francoists), who had very little popular support and had already lost control of some of the country's main institutions; it was opening up to the Center and the Left. Suárez and the king proceeded to engineer a political opening that was far broader than the one initiated earlier. The young prime minister began holding meetings with the even younger head of the Socialist Workers party, Felipe González, who would soon come to fill the prime minister's own chair. These meetings paved the way in early 1977 for the legalization of opposition political parties that had been forbidden under Franco. A few weeks later even the Communist party was legalized, a step that provided some considerable consternation among the old guard. At the same time the government dealt adroitly with the economy and with the desires for regional autonomy.

Meanwhile, the Suárez government and the king had pushed through the Political Reform Act of 1976. It provided for the holding of elections for a new bicameral Cortes, or parliament, which would also have the authority to write a new constitution. The Cortes would have a Chamber of Deputies of 350 members elected by proportional representation and a Senate of 270 members elected by plurality. In an adept political move, Suárez and the king got the old Cortes to approve the Political Reform Act even though it meant the end of the old Cortes's existence. This maneuver established the legal basis for the country's new democratic institutions and furnished them with sorely needed legitimacy.

Elections were scheduled for June 1977. Three major groups contested the elections. The Right (the old *Franquistas*) came together as the *Alianza Popular* (Popular Alliance) headed by Manuel Fraga, who had been considered a liberal in an earlier Franco cabinet. The Center was brought together under the banner of the *Unión del Centro Democrática* (Union of the Democratic Center, or UCD) headed by Suárez, a loose coalition of a dozen political factions and bureaucratic interests. The main force on the Left was Felipe González and the *Partido Socialista Obrero Española* (PSOE—Spanish Socialist Workers party). The *Partido Communista Española* (PCE—Spanish Communist party) headed by Santiago Carillo also contested the election. Suárez and the UCD won the largest plurality with 34 percent of the vote, but augmented by the d'Hondt system of representation, which favors large parties at the expense of smaller ones, the number of UCD seats in the Cortes was 47 percent—enough to form a governing bloc.

More important legislation followed. A constitutional committee of the Cortes drafted a new, democratic constitution in 1977–78 that was overwhelmingly approved (over 90 percent) by Spanish voters in a referendum of December 1978.[10] Suárez also called the leaders of all the political parties to his residence, where they hammered out an accord (the Moncloa Pact) providing for an economic stabilization program to be accompanied by increased social programs. Neither Left nor Right, neither business nor labor, was entirely happy with all aspects of the pact; but they were in remarkable agreement that the economy had to be managed successfully if democracy was to survive, and that served as the basis of the accord. The Suárez government had also enacted major legislation dealing with labor's organization and rights, and had entered into negotiations to arrive at autonomy agreements with the more independent-minded regions, such as Catalonia and the Basque provinces. These impressive accomplishments were later reflected in the March 1979 parliamentary elections, when the UCD and Suárez slightly increased their percentage of votes and seats, and then again in April 1980, when the UCD candidates won twice as many municipal positions as those of any other party.

Despite the impressive policy accomplishments of Suárez and the solid electoral approval for his party, trouble was beginning to mount for the young prime minister. The effectiveness of his leadership was increasingly questioned because of the continuing problem of Basque terrorism, the poor performance of the economy in the late 1970s (when the second "oil shock" hit), the political differences over educational and religious issues, and the increase in crime and immorality. In addition, with the basic accomplishments of the democratization carried out successfully, there was no longer such a strong sense of the need for national unity as there had been earlier, and the political debate now turned more partisan and rancorous. Finally, the UCD was a coalition that electorally had done well so far, but now it began to split up into quarreling factions that often criticized Suárez and would no longer take direction from him.

Apparently fed up with the carping and wishing to build his own political base without such fractious disputations, Suárez resigned abruptly in January 1981. He was succeeded as prime minister and head of the party by Leopoldo Calvo-Sotelo. But the economy continued to slide downhill and Basque terrorism remained unabated. These events provided ammunition to a number of reactionary military officers who became disillusioned with the course Spanish democracy was taking. They plotted several coup attempts, the most serious of which occurred in February 1981, when a handful of soldiers invaded and shot up the Cortes and appealed to other military forces to join them in revolt. But the king, in a long night on the telephone, rallied his military commanders (many personal friends from his military school days) and urged them to remain loyal. Later, he put on his military uniform, went on national television, made it clear that *he* was the commander-in-chief and that he supported democracy, and appealed for national calm. The coup attempt galvanized wide sections of the population into demonstrating for democracy and the constitution; the rest of the officer corps stayed loyal, and the coup failed.

Calvo-Sotelo proved to be an unpopular and ineffective prime minister. In addition, González's Socialist party (PSOE) had been increasing in strength in recent elections and in the polls. Some Spaniards were convinced their democracy could not be thought of as consolidated until the opposition had actually won and a peaceful transfer of power had taken place. On the Left sentiment was also increasing that while Spain had successfully achieved political democracy, now it was time to take the next step to economic democracy. Only the Socialist party could achieve that, they said. There was an air of Marxist determinism about these arguments that some Spaniards found disturbing, especially if the process had to work the other way. That is, if the Socialists did come to power, would they then be willing to give up power if they were subsequently defeated in an election, or would that same "historical inevitability" previously described imply that they would have to stay in power *regardless* of the popular vote?

Actually the PSOE had been undergoing a considerable transformation. In the 1930s republic, the Socialists had on some issues been more radical than the Communists. In exile under Franco, the Socialists retained their Marxist militancy. But now with Felipe González as their head and with the prospect of democratic electoral victory, the Socialists began moderating their positions. Not without some major fights from the militant wing, the party at its conventions in the late 1970s had excised Marx and the Marxist lexicon from its platform, moderated its foreign policy stands, and came to accept capitalism and private property. The party went from a socialist to a more moderate social-democratic position. On that basis Felipe González and the PSOE decisively won the parliamentary election in 1982, with González becoming prime minister, and then won again—overwhelmingly—in 1987. As yet, however, the test has not occurred of what would happen if the PSOE were to lose an election, but most observers are agreed that it is now a fully democratic party that would also peacefully transfer power back to the opposition should it be defeated.

González proved to be an effective and popular prime minister. Only in his thirties when he came to power, González was handsome and politically shrewd. He recognized the need to give the left wing of the PSOE some positions in his government (for example, in the Foreign Ministry headed by Fernando Moran), but for the most part he governed pragmatically and adeptly. Although his party was on the left of the political spectrum, González moved to occupy the broad center—as had Suárez for a time before him.

González's policies were also prudent and pragmatic. In foreign affairs, where he had little experience, González started by following the advice of the Socialist International, an association of the world's Socialist parties, and of his Foreign Ministry officials who represented the PSOE's more militant Marxist wing. But this stance earned him criticism from the United States, NATO, and even other Socialist governments in Europe; and hence the flexible González backed away from the Left's positions and began following a more Centrist course—as in his campaign to have Spain join NATO. On the domestic front González assured business leaders of his nonrevolutionary credentials; moved to reform the military; backed away from nationalization and Socialism, which the PSOE's militants wanted to carry out; and followed an orthodox economic policy—including implementing a strict austerity policy whose incidence fell hardest on the shoulders of González's own followers in the unions and the PSOE. He continued the policy of his centrist predecessors by renewing the social pacts between labor and business under which labor largely abandoned its strike weapon in return for employer-financed benefits. González faced criticism from his own party for abandoning the Socialist agenda and following such a Centrist course, but the PSOE militants had no one other than González to vote for, and, besides, by this strategy González picked up far more votes in the center than he lost on the left.

By 1992 González had been in power for a full decade. He was the senior member of the European democratic prime ministers. Inevitably over the course of this decade some domestic disillusionment with González had set in, there had been some defections from the party, corruption had become more widespread, and González's popularity had declined. But it had not flagged enough for González to be threatened with a loss of power, either at the polls or from within the PSOE. Besides, the opposition was still divided, had not managed to build up its popular support, and had not been able to turn Centrist voters (where elections would be decided) away from González.

HAS IBERIAN DEMOCRACY BEEN CONSOLIDATED?

As the narrative history recounted here indicates, Spain and Portugal have taken some important and impressive steps toward democracy. There are a series of analytical issues that need to be addressed, however, before we can arrive at final assessments about these developments. Here we raise the issues; subsequent chapters try to answer them, and the conclusion attempts to put the whole picture together.

The "Explosion" of Political Participation

Spain and Portugal have moved very quickly from being closed, backward, almost "sleepy" nineteenth-century societies to highly mobilized ones in which virtually everyone got interested in politics and voter turnout was in the 80 to 90 percent range (as compared with less than 50 percent in the United States). Recall that Franco and Salazar had run their regimes on the basis not of mass mobilization but of mass apathy and demobilization. Now that has been radically changed: *Everyone* is involved and politicized. Such citizen involvement is good for democracy, but history teaches us that when the politically active population increases too rapidly rather than gradually as in the British and U.S. historical experience, it can be a formula for instability. Expectations and demands get raised before the political systems can fully satisfy them, and the result is often disillusionment, despair, and the undermining of democracy. We shall have to weigh whether that is possible in the two Iberian countries.

Has the Political Culture Changed?

Spain and Portugal now have all the institutional paraphernalia of democracy: political parties, regular elections, parliament, and so on. The question is, Has the more fundamental political culture—the beliefs and values of their peoples—also changed? Spain and Portugal, we know, have long traditions of authoritarianism, elitism, and patrimonialism—none of which are conducive to democracy. Since the mid-1970s the formal institutions have changed to a more democratic type—that is the "easy" step. But if the underlying values remain authoritarian and inegalitarian, that does not auger well for Iberian democracy. We shall have to weigh carefully how much the traditional Spanish and Portuguese values have changed toward a more democratic ethos and, alternatively, to what degree these countries have retained the authoritarian attitudes of the past.

The Socioeconomic Underpinning

A rich literature suggests that there is a close correlation between socioeconomic development and democracy.[11] As the levels of literacy and urbanization rise, and as economic development goes forward and a larger middle class is created, the possibilities for democracy increase. Note that these are tendency statements, however, not statements of cause and effect. There is no necessary or automatic relation between socioeconomic development and democracy; instead, what we can say is that democracy has a better chance of flowering and becoming institutionalized in developed, literate, middle-class societies than in poorer countries.

So we will need to know how successful the Spanish and Portuguese development efforts of recent decades have been, how urban and literate their populations are, what the size of their middle class is, and whether they have overcome their historically deep class divisions, overcome poverty, and solved the problems of land ownership and vast inequalities of income. Also, what about the considerable socioeconomic differences between the two countries? Once we have answers to these questions, we will be in a far better position to assess the prospects for Spanish and Portuguese democracy.

Vestiges of Authoritarianism

Some institutions in Spain and Portugal have undoubtedly become democratic. The political parties, the parliament, the electoral machinery are also functioning in a democratic fashion. In addition, the manifestly authoritarian institutions of the old regime—the secret police, the censorship, the social and political controls—have been largely abolished or changed drastically.

But many other important institutions have not changed very much since Franco and Salazar. They include the judiciary, the police, the bureaucracy, and the military. These institutions are still staffed in part by the same persons as under the old dictatorships; similarly, their internal practices and institutional mores (closed, top-down, authoritarian) are still largely the same. Does this imply a danger for democracy?

Then too, there are society's basic underlying institutions. These include the family, gender relations, religion, and the Church. Historically, all these societal institutions have been governed in Spain and Portugal by authoritarian, conservative, and traditional principles. Is that still true today? To what extent have these underlying societal institutions also been democratized, or are they still dominated by authoritarian principles, and what are the implications of that for Spanish and Portuguese political democracy?

Democracy's Consolidation

Both Spain and Portugal have made some impressive strides away from dictatorship and toward democracy. They have done this very rapidly. But the question is, How do we know when the transition from authoritarianism to democracy is complete? Moreover, how can we tell when democracy has been fully consolidated and is well institutionalized?

One rule of thumb is to say that when a country has had at least two transfers of power from one ruling group to another through democratic and electoral process, then democracy is well consolidated. By this measure Portugal has succeeded whereas Spain (only one change of government so far) has yet to pass the test. Another measure is to survey attitudes toward the main political institutions (parliament, parties, unions, and so on) to find out how much they are accepted and admired, and whether pluralism has been fully ingrained. Here, in both countries, we get some mixed results.

So let us leave open for the present the overriding question of whether Spain and Portugal have by this point fully and completely made the transition to democracy. At the level of the main political institutions—parties and the like—they certainly have; but at a deeper and more fundamental level there are still very mixed signals and results. These are themes that we address and seek to answer in succeeding chapters, and that we return to in the conclusion.

NOTES

1. Philippe C. Schmitter, "Corporatist Interest Representation and Public Policy-Making in Portugal," Paper presented at the Annual Meeting of the American Political Science Association, Washington, D.C., September 5–7, 1972; and Howard J. Wiarda, *Corporatism and Development: The Portuguese Experience* (Amherst, Mass.: University of Massachusetts Press, 1977).
2. Wiarda, *Corporatism and Development*, chapter 9.
3. Among the best studies is that by Neil Bruce, *Portugal: The Last Empire* (New York: Wiley, 1975).
4. The interviews with Caetano took place in the spring of 1973. This author had approached the prime minister to discuss the early origins of the Portuguese corporative system, of which Caetano was one of the architects. But once the interviews began, it became clear that Caetano really wished to talk about current politics. These interviews have never been published, but they are so revealing that they should be.
5. For a report on some of these interviews see Howard J. Wiarda, "The Portuguese Revolution: Toward Explaining the Political Behavior of the Armed Forces Movement," *Iberian Studies*, 4 (Autumn 1974).
6. António de Spínola, *Portugal e o Futuro* (Lisbon: Arcádia, 1974).
7. Among the better accounts of the Revolution are Douglas Porch, *The Portuguese Armed Forces and the Revolution* (London: Croom Helm, 1977); and Lawrence S. Graham and Harry M. Makler (eds.) *Contemporary Portugal: The Revolution and Its Antecedants* (Austin, Tex.: University of Texas Press, 1979).
8. Among the many books see Samuel D. Eaton, *The Forces of Freedom in Spain, 1974–1979* (Stanford, Calif.: Hoover Institution Press, 1981); and José Maravell, *The Transition to Democracy in Spain* (New York: St. Martin's Press, 1982).
9. Howard J. Wiarda, "Toward a Framework for the Study of Political Change in the Iberic-Latin Tradition: The Corporative Model," *World Politics*, 25 (January 1973): 206–35. A Spanish language version was presented at a conference in Madrid in March 1974.
10. Andrea Bonine-Blanc, *Spain's Transition to Democracy: The Politics of Constitution-Making* (Boulder, Colo.: Westview Press, 1987); also Robert A. Goldwin and Art Kaufman (eds.), *Constitution-Makers on Constitution-Making: The Experience of Eight Nations* (Washington, D.C.: American Enterprise Institute for Public Policy Research, 1988), chapter 6.
11. W. W. Rostow, *The Stages of Economic Growth* (Cambridge, England: Cambridge University Press, 1960); and Seymour Martin Lipset, *Political Man* (New York: Doubleday, 1960).

Chapter 5

Political Culture in Iberia

Spain and Portugal have by now made some remarkable *political* transitions to democracy. In the years since the death of Franco and the deposition of the Salazar/Caetano regime, political parties have competed for elective office, elections have been held regularly, the parliament has developed, and all the institutional machinery of democracy has been put in place. There is no doubt that Spain and Portugal are now governed more democratically than at any time in the preceding 40 years—or maybe ever.

The question we must now ask is, How much has the underlying political culture of Iberia changed? Granted that the institutions of democracy have been put in place, but does that mean that historic Spanish and Portuguese attitudes and behavior have been altered? Spain and Portugal have long been known as countries where authoritarianism, elitism, and paternalism are deeply imbedded, not only in the political tradition from Isabella and Ferdinand through Franco and Salazar but in social and cultural attitudes and institutions as well. Personal values, the Church, the family, the social order, and other institutions have long been based on mores and beliefs that are as authoritarian as those in the political realm. Indeed, these authoritarian belief systems have long undergirded the authoritarian political order. So, while Spain and Portugal have put the formal institutions of democracy in place, unless underlying attitudes change correspondingly, Iberian democracy could quickly be in deep trouble. That is the question we explore here: Just how much have Spanish and Portuguese attitudes, belief systems, values, and political behavior been altered to go along with the obvious changes in the political-institutional realm? The answer is crucially important to our assessment of the prospects for Iberian democracy.

POLITICAL CULTURE AS AN EXPLANATORY DEVICE

Anthropologist Clifford Geertz has defined culture as "the structures of meaning through which men give shape to their experience."[1] Edgar Schein also provides a good summary definition of culture as "a pattern of basic assumptions—invented, discovered, or developed by a group as it learns to cope with its problems of external adaptation and internal integration—that has worked well enough to be considered valid and, therefore, to be taught to new members as the correct way to perceive, think, and feel in relation to these problems."[2] Especially noteworthy in this second definition is not just the concept of shared assumptions within a culture but how these may be passed on from generation to generation, often for hundreds of years.

Here we are concerned mainly with *political* culture—that is, with those attitudes and orientations within the general culture that specifically affect political institutions and behavior. We will be examining the shared assumptions of the Iberian nations, the beliefs and values that shape the political system, the artifacts and symbols (flags, anthems, agencies of national identity), and the patterns of political behavior of the Spanish and Portuguese. We will also discuss subcultures that may exist within the overall political culture, as well as the processes of cultural continuity and change.

Political culture has sometimes been a troubling concept in the field of comparative political studies.[3] We can talk of, examine, and measure *patterns* of political culture, but we need to guard against that tailing off into dangerous national stereotyping or even racism. At the same time, advocates of economic determinist approaches often dismiss political culture as merely a part of the "superstructure," a reflection of underlying economic or class interests without explanatory power of its own. Another problem is that political culture can become a residual category, a "dumping ground" of explanations ("Oh, it's because they're Spanish!") when we have no other means of explanation.

Most serious scholars, however, argue that we cannot understand Iberia without taking into account Catholicism and the historic role of the Catholic church, the educational and family systems and how values are taught, the historical tradition of Spain and Portugal, social attitudes among the classes (i.e., the traditional upper class disdain for manual labor), the role of law and the code law legal system, political institutions and attitudes toward authority, and other features long dominant in Spain and Portugal. But, of course, as soon as we talk of *any* of these things, we are necessarily talking of political culture. Political culture is undoubtedly important; the only real question is *how* important.

Is it the political culture that shapes or determines the economic processes and political institutions of Iberia, or is it economic and institutional forces that shape and determine the political culture? Put in social science terms, is political culture a *dependent variable* (dependent on economic or institutional forces) or an *independent* one, standing on its own? Which came first, the chicken or the egg?

The answer is both—and at the same time it may be a silly and unnecessary question. It is very obvious in Spanish and Portuguese history that at some points the political culture variables (let us say Catholicism and the Catholic church) shaped political and economic outcomes, whereas at other times (the last three decades) socioeconomic forces have been determinant in altering the culture.[4]

Political culture is, therefore, both an independent and a dependent variable at the same time: Political culture both helps determine economic and political outcomes and at the same time is itself changed by them. Nor is it necessary to answer the chicken-egg problem; rather, we should see political culture, geographic factors, economic forces, political forces, and international pressures all interacting in interrelated, complex, and dynamic ways. Political culture is, thus, a useful and necessary but not a complete or sufficient explanatory factor; we must also recognize that it is not fixed in place. Rather, the political culture may change over time, sometimes slowly and sometimes rapidly depending on the circumstances. Clearly Spanish and Portuguese political culture today is quite different from what it was historically or even 30 years ago. It is more open, more democratic, less religious, more liberal, more secular, more modern and European. Does that mean that Spain and Portugal have definitely left their authoritarian pasts behind and consolidated pluralism and democracy? It could be. But while the recent changes in Iberian political culture have been impressive, there are also many continuities with the past. That is why we need to examine the political culture carefully, because it provides *one* of the key indicators as to whether or not Spain and Portugal have successfully bridged the transition to democracy.

HISTORIC POLITICAL CULTURE

Spain and Portugal are old societies, old cultures. Their known histories go back over 2000 years; the weight of this long history, the heavy hand of the past, still hangs ponderously over both countries.[5] During these two millennia they have been powerfully shaped by indigenous, Roman, Visigothic, Christian, and Islamic influences, as well as by more modern European trends including rock music, dress styles, and—not least—democracy. Here we analyze some of the historic elements of Iberian political culture; later in the chapter we talk about the change process.

Catholicism

Iberian Catholicism has long been more intolerant, more absolutist, and more fanatical than Catholicism in many other parts of Europe or in the United States. It was Spain, after all, that fought a long, five-century crusade against Islam and the Moors during the Middle Ages, established the brutal and repressive Inquisition to root out heretical ideas, drove out the Jews in 1492, and carried out the bloody—but ultimately unsuccessful—Counter-Reformation against rising Protestantism in the sixteenth and seventeenth centuries. Portuguese Catholicism has not usually been so absolutist, intolerant, and forceful as Spanish Catholicism, but it has been similarly monopolistic and authoritarian.

The main reason Spanish Catholicism has been so intolerant is that it has long felt threatened. It was threatened by the strength of Islam during the seven-century period of Moorish domination of Iberia; it felt threatened by and jealous of the power, money, and influence of the Jews in the late Middle Ages; and it felt threatened in the sixteenth century by Protestantism and the breaking of

Catholic unity and monopoly in Europe. Hence, Spain took upon itself the role of defender of the faith, seeking to drive out and suppress what it regarded as heresies; it embarked on a new crusade that helped ruin Spain financially and drove out some of her most talented and able people. Since the French Revolution of 1789, the Spanish church has felt most threatened by liberalism, pluralism, and republicanism, and long took vigorous action to stamp out these more recent "heresies." Marxism and Bolshevism have also been anathema to the Spanish church.

The reason Iberian Catholicism is of so much interest to us here is that Catholicism was not only a body of religious beliefs, but it undergirded the educational system, the legal system, the pattern of social relations, and the political structure as well. The same religious beliefs that stressed order, discipline, hierarchy, and authority also provided the foundation for the political system. Catholicism was not just something that could be compartmentalized and confined to the religious sphere, as in the American doctrine of the separation of Church and state; it infused legal, educational, social, political, even economic relations as well. All walks of life were informed by Catholic principles; the religious, social, and political spheres could not be separated. Spain and Portugal were not only Catholic countries in their religious beliefs, but they were also Catholic cultures, Catholic societies, and Catholic polities.

Now this is all changing. The Church is less influential in Spain. Vocations are down, attendance at Mass is down, and fewer Spaniards consider themselves Catholic. Even fewer participate in the sacraments regularly. As Spain and Portugal have modernized, they have also become more secularized, materialistic, and nonreligious. Hence, as the Church has become less powerful, the political-cultural values associated with it—conservatism, traditionalism, intolerance, and so on—have also declined in influence.

Authoritarianism

Authoritarianism has long been associated with Spanish and Portuguese political culture. Authoritarianism implies top-down rule, power emanating from above, and the absence of grass roots participation and democracy. Authoritarianism often means dictatorship. Interestingly, authoritarianism in Spanish and Portuguese life is not just associated with the national political sphere; it also pervades the family (domination by the father), the educational system (knowledge imparted from on high), the workplace (domination by bosses), the social structure (elitism and inequality), and virtually *all* areas of life. Authoritarianism in Iberia is, thus, a general rather than a solely political phenomenon.

Authoritarianism in Spain and Portugal stems from the same medieval and traditional Catholic beliefs analyzed earlier. Historic Catholic political doctrine provided Christian legitimacy for a strong but just prince and the need for order, discipline, stability, and hierarchy. These are all profoundly conservative principles. "I need authority for my cattle," said one recent Portuguese politician out on the stump, "and I will need authority for my people." The crowd cheered. One cannot imagine a North American or North European audience expressing approval for such rank authoritarian sentiments. And recall that Franco was the *Caudillo de España* (the authoritarian man on horseback of Spain) *por la gracia de díos* (by the grace of God)—not by the grace of the majority or of demoracy or one-person-one vote.

If power emanates from God and is therefore, presumably, good, there is no reason to limit or check and balance it. Nor is there a need for elections, separation of powers, or a bill of rights. It is the ruler, as the chosen instrument of God, who grants all such rights. They are not inalienable or indivisible. The ruler may govern absolutely—may suspend all rights. He or she should not govern as a tyrant, but his or her authority remains strong. Nor, if the ruler's power and authority stems from God, should one resist that authority, let alone rebel against it. Authority is God-given and to rebel against it is to resist God, to rebel against His authority. If one is a serious Catholic, as most people in Spain and Portugal have been historically, one does not violate these injunctions lightly. For to do so is not only to tempt the ruler's wrath but God's wrath as well. For a believer, rebelling against God's Holy Word is inviting damnation. So given these ethical and religious imperatives, it is not hard to understand why the principles and institutions of authority have been so powerful and long-lasting in Iberia and why the resistance to that authority has most often been feeble.

Authoritarianism in Spain and Portugal stems not just from culture, but also from institutions—or, better, the lack thereof. Historically Spain and Portugal have long been characterized by the absence of institutional infrastructure—political parties, interest groups, neighborhood and community groups, civic associations, and associational life of all kinds—that is the essence of pluralist, grass roots democracy. In the absence of such intermediaries, and given the centrifugal or "invertebrated" forces in Spanish and Portuguese society that have often torn these countries apart, strong, authoritarian leadership, it is reasoned, is what keeps these two countries from disintegrating. In more recent times (the Franco and Salazar eras), the need for a strong state has also grown out of the desire for rapid economic growth and central state planning. But now all this—and the political culture—is changing.

Elitism and Social Hierarchy

It is not just the rulers who receive their authority from God, but in the Spanish and Portuguese tradition the entire social hierarchy and class structure are ordained by God. The system is fixed and immutable, providing few opportunities for moving up the social scale. And once again, since this hierarchy is God-given, one should not, except in the most grievous of circumstances, rebel against it. Instead, one *accepts* one's station in life, for this is in accord with God's law and will. Rebelling against either a ruler or against those higher up in the social hierarchy is to risk violating God's law and invite the punishment that will surely follow, as well as eternal damnation. How old-fashioned, reactionary, or maybe just quaint this all sounds to modern, secular, non-Hispanic ears; but to understand Spain and Portugal we need to place ourselves in their people's shoes and to comprehend these societies on their terms, not ours.

The best way to understand the pervasive notion of elitism, inegalitarianism, and social hierarchy in Spain and Portugal is to go back to the Catholic foundations of Iberian life: St. Augustine, St. Thomas Aquinas, maybe Dante, and the Jesuit writers of the sixteenth century (Suárez, Soto, Vitoria, Molina). All of them have pictured society as organized on an authoritarian and hierarchical basis. At the top, as shown in Table 5.1, is God, from whom all power flows. Then come seraphim, cherubim, archangels, angels, and other heavenly beings. (Those readers who attended catechism as children will understand this better than others; suddenly, those catechism classes that bored you as a youth will now help you in understanding Spain and Portugal.)

Table 5.1. THE SPANISH AND PORTUGUESE SOCIETAL HIERARCHY*

God	
Seraphim	
Cherubim	Heavenly beings
Archangels	
Angels	
Other heavenly beings	
Kingdoms	
Principalities	The powers
The nobility	
The clergy	
Soldiers	
Artisans	The "old" middle class
Craftsmen	
Merchants	
Workers	Laboring classes
Peasants	
Gypsies	
Indians	Questionable if human or not
Blacks	
Lions	
Foxes	The higher animals
Dolphins	
Other animals and living and creeping things	Other animals and living things
Trees and bushes	
Rocks and "inert matter"	Nonliving things

*Adapted from Dante and St. Thomas Aquinas.

Eventually, in this social hierarchy, one gets to people; but only certain kinds of people. At the top come monarchs whose authority, like Franco claimed his to be, is derived from God's divine will for the universe. It is probably no coincidence that the political concept of "divine-right monarchy," which stood against the emerging principle of popular sovereignty, had its origins and strongest expression in Spain and Portugal. After the monarch comes the nobility, with its various ranks, whose authority, position, land, and peasants are also God-given. One can no more rebel against this level of authority than one can against princes. Next comes the "old" middle class occupying an indeterminate and insecure rung on the social hierarchy: soldiers, artisans, craftsmen, merchants. Then come workers and peasants, who were obliged to work with their hands and to accept their station in life. Finally come the lower orders—African slaves, gypsies, eventually (in the New World) Indians—of whom it was not clear whether or not they had souls. And if they had no souls, they had no legal rights as even the lowest class Spaniard or Portuguese possessed and could, therefore, be treated as animals whose higher orders (lions, foxes, dolphins) they approximated in the social hierarchy.

It is important to emphasize how fixed and immutable this hierarchy was. One was born into a certain station in life; one grew up in that station, married there, died there; one's children occupied the same station. Generation after generation and century after century the same social hierarchy, with only slight variations, was perpetuated. Spanish and Portuguese children would never grow up and hear, nor would they believe them if they did hear, the same Ben Franklin/Horatio Alger myths as their North American counterparts: work hard, save your money, study hard, get ahead. For the Spanish and Portuguese that was not possible. Life for them was unchanging, static, not improvable; one accepted one's station in life rather than trying to overcome it; the social hierarchy remained closed, and there were few if any upward escalators.

Family and Clan Groups

Spanish and Portuguese society has long been a society of clans and families. Some call them almost "tribal" in nature, a term that connects Iberia to Africa via the long Moorish occupation, and that doubtless carries the implication of an ethnic slur. Spain and Portugal are, of course, sensitive to these slurs and have sought to avoid them. But even today what passes for a "political party" or an "interest group" in Spain and Portugal are often really modern-day reincarnations, or sometimes disguises, for a family or a clan group.

When we speak of the continuing importance of the "family" in Spain and Portugal, we are referring to the extended family and not just the nuclear family. It includes brothers, sisters, uncles, aunts, cousins and second-cousins—and their children. It also includes ritual family members—godparents, godchildren, and their families. In addition, it may include political relations: members of one's graduating class (civilian or military); close friends and their families; persons linked to one over the years by employment, favors, patronage, or business deals. Such extended families may number several hundred or even thousand persons. They are held together by ties of blood, favors, trust, and mutual obligations.

Portugal was long dominated by seven or eight of these major families—or *grupos*. Spain, a larger and more complex society, has similar clans at both the regional and the national level. Typically, one of these elite clan groups will have diverse investments: a bank (both as a commercial venture and to handle the family's finances), a newspaper (to get the family's point of view across), a construction company (to take advantage of government public works projects), an insurance agency (to take advantage of compulsory insurance laws), a travel agency, a hotel and/or apartments, an office building, and land and cattle. Typically, too, the clan will have several of its members in each of the main political parties so that no matter which is in power, the family will be eligible for high government positions and will have its interests protected. Through its banks the clan may make loans to the government or help facilitate international financial transfers—a favor that, it is expected, would be returned with another favor.

Knowledge about these family and clan groups is limited. Unlike parties or interest groups that are studied much more because their activities are far more public, the clan groups are far more difficult for outsiders to penetrate. They often hide their activities, jealously guard their privacy, disguise their true nature behind other labels (if you scratch a political party in Spain or Portugal, it is often said, you discover one of these extended families), shield their members from scrutiny, block access to nonmembers, alter their surnames to hide their family connections, and close ranks around their own. This makes it very hard for outside investigators to understand them. Yet most close observers of Spanish and Portuguese society and politics are convinced these groups are very important, maybe even more so than the visible and public political parties and interest groups. Unless we understand these extended families, clans, and "tribes," we may be missing one of the most important institutions in Spanish and Portuguese life.

Patrimonialism

The phenomenon of patrimonialism is closely related to the family and clan network system just described. Patrimonialism refers to a society dominated by mutual obligation, by patronage, by gifts and favors granted in return for loyalty and service. In ancient Roman usage, a *patrón* was a master or landowner who had freed his slaves but still had some rights over them—rights to a certain number of days of labor, for example, or to military service on behalf of the patron or, more recently, to support his candidates at election time. The patron is often a landowner and has seignorial, or quasi-feudal, rights over those who work on his estate—hence the Spanish term *señor*, which is both a form of respectful address and an indication of the person's social importance. The patron has certain preeminent rights, but he also has the obligation to take care of those less fortunate than he. Just as God looks after His flock, so a patron must take care of those of lower rank in society: serving as godfather to their children, bailing them out of trouble, helping them along when the opportunity arises. Of course the recipient of these favors is expected, when called upon or the opportunity arises, to return the favor.

A patrimonial society, in this sense, is one dominated by the granting of favors in return for favors, of obligations in return for obligations, in ways that can become quite complex and that may go on for generations. Patrimonialism has feudal and medieval origins deriving from the historic relationship between lord and peasant. Patrimonialism is usually pictured as a form of traditional authority in contrast to a modern society based on contract, mutual consent, and merit. But patrimonialism in Spain and Portugal, although having ancient origins, also has modern-day political expressions: a government job in return for a vote or other favor, a patron who carries his followers with him into office, political parties that mainly dispense patronage rather than standing for issues and ideology, a particular government office or interest group that is dominated by a single family clan, the hiving off of government programs so that they benefit not the general public but only a private or clan interest, and so on. Patronage has by no means disappeared as Spain and Portugal have modernized, but it now has to be exercised more discreetly; it is no longer the only coin of political power (elections and merit also count), and the patronage system itself has become more complex and "modern," centering no longer around land but on government jobs and programs.

Organicism and Corporatism

Organicism and corporatism stem from the self-same Christian, Catholic, and Thomistic origins as do so many other political-cultural features of Spanish and Portuguese social and political life. When we say a society is "organic," we mean that it is unified, integral, closely tied together. All its parts are harmonized and in the proper relationship—as God has ordained in I Corinthians 13. Just as God designed His universe in perfect order, so the proper society must also have an integrated and proper plan. And just as God created men and women in His perfect image, so the body politic must also reflect the integrated unity of the human body, with its parts all interrelated, in perfect harmony, mutually interdependent, and so on. There is little room in such a conception for political pluralism and the complex competitions for power and the separation of powers of democracy.

Corporatism in this conception refers to the several natural, integral units that make up society: the family, the Church, the parish, the towns, the military, the bureaucracy, the university, and eventually organized business and labor. Earlier it was suggested that there was both an historic political-cultural sense of corporatism and a modern, political-institutional form. Under Franco and Salazar, Spain and Portugal sought to combine these two senses of corporatism, but here we are concerned with corporatism in its "natural" or political-cultural form.[6]

The corporate units that make up society are also to be organized in an integral and organic fashion, again corresponding to God's just ordering of the universe. The Church has its place in society, the army its place, labor its place, and so on. There is little room for change in such a conception, or for much overlapping membership, or for much competition and pluralism of ideas. Nor is there supposed to be "rebellion" (strikes by labor or lockouts by management) against this corporate system. Rather, society is supposed to be tied closely together into an organic whole with all its parts (individual as well as corporate) intermeshed in accord with God's just and harmonious ordering of the universe. In this way the organic and corporate conceptions of society are closely intertwined.

We now have in these preceding pages at least three ways of conceptualizing Spanish and Portuguese society. First, we have a system of social categories, rank orderings, and hierarchy—a system derived in part from history, political culture, and the writings of the Church fathers, but also created in part and certainly reinforced by an emerging structure of class relations. Second, we have the system of family and clan relations, dominated by patronage considerations and patrimonialism—a system in which various elite families and their retainers and clientele may compete for power and political spoils, and that overlaps with the social and class structure in various ways. And third, we have the system of corporations—a vertical structure that is distinct from the horizontal class-based one, but that also overlaps with the social hierarchy in various ways.

Figure 5.1 presents these three conceptions of society graphically. If we understand these three graphics and how the system that each depicts works, then we are a long way toward understanding Spanish and Portuguese politics. But now if we superimpose the three representations on top of each other, as in Figure 5.2 (p. 104), we can begin to envision Spanish and Portuguese politics in all their multifaceted complexity. If we then superimpose on top of that a political party system, a modern interest group system, and a political or governmental system, we are *really* beginning to comprehend Spain and Portugal. But it is almost impossible to depict such a schema graphically and still make sense of it. If we cannot understand it all, we should not feel alone, for the Spanish and Portuguese cannot always comprehend it either—and they were born to the system.

A few illustrations may help provide a sense of the interrelatedness and complexity of the system. For example, those at the top of the social and economic class structure tend also to be the heads or "godfathers" of the main family or clan groups. They relate to those below them in the social scale not only by considerations of class rank but also by the system of patronal or godfather relations that are at the heart of the family network. By the same token, these family elites may dominate or be in control of one of the main corporate or interest groups, or one of the political parties, or have an influential family member in place there. They may now relate to

(a) The Social and Class Structure

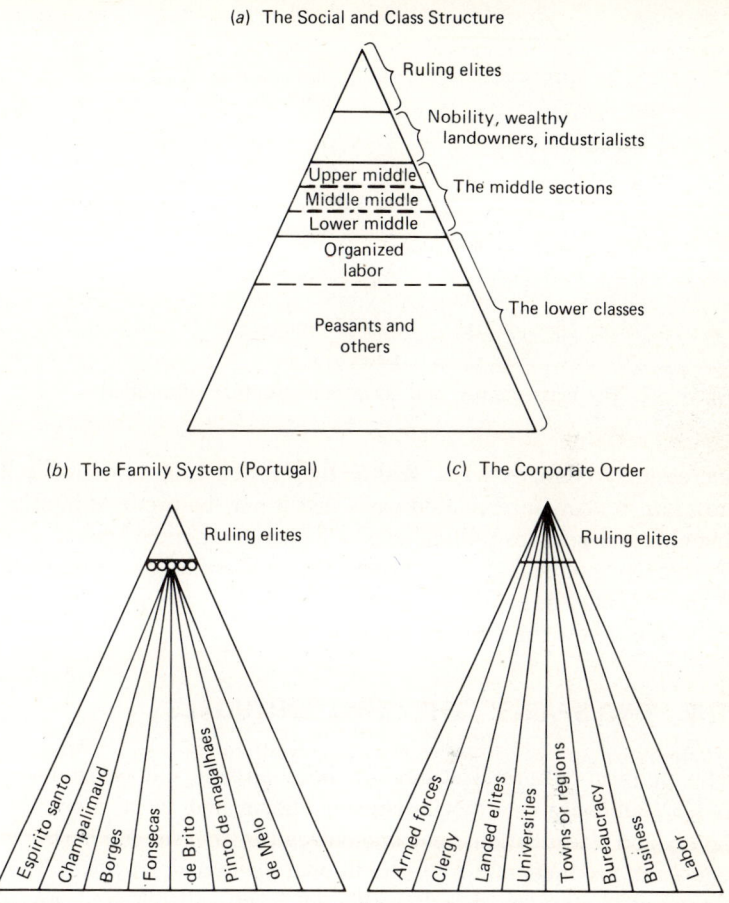

- Ruling elites
- Nobility, wealthy landowners, industrialists
- Upper middle / Middle middle / Lower middle — The middle sections
- Organized labor
- Peasants and others — The lower classes

(b) The Family System (Portugal)

Ruling elites: Espirito santo, Champalimaud, Borges, Fonsecas, de Brito, Pinto de magalhaes, de Melo

(c) The Corporate Order

Ruling elites: Armed forces, Clergy, Landed elites, Universities, Towns or regions, Bureaucracy, Business, Labor

Figure 5.1. Graphic representations of the Spanish and Portuguese systems.

those below them in the social scale no longer by ties of interpersonal patronage and mutual obligation but also by the new relations of impersonal employer-labor relations or as government program director to lower employee. An effective "player" in the political game seeks to mobilize as many of these resources—class standing, wealth, family connections, institutional position—as possible.

The system becomes more like a lattice, with various interconnecting parts, rather than the simpler, old-fashioned hierarchy. It consists of different conceptions of society pertaining to different historical and cultural epochs superimposed on each other in

The class structure depicted with solid horizontal lines

The corporate structure depicted with vertical broken lines

The family structure depicted with circles and dotted lines

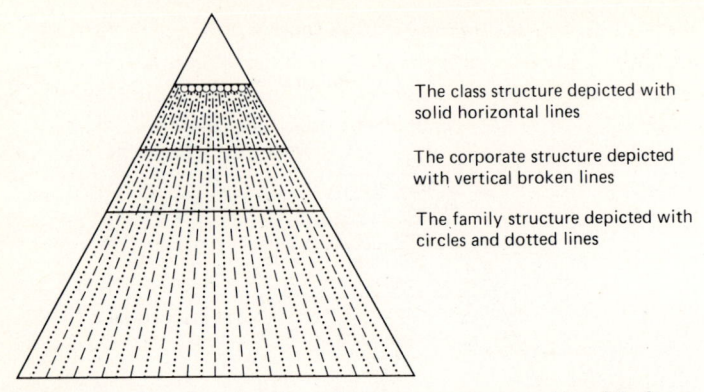

Figure 5.2. The class, family, and corporate structure (simplified).

increasingly complex ways. Rather than functioning effectively, it now has so many interrelated parts that it may be prone to ineffectiveness and perhaps pulling apart. The contemporary Spanish and Portuguese political systems are all but impossible for coordinated management. But before we go too far with this tangent we need to know more how the systems got that way.

THE "TWO SPAINS"; THE "TWO PORTUGALS"

The political-cultural features we have already emphasized—an older Catholicism, authoritarianism, elitism and social hierarchy, family and clan relations, patrimonialism, organicism and corporatism—are products of a more traditional Spain and Portugal. They grew out of a medieval and semifeudal Spain and Portugal, out of the Reconquest and possibly from an even earlier (Roman, Islamic) history. These historic political-cultural traits have deeply and profoundly shaped the Spanish and Portuguese people, their social and political attitudes, and—just as important—what other people think about them. Some of these political-cultural traits are still alive and vibrant today; the degree of their being so is open to some dispute among scholars, although there can be no question of the importance of the issue for the survival of Spanish and Portuguese democracy.

But beginning in the eighteenth century, recall, a split occurred in the Spanish and Portuguese "soul" or political culture that made the issue more complicated. One part of Spain and Portugal (the traditional groups—Church, army, nobility—and the countryside) remained conservative, traditionalist, and grounded in the hierarchical, elitist, and authoritarian conceptions already described. But the other part (mainly urban and middle class) was infused with the new and more liberal spirit of the Enlightenment, was more rationalist in its thinking, and was outward and European-oriented rather than closed and inward-oriented.

This conflict was reflected in the controversy over some of the Bourbon monarchy's modernizing reforms in the eighteenth century, most of which the liberals supported and the conservatives opposed as "anti-Christian" or "anti-Spanish." It was reflected in the intense debate over the liberal Spanish constitution of 1812 and the long argument over constitutionalism that followed. It was reflected in the intermittent but bloody and hate-filled Carlist civil wars of the nineteenth century, which again pitted conservatives against liberals. And it was reflected in the polarized politics of the 1930s republic and in the bitter civil war of 1936–39, one of the nastiest, bloodiest, and most brutal conflicts of the twentieth century. In Portugal this same fundamental split between liberals and conservatives was present, even though its expressions were not quite so bloody.

From the eighteenth century onwards, therefore, two Spains and two Portugals grew up. There now existed two political cultures, side by side. These two political cultures were like two gigantic "families," two parallel pillars of power. Each had its own values, its own ways of behaving, its own society, eventually its own clubs and newspapers. The two parallel cultures touched each other from time to time but rarely associated or communicated. Rather, they were most often in conflict, competing to be the dominant force in their countries. The differences between them were not ameliorated or compromised over time; instead they stood apart as two wholly distinct ways of life. It was a liberalism that the conservative side saw as anarchism, libertinage (liberty without restraints), and anti-Christian, and a conservatism that the liberal side saw as reactionary, antimodern, and antidemocratic, for which there could be no accommodation.

To complicate the situation more, during the early decades of the twentieth century, roughly 1900 through the 1930s, a third unsettling ingredient was added to this already simmering cauldron.

The new force was Marxism, often in its revolutionary forms. Recall that Marxism in Spain and Portugal in these early years was not always of the parliamentary sort; rather, its dominant currents were radical, anarchist, syndicalist, Trotskyite, and Leninist. These movements did not generally believe in democracy but were often dedicated to revolutionary change and violence. Hence, there grew up in Spain and Portugal not just another social cum intellectual movement—another "family" often with *its* own clubs, newspapers, bars, and political parties—but one that again brooked no compromise with the other two. For radical Marxism in Spain and Portugal not only denounced conservatives as reactionary but also denounced liberals and republicans as "bourgeois."

Hence, by the 1930s we had no longer just two Spains and two Portugals, but *three* Spains and *three* Portugals. The one was so conservative as to be reactionary and traditionalist and saw the other two as evil, sinful, and anti-Christian. The liberal strain was similarly exclusivist, often anticlerical, and opting for the most advanced and radical forms of republicanism. The Marxist strain was antiliberal and antirepublican, and despised the other two. These three ideological currents or "families" in Spain and Portugal were so far apart as to rule out compromise; they represented wholly different ways of life that we can summarize as (1) feudal and medieval, (2) bourgeois and capitalist, and (3) socialist and revolutionary. In the Marxist formula these stages were supposed to follow successively upon one another, but in Spain and Portugal all three political cultures were present at once, approximately equal in strength, and with no inclinations toward compromise among them. Thus, even when civil war was not actually being waged between and among these three main ways of life (and several smaller currents), the *conditions* of endemic or potential civil war were always present.

AUTHORITARIANISM, REPRESSION, AND A SUBJECT POLITICAL CULTURE

Both Franco and Salazar had plans to deal with this problem in their two countries—the problem of such deep divisions as to make Spain and Portugal all but ungovernable. Once again the parallels between these two regimes are quite remarkable.

Both Franco and Salazar moved to illegalize, wipe out, and completely eliminate the Marxist or radical "virus," as they called it. To that end Salazar and the preceding military regime that had named him prime minister took harsh measures in the late 1920s and early 1930s against the Marxist and communist "family." They illegalized the Marxist political parties and sent their leaders into exile or to jail; shut down their newspapers and printing shops; suppressed the Marxist labor and peasant movements; and killed, jailed, silenced, or exiled all opposition leaders. Franco had come to power through other means, in a civil war that was waged as a crusade against the Republican forces. Those who had not been eliminated in the civil war were killed, sent abroad, or imprisoned in the war's immediate aftermath. The first years of the Franco regime were quite brutal—far more so than those experienced in Portugal. However, for both Franco and Salazar, Marxism and socialism were not expressions of pluralism that needed to be accommodated; they were "alien" and "cancerous" forces that required elimination. Some Marxist and communist groups continued to exist in both countries, mostly underground, but as a main contender for power, Marxism and communism had largely been eliminated. The radical strain had been expunged from the body politic.

Liberals and republicans did not fare much better. In Spain many republicans were killed in the 1930s civil war or assassinated in its immediate aftermath. In both Spain and Portugal the liberal and republican political parties were illegalized, their trade unions were similarly illegalized and forced to reorganize as state-directed corporative agencies, and their leaders were jailed or forced into exile or underground. Franco and Salazar, in general, did not deal quite so harshly with the liberal current as with the Marxist one: The liberals were silenced but they did not necessarily have to face life imprisonment, permanent exile, or the firing squad. Instead, most of the liberal and republican politicians were allowed to return to their homes and their private pursuits; as long as they stayed silent, did not criticize Franco and Salazar, and kept out of politics, the regime largely left them alone.

With the two other main "families" and political cultures in Spain and Portugal now eliminated or silenced, Franco and Salazar moved to resurrect, revitalize, and give a monopoly to the more traditional political culture. The Franco and Salazar regimes did not try (as did Hitler and Mussolini) to invent a fully totalitarian ideology to stuff down the throats of their populations, but they did have distinct ideas or "mentalities" for which they stood. These ideas included a strong defense of traditional Catholicism, authoritarianism, conservatism, social hierarchy and the obligation to accept one's station in life, organicism and corporatism, and nationalism and the idea that Spain and Portugal represented a "third way," distinct from either liberalism or Bolshevism. All these ideas were at the heart of Spanish and Portuguese traditionalism and reaction.

The Franco and Salazar regimes used a variety of instruments to carry out this program. They employed censorship to blot out alternative views (those of the other two "families"). The corporative system was not only a way of organizing the new society but also a way to disseminate regime propaganda. The press, radio, and television were all controlled by the regime and published or broadcast only what it wanted. The single party machinery of both regimes was also used as an instrument of indoctrination. Virtually all national institutions were enlisted in this campaign to instill only one belief system, one political culture—the traditionalist one—in the Spanish and Portuguese populations, and to discredit or eliminate other points of view.

Especially important as an agency of this kind of conservative political socialization was the school system. Teachers were carefully screened, and efforts made to eliminate dissenters. Textbooks were infused with the political culture ideas that the Franco and Salazar regimes wished to disseminate. In these texts, the family and the Catholic church were pictured as the primary units of society. Children were taught to obey their parents and all those in authority over them. The contrary notions of liberalism and Marxism were strongly attacked. Class conflict was criticized, and the class harmony of corporatism was praised. Liberalism was painted as bankrupt and contrary to Spanish and Portuguese values.[7]

Franco and Salazar were pictured as the saviors of their nations. The principle of authority was enshrined in all areas: the political as well as the social and familial. The "social peace" of the Franco and Salazar eras was much praised, as contrasted with the "anarchy" of republicanism. Catholicism and its values were vigorously taught in the public school system so that even public education was infused with religious education. In this way the Franco and Salazar regimes used the educational system to inculcate the belief that their values were the only legitimate national values and that all contrary beliefs were not only evil and immoral but also non-Spanish and non-Portuguese.

No one is quite sure how effective these socialization campaigns were in Spain and Portugal. Undoubtedly they were effective—for a time. For many years in the 1940s, 1950s, and 1960s Spain and Portugal had no really serious opposition movements that threatened the regime. There was a remarkable conformity, no mass rebellions occurred, and social peace reigned—more or less. Dissent was rare, and the Franco and Salazar regimes seemed to be sailing on. The effectiveness of this form of socialization seemed to be supported by the public opinion surveys of the late 1960s–early 1970s that showed the Spanish population as *even more* conservative than the regime itself.[8]

In these ways Spain and Portugal were progressively depoliticized. They became *subject* political cultures rather than informed, civic, or participatory ones.[9] The Spanish and Portuguese populations were demobilized from the frenetic and intensely politicized period of the 1910s into the 1930s. Along with the effort to infuse the two countries with the traditional values, apathy was used as a further instrument of depoliticization. Spain and Portugal were, in a sense, tucked in and put to sleep—told not to worry because Franco and Salazar would paternalistically take care of them. An effort was made to turn back the clock and restore the more traditional, peaceful, "sleepy" society of the nineteenth century—or even earlier. The traditional "Hapsburgian Model" had been resurrected in newer corporatist and authoritarian forms.

But eventually all the regime propaganda began to wear thin. Many Spaniards and Portuguese stopped listening. Or they didn't believe it anymore. Or they became bored. New ideas filtered in. The population had other things on their minds—living like Europeans, greater freedom, opportunities for travel and alternative points of view, eventually democracy. A new generation had grown up that didn't remember or care about the ideological wars of the 1930s. Spain and Portugal under Franco and Salazar had been gigantic catechism classes; "public" education there was like being in parochial school all one's life. Although many Spaniards and Portuguese stayed on the "straight and true" path, many others—as sometimes happens with catechumens—grew up, lost interest, joined trade unions or the illegal underground organizations, or migrated to the centers of "sin and iniquity" in the cities or abroad. It was like, on a national scale, the child in America who grows up in a small town, for many years has the shelter of the family and the local community, attends church or synagogue regularly and maybe even goes to a parochial school—and then goes to a far-off secular university where his or her beliefs are challenged for the first time, alternative points of view are presented, and new and maybe potentially subversive ideas begin to creep in.

On a national scale, that is what, in essence, happened in Spain and Portugal. After all the years of socialization in the regimes' values, their peoples eventually lost interest and wanted to listen to other drummers, other points of view. As that began to occur on a larger and larger scale, the Franco and Salazar regimes—themselves becoming old, boring, and dinosauric—lost their hold on public opinion and on the political culture. By the time the Salazar regime was overthrown and Franco died, a post-Salazar and post-Franco political culture had already begun to emerge.

SOCIAL CHANGE AND CULTURE CHANGE

Eventually Spain and Portugal awakened from the torpor of the Franco and Salazar regimes. They again became, by the late 1960s–early 1970s, vibrant and alive. Once more they were becoming mobilized and politicized, but not always in accord with the wishes of their reigning regimes. They began to turn their backs on the official ideology of the Franco and Salazar regimes and to go off in new directions. A new political culture began to emerge, replacing or again standing alongside the older, official political culture of Franco and Salazar. What were the causes of this major shift, this "sea change" in political culture?

The first and most important cause was industrialization and the vast social changes to which it gave rise. In Spain the economic growth rate was about 7.3 percent per year in real terms between 1961 and 1973; in Portugal the growth rate during this same period was around 5 percent. In Spain in 1930, the percentage of the population employed in agriculture was about 50 percent; in Portugal it was 70 percent. But by the end of the 1960s (near the end of the Franco and Salazar eras) these figures had changed dramatically: only 30 percent agricultural in Spain and about 48 percent in Portugal.

Industrialization and rapid economic development from the 1950s through the 1970s dramatically changed the face—and the political culture—of Spain and Portugal. The shift from agriculture to industry led to rapid urbanization. In the cities, the new working class had access to television, movies, newspapers, radio, and ideas unavailable in the countryside. These new ideas and media helped change the way people think, altered their outlook on life, and made them more secular and nationalistic and less attracted to Catholicism and the older values.

Industrialization and economic development also led to vast social changes. The middle class doubled in size in both countries between the 1950s and the 1970s, and their outlook changed—toward modernization and democracy—as well. A new business-industrial class grew up that was more sophisticated, cosmopolitan, and European-oriented. The working class grew and so did working class consciousness. In the urban areas also, a large *lumpenproletariat* of semiemployed and underemployed peddlers, cigarette vendors, and penny capitalists also saw the city lights for the first time. Along with the class changes, therefore, came a growing change in political ideas.

Another cause of change was emigration. So many Portuguese and Spaniards were leaving the countryside that the domestic job market could not absorb them all. Millions emigrated to England, Holland, Switzerland, France, West Germany, and Belgium where they took menial jobs as waiters, dishwashers, construction workers, and garbage collectors. Although their pay was low by North European standards, it was high by Iberian standards. Many of these workers, who lived abroad for extended periods and then returned to Spain and Portugal, brought back with them advanced ideas of trade unionism, social welfare, and democracy.

Another important influence was tourism. By the early 1970s over 40 million tourists were visiting Spain annually. The number of tourists equaled the total population of Spain. The comportment of these tourists, their affluence, their lifestyles, and the freedom they enjoyed undoubtedly had a strong influence on Spanish values. Portugal had far fewer tourists than Spain, but eventually the broader European influence was felt there too.

The European influence was stronger than just tourism and emigration, however. By the early 1970s many more Spaniards and Portuguese had traveled in Europe, had business dealings there, went there on holidays, and kept abreast of European events. The desire to be or live like the other, developed Europeans was powerful. That meant not just European affluence but European democracy and freedom as well.

In both countries literacy rates and access to education also began to rise. As Spain and Portugal became more affluent in the 1960s and 1970s, their educational systems improved; a higher percentage of children went to school, they stayed in school for more years, and even some adult literacy programs began. Education expanded people's vistas, taught them new ideas, and made them more aware of the institutions around them. For the Franco and Salazar regimes, "a little education" proved ultimately to be dangerous and subversive.

Finally—and it is a vague thing—values just changed. The Franco and Salazar regimes got old and ran out of gas. People no longer felt passionately about them, one way or another. In earlier decades many had been either strongly in favor or strongly opposed, but later apathy and indifference had set in. As Franco and Salazar got older, infirm, and less full of vim and *machismo*, people realized that they would go soon too, that they were not immortal. Everyone was sitting around waiting for the Franco and Salazar regimes to pass from the scene, which they eventually did. But by the time they did disappear, the values and political culture of their peoples had already changed.

In the 1960s, the Franco and Salazar regimes had been portrayed as perhaps *permanently* authoritarian-corporate regimes. They had been seen by many observers as models of how to achieve economic change and social modernization without those being accompanied by value changes leading to democratization. But as we have seen here, that was not an accurate portrayal. In fact, the value changes—changes in the political culture—were also occurring concomitantly with socioeconomic changes. But for a long time, while Franco and Salazar were still alive, they were hidden, disguised, below the surface, not immediately visible. In fact, Spanish and Portuguese political culture had changed considerably in recent decades; those changes, however, became apparent only after the Salazar regime and Franco had passed from the scene.

A NEW SPAIN, A NEW PORTUGAL?

Spain and Portugal have undoubtedly undergone major changes in recent decades, including changes in their political cultures. The key question is whether these changes have been sufficiently thorough that we can now say Spain and Portugal have become full, consolidated democracies and are safely in the democratic camp.

To begin, let us examine the changing nature of Iberian Catholicism. Spain and Portugal have long thought of themselves as Catholic societies, cultures, and countries—often more Catholic than the Vatican. Franco and Salazar, in part, resurrected the idea of a confessional state, and survey data from the 1960s and early 1970s show Spain and Portugal as more Catholic than other historically Catholic countries of Europe (Italy, France, Belgium) and roughly at the same level as Ireland.[10]

Whereas in the mid-1960s 80 percent of the Spaniards described themselves as practicing Catholics, by the mid-1980s the figure was below 30 percent. Fewer and fewer Spanish and Portuguese Catholics attended Mass or participated in the sacraments. They have almost no contact with the Church. They may still want their children baptized in the Church, they prefer to be married in the Church, and they would like before dying to receive the last rites of the Church, but these "hatch'em, match'em, and dispatch'em" functions do not speak of a strong and powerful religious influence still able to shape, if not determine, the overall political culture. The Church in both countries has also experienced a decline in its institutional infrastructure—schools, hospitals, vocations. The Roman Catholic church itself, since Vatican II, has also changed, becoming more liberal and open. Spain and Portugal, meanwhile, have become less religious, more secular, more indifferent toward the Church, and even atheist. Along with this decline in the Church's influence has also come a diminution in the strength of the values associated with historic Catholicism: unquestioned authority, social hierarchy, elitism, and political absolutism.

A second trend is that the Spanish and Portuguese have become strong supporters of democracy. By percentages that range from the low eighties to over 90 percent, overwhelmingly Spaniards and Portuguese have expressed a preference for liberal, democratic, representative rule. By the same token, the support for democracy's main alternatives, Marxism-Leninism and authoritarianism-corporatism, has dropped to less than 10 percent each.

These figures make democracy seem popular and secure, but there are some disturbing subthemes that make the prospects appear less rosy. First, if we ask Spaniards and Portuguese what they mean by democracy, the answer comes back as "strong government"—which seems to imply the still-present possibility of an authoritarian "out," particularly if there should be a crisis or the economy should go into a downturn. Second, although democracy in the abstract is strongly supported, support for what we think of as democracy's essential supporting institutions—such as labor unions and political parties—is very weak, in the neighborhood of 20 to 30 percent. Third, while expressing support for democracy, when asked which was the best government they had in the last 25 years, more than 50 percent of the Portuguese said that of Salazar/Caetano. Finally, in both countries in recent years, there has been a certain disillusionment with ("it hasn't delivered") and decline in support for democracy, but it is uncertain whether this reflects unhappiness with the particular government-of-the-moment or if it is a more fundamental disillusionment with democracy itself.

A fourth change in the political culture relates to the declining influence of *amiguismo* (friendship, personal ties), *caciquismo* ("bossism"), and patrimonialism (government by mutual favors). Increasingly, it is merit and achievement that count in Spain and Portugal—*along with* personal ties and friendships. As Spain and Portugal have become more *national* political regimes, the power of the local bosses has also declined.[11] In addition, the patrimonialist features that were dominant in earlier decades are no longer so strongly present; now real public policies (housing, education, health care) must be carried out *in addition to* finding a place on the public payroll for one's friends and cronies. All this means that change has taken place in these areas of historic political culture, but it is by no means complete.

Fifth, Spain and Portugal have become increasingly materialistic and consumer goods–oriented. It used to be said in some quarters that Spain and Portugal were "different" because they were more spiritual, more humanistic, more artistic, more idealistic than their presumably crass, money-grubbing, and materialistic North American and North European counterparts. Some of this may still be true; Spain and Portugal may still be "different" in certain respects. But the evidence indicates that by now Spain and Portugal have become just as materialistic as the rest of the world. That may or may not be good, but it does show that in this area as in others Spanish and Portuguese political culture has become less distinctive.

Another area of change, sixth, is in gender roles. Spain and Portugal have been, historically, male-dominated societies. But now middle class women are increasingly joining the professions, while lower class women are working in the thousands of factories, often foreign-owned, that have been established in the last 30 years. Although politics is still male-dominated, some women have occupied cabinet, foreign ministry, and parliamentary positions—even the position of prime minister of Portugal for a brief time. Children have also become much more independent and have adopted a freer lifestyle. All these changes have given rise to a variety of problems that are familiar in other advanced industrial countries (rising rates of divorce, delinquency, absence of child care, breakup of the family, and so on) but that are new to Spain and Portugal. In these as in other areas, the institutions that supported the historic political culture, and hence the political culture itself, are undergoing fundamental transformation.

Seventh, Spaniards and Portuguese have shown a marked inclination toward moderation and centrism. This stands in stark contrast to the period of the Second Republic in Spain, when public opinion became polarized, the extremes gained ascendancy, and the country broke down into civil war. No one wants to repeat that experience again. Portugal, too, after its conservative-versus-republican conflicts earlier in the twentieth century and the extremism of the revolution in 1974–76, has similarly calmed down and become more centrist. The extremes have been repudiated electorally and moderate regimes are in control. As we see in greater detail in Chapter 7, outside of the Spanish Basque area, today there are no significant political movements of either the extreme Left or the extreme Right. Once again, Spain and Portugal have become "just like us"; the radicals are out and moderation and centrism are in.

Finally, what may save Spain and Portugal is apathy. In neither country are people so passionate about politics as they were earlier. Party identification is down compared with the rest of Europe and so is the percentage of persons who vote. More and more Spaniards and Portuguese are concerned primarily with jobs, getting ahead, consumer goods, money, and affluent lifestyles. Their interest in the great political issues has waned. These attitude changes had been building for some time, but a qualitative change came in the mid-1980s. From 1975 to 1985 politics was at the center of Spanish and Portuguese preoccupations, but by the mid-1980s democracy had been more strongly consolidated and attention began to shift away from political concerns toward economic concerns. The apathy, declining party identification, and lower voter turnout may be worrisome for Iberian democracy in the long run, but in the short term the decline of passionate politics may have helped stabilize these two still somewhat uncertain democracies.

A good way of summarizing all these political-cultural changes is to say that Spain and Portugal have become more like Europe. That is, institutionally and in terms of their values, the two Iberian nations are closer to Europe than ever before. They are no longer "different," no longer "Third World," no longer "African" or "Latin American." At the same time, it must be remembered that Spain has a per capita income of only a third to a quarter of the rest of affluent Europe, and Portugal lags even farther behind. Furthermore, the process of "Europeanization"—in part because of these and other socioeconomic differences (levels of literacy, poverty, and so on), and in part because of political-cultural traits from the past—is still only partial, still incomplete.

SO, IS DEMOCRACY FULLY CONSOLIDATED?

There is no doubt that Spanish and Portuguese political culture is changing; the question is how broadly and how deeply. Spain and Portugal had a political culture strongly shaped by Roman, Islamic, and medieval Catholic precepts—authoritarian, hierarchical, elitist, organic, corporatist, patrimonialist. But a parallel liberal structure emerged in the eighteenth century and grew up in the nineteenth and twentieth centuries, and along with it a Marxist sector began to emerge as well. Recent socioeconomic change has begun to ameliorate the sharp divisions of the past and have led to a more moderate, middle-of-the road, and democratic regime.

And yet there are worrisome aspects and conflicting crosscurrents in Spanish and Portuguese political culture as well. The survey and other data often lead to conflicting conclusions. Estimates are that fully one-third or more of the population still supports the old values: discipline, order, hierarchy, authoritarianism. These values could easily be translated into support for a strong, nationalistic, conservative government. Recall that when Spaniards and Portuguese say they prefer democracy, they mean by that strong, forceful government. In addition, Spaniards and Portuguese have strong anticapitalist sentiments, which means liberalism in the political sphere has not yet been translated into liberalism in the economic sphere. But many social scientists believe you can't have a liberal polity without having a liberal, open market economy as well. And if you do not, conflict is liable to arise. Put together, these sentiments imply the still-present possibilities for a demagogue, a populist strongman, a statist and nationalist, like Juan Perón in Argentina, to come to power. Such an outcome does not seem imminent, but in times of economic trouble, social unraveling, or political instability, one could still see Spain or Portugal reaching for such a solution.

In addition, there are still powerful elements in Spain and Portugal—leftovers from the 1930s—who are antiliberal and antidemocratic. These groups are not just indifferent to democracy; they tend toward the values of fascism. They are not just conservative but reactionary and wholly traditionalist. These elements are not presently numerous but they could combine with the statist, nationalist, and strong-government advocates mentioned previously; recall that over 50 percent of the Portuguese population still think of the Salazar regime as the best government they've had in the last 50 years. Or they may enlist the decisive influences of the army on their side.

Many Spanish and Portuguese institutions have hardly been touched, and certainly not purged or reformed, by the democratizing changes following the Portuguese revolution and Franco's death. These institutions include the armed forces (still wary of civilian politicians and wanting to continue to play a "moderating" role—see Chapter 6), the bureaucracy (where the same persons who served Franco and Salazar are still often in control), the Church (now more moderate but still with strong right-wing elements), and the elite business community which is still not fully reconciled to democracy. We are cheered by the expressed preference for democracy by over 80 percent of the population in both countries, but we should worry about the lack of support (20 to 30 percent) for what we think of as democracy's and pluralism's essential mediating institutions: political parties, labor unions, and peasant associations. We should also worry about some subcultures in Spain, such as in the Basque country, where well-armed and well-organized terrorists are plainly not reconciled to democracy. And finally we should worry about the so-called success democrats in Spain and Portugal, who are inclined to support democracy in prosperous times but in a social or economic crisis could easily be persuaded to opt for other solutions.

Substantial changes have thus occurred in the political culture of Spain and Portugal since the 1950s, but these changes are still incomplete. The trend has been toward democracy and liberalism, but there are just enough uncertainties present that we cannot yet close the door definitively on other possibilities. In earlier writings,[12] this author has suggested that it has historically been dangerous for one part of Spain or one part of Portugal (presently the liberal part) to try to rule completely without the other part, as if the other part did not exist. In the past that uncompromising attitude has been a formula for conflict and civil war.

The author now thinks that there has been sufficient change in Iberian society and political culture that the prospect for severe conflict is unlikely. But this author still sees the need for an accommodation with the older Spain and the older Portugal. The old society and the old values cannot just be wished away. Hence, instead of their trying simply to imitate the parliamentarism of the rest of Europe, the Spanish and Portuguese could perhaps use a political formula that combines liberalism and democracy with the still-valued traits from their own historical and cultural traditions. Such a formula might imply strong presidential leadership *à la* de Gaulle in France, a form of Rousseauian democracy (free but organic), or perhaps a form of neocorporatism (as distinct from the older, discredited form). The precise nature of these compromises needs to be worked out by the Spaniards and Portuguese, but if democracy is to not only survive but thrive, some form of accommodation with the past is likely still necessary.

NOTES

1. Clifford Geertz, *The Interpretation of Cultures* (New York: Basic Books, 1973), p. 312.

2. Edgar Schein, *Organizational Culture and Leadership* (San Francisco: Jossey-Bass, 1985) p. 9.
3. See Gabriel A. Almond and Sidney W. Verba, *The Civic Culture* (Princeton, N.J.: Princeton University Press, 1963); Gabriel A. Almond and Sydney W. Verba, *The Civic Culture Revisited: An Analytic Study* (Boston: Little, Brown, 1980); and Lucian W. Pye and Sidney W. Verba (eds.), *Political Culture and Political Development* (Princeton, N.J.: Princeton University Press, 1965).
4. An excellent statement is Samuel H. Barnes, *Politics and Culture* (Ann Arbor, Mich.: Center for Political Studies, Institute for Social Research, University of Michigan, 1988).
5. See especially the essays dealing with Spain and Portugal by Richard M. Morse in Howard J. Wiarda (ed.), *Politics and Social Change in Latin America: The Distinct Tradition* (Amherst, Mass.: University of Massachusetts Press, 1982; revised edition, Boulder, Colo.: Westview Press, 1992).
6. Ronald C. Newton, "Natural Corporatism and the Passing of Populism in Spanish America," in Frederick B. Pike and Thomas Stritch (eds.), *The New Corporatism: Social-Political Structures in the Iberian World* (Notre Dame, Ind.: Notre Dame University Press, 1974) pp. 34–51.
7. The best study is by Richard M. Nuccio, Socialization of Political Values: The Content of Official Education in Spain (Ph.D. dissertation, Department of Political Science, University of Massachusetts, 1977).
8. See especially the early surveys by the Spanish polling agency FOESSA, *Estudios Sociológicos sobre la Situación Social de España* (Madrid: Euramerica, various years).
9. The distinctions are elaborated in Almond and Verba, *Civil Culture*.
10. José Ramón Montero Gibert, "Iglesia, Secularización y Comportamiento Político en España," *REIS*, 34 (1986): 131–59.
11. Richard Gunther, *Politics and Culture in Spain* (Ann Arbor, Mich.: Center for Political Studies, Institute for Social Research, University of Michigan, 1988).
12. Howard J. Wiarda with Iêda Siqueira Wiarda, *The Transitions to Democracy in Spain and Portugal* (Washington, D.C.: University Press of America for the American Enterprise Institute for Public Policy Research, 1989).

Chapter 6

Interest Groups and the Political Process

*I*t is often said that "interest group pluralism" (as compared with socialism, communism, and other ideologies, the term seems to lack grandiloquence) is *the* ideological foundation of the American polity.[1] If that is so, the same cannot be claimed for Spain or Portugal. To be sure, Spain and Portugal have interest groups and, since Franco and Salazar, a considerable degree of pluralism. But it cannot really be said as yet that interest group pluralism provides *the* political or ideological basis for the Iberian polities.

Although it is usually translated as "interest group," the term *"interes"* in Spanish and Portuguese implies something different from the English language term. An *interes* in Spain and Portugal is usually thought of as a group that is part of the regime, part of its backbone, not separate or independent from it. Such *intereses* as the military and the Catholic church, as we will see in more detail, are integral, organic elements *within* the state system of power and authority in Iberia (and are often shaped or even created by it), not bodies created and sustained only by their own independent grass roots memberships. Such *intereses* deal with each other most often indirectly, bureaucratically, through the state structure, rather than in direct competition as in American-style interest group activities. Hence, to understand Spain and Portugal we need a model of the relations between the state and its component societal or interest groups derived not just from the system of interest group pluralism as it exists in the United States but from the peculiarities and special forces in Iberian history as well. At the same time, in order to fully understand Spain and Portugal, we have to take into account the strong influence of extended families, clan groups, and patronage networks operating there.

The issue is complicated by the fact that Spain and Portugal now have *both* an emerging system of independent interest group pluralism in part shaped and patterned after those of the United States and Western Europe, *and* a system of what we have called state-conditioned, organic, or corporate groups that is reflective of an earlier—and ongoing—history. At one level, therefore, it is appropriate, as in the United States, to talk about interest group competition or the interest group struggle over public policy issues in both Spain and Portugal; while at another level we need to construct a model of what we here call an organic or "contract state" to deal with those *intereses* that are integral parts of the regime rather than separated from it.[2] In the chapter's conclusion we seek to tie these two conceptions of interest groups together to see how they interrelate and how the whole system works, *and* to assess the overall influence of the interest group system on Spanish and Portuguese politics as compared with other arenas of politics. We also try to show the relations of these formal interest groups to the more informal patronage and clan groups.

BASIC SOCIAL AND ECONOMIC DATA

Several times in this book we have had occasion to refer to the immense differences between Spain and Portugal. Nevertheless the very fact of treating the two countries together for comparative purposes in one book tends to blur these differences. There are, in fact, striking parallels and similarities between the two countries; but in this section, by representing their basic socioeconomic profiles, we reemphasize the differences—as well as where Spain and Portugal fit in the global rank-ordering of nations (see Table 6.1).[3]

To begin, Spain occupies an area of 194,896 square miles (approximately 504,781 square kilometers), a territory that is slightly smaller than France, larger than Italy or the United Kingdom, and approximately one-eighteenth the size of the United States (and smaller than Texas). Portugal has a territory of 35,553 square miles (approximately 92,082 square kilometers)—slightly larger than Austria or Hungary, about the size of Maine. On the Iberian Peninsula,

Table 6.1. PORTUGAL AND SPAIN COMPARED WITH SELECT OTHER COUNTRIES; PER CAPITA INCOME AND LIFE EXPECTANCY (1986)

Countries	Per capita income	Life expectancy
Low-income		
India	290	57
Middle-income		
Guatemala	930	61
Upper-middle-income		
Brazil	1,810	65
Poland	2,070	72
Portugal	2,250	73
Greece	3,680	76
Industrial market economies		
Spain	4,860	76
Ireland	5,070	74
Italy	8,550	77
France	10,720	77
United States	17,480	75

Source: *World Development Report 1988* (New York: Oxford University Press for the World Bank, 1988).

Spain takes up over four-fifths of the total territory and Portugal takes up somewhat under one-fifth.

These same proportions are roughly repeated with regard to population. In 1990 Spain had a population of approximately 40 million, somewhat lower than that of France, England, or Italy and approximately one-sixth that of the United States. Portugal in 1990 had a population of just over 10 million—about that of Greece, Cuba, or Belgium and one-quarter that of Spain.

Spain's gross national product in 1988 was approximately $300 billion. Its per capita income (gross national product divided by population) in 1988 was about $7,740. Spain, therefore, falls into the category designated by the World Bank as an "industrial market" or "high-income" economy, but at the lowest end of that advanced category. Spain ranks close to Ireland in per capita income, but its wealth per person is only one-half that of Austria, the Netherlands, and France, and only about one-third that of Norway, the

United States, and Switzerland. Further comparisons are provided in Table 6.1.

In 1988, Portugal had a gross national production of $38 billion, about one-eighth that of Spain. Portugal's per capita income was $3,650—less than half of Spain's. Portugal ranks with what the World Bank calls "middle-income" countries, but at the upper end of that category. Its per capita income is close to that of Poland, Yugoslavia, Panama, and Argentina. Like these others, Portugal is not yet a fully developed country nor anymore an underdeveloped one; it lies somewhere in between.

In both Spain and Portugal the rate of recent economic growth has been very fast. Between 1965 and 1980 Spain's growth rate was 5.2 percent per year, one of the highest in the world, though during the recession years of 1980–86 the rate was only 1.8 percent. Portugal grew even more impressively, at a yearly rate of 5.5 percent between 1965 and 1980, and then also tailing off to 1.4 percent in the 1980–86 period. Since joining the European Common Market in 1986, both countries have experienced impressive renewed growth.

If we turn from these economic indicators to some social indicators, the differences between the two countries are also quite striking. Portugal has a life expectancy at birth (1988 figures) of 74 years, whereas that of Spain is 77. These figures reflect the significant improvement in nutrition and health care in both countries in recent decades. In Portugal the population growth rate is down to 1.7 percent per year (from 3.1 percent in 1965); in Spain the present rate is 1.8 percent, down from 2.9 percent in 1965. In Spain the daily caloric supply per person (1986 figures) is 3,359 while in Portugal it is 3,151.

Spain had one physician for every 320 persons in 1984, and Portugal had one for every 410 persons. In 1985 Portugal had 47 percent of the children of secondary school age actually enrolled in school, while in Spain it was 91 percent. The percentages enrolled in tertiary education (high school) were 13 percent for Portugal and 27 percent for Spain. Portugal in 1980 had 26 percent of its working population employed in agriculture (down from 38 percent in 1965) and 37 percent employed in industry (up from 30 percent in 1965). Spain had only 17 percent of its work force employed in agriculture in 1980 (down from 34 percent in 1965) and 37 percent in industry (up from 35 percent in 1965). Portugal was 31 percent urban in 1985, up from 24 percent in 1965; and Spain was 77 percent urban in 1985, up from 61 percent in 1965. In both countries the percentage of women attending school is now equal to the number of men attending school.

These figures make it clear that Spain is not only a bigger country than Portugal with a much larger population, but it is also considerably more modern and developed. Literacy, levels of education, and per capita income are all considerably higher in Spain. In addition, Spain has more resources, a far larger internal market, and a larger middle class. All these conditions make it more likely that Spain can sustain stable democracy better than can Portugal. Spain has "made it" into the modern world, whereas Portugal is still struggling, still closer to the Third World. These conditions help make Portugal more volatile politically than Spain.

THE SOCIAL BASIS OF POLITICS

Spanish and Portuguese politics tend often to have a social or class basis. In this regard they are far closer to the European pattern than to the United States. Americans don't talk much about class and class structure, in part preferring not to, in part because Americans believe so strongly in an ethos of upward mobility that erases class barriers, and in part because the United States lacked a feudal past that would have created a rigidly hierarchical class structure. But in Europe, and especially in Iberia where feudalism and a hierarchical social structure were long presumed to be divinely ordained, the class and social group to which a person belongs are critically important in explaining political behavior.[4]

It is not our purpose here to fully explore this thesis or the reasons for it, but only to introduce the subject and to show the strong social basis of Iberian politics. For example, as we will see in detail in Chapter 7, there is a very close correlation in both Spain and Portugal between class standing and voting behavior. Those who are working class tend *strongly* to vote for the Left and Marxist (Socialist or Communist) parties, and those who are middle class, or "*bourgeois*," to use the Marxist term, tend *strongly* to vote for the centrist and conservative (social-democratic or Christian Democratic) parties. The correlations are not one-to-one but they are strongly present and they are far stronger than in the United States.

Another factor is the rigid social hierarchy that still exists in both Spain and Portugal—and the political implications flowing from this. There is now in these two countries more upward social mobility than ever previously, as new jobs, careers, and educational opportunities have opened; but these are still limited, and in many respects the old social hierarchies are still in place. High school and especially university education is still limited to a small elite; the rest of the population is consigned to more menial pursuits. Persons are born into a certain station in life and, the odds are still quite good, they will remain there, marry there, their children will grow up in the same class, and so on. Far more so than in the United States, persons identify with their class, they feel solidarity toward it, and they vote and behave in accord with their class dictates and interests.

Political party identification reflects these prevailing class attitudes, perhaps more in Portugal—because of its revolution and class struggle in 1974—than in Spain. That is, membership in a party is almost like membership in an extended family—and may serve as a substitute for it. For example, if one is a member of the Communist party in Portugal, one's whole life can be enveloped in the party. There are Communist bars, Communist grocery stores, Communist barber shops and hair salons, Communist clubs, Communist neighborhoods, Communist unions, even Communist funeral homes. All one's friends are Communists. One can almost literally go through his or her entire life and have contact with only fellow Communist party members. The same kind of close, cradle-to-grave party ties have developed for the Socialists and, increasingly, for the Christian Democrats. Italy, with its strong two-party system (Communists and Christian Democrats), is perhaps the country where such party-as-family ties are strongest, but in Iberia similar kinds of identifications are often present. Such close identification between class and party are not as powerful in Spain and Portugal as in Italy but they are certainly far stronger than the relations between party and society in the United States.

With regard to class and interest groups, several things ought to be said as an introduction to the analysis that follows. First, neither Spain nor Portugal has the plethora of interest groups—church groups, neighborhood groups, scout groups, school groups, national interest groups, professional and alumni associations, and so on—that the United States has. In contrast, Spain and Portugal have been marked by the absence of such a vast network of associations, of intermediary or secondary groups, that serve as both a buffer and a transmission belt between the state and individual persons. Second, Spain and Portugal do not have the system of cross-cutting loyalties that serve to ameliorate group conflict in the United States. That is, if one is a member of several interest groups (labor union, church, neighborhood association), such overlapping memberships tend to moderate one's adherence to any one of them and, thus, produce more moderate, compromising politics. Because Spain and Portugal do not have so many interest groups and, therefore, fewer cross-cutting loyalties, they have less moderate, less accommodative, less middle-of-the-road politics.

With the absence of cross-cutting loyalties, one's loyalty to the single group that a person does belong to tends to be absolute. One goes all out for that group with little willingness to compromise. Politics often becomes an all-or-nothing affair—zero-sum politics—where one either wins everything or loses everything, and there is nothing in between. Politics tends also to be absolutist, stereotypical, a society of stock types. If one is a military person, one is expected to have *all* the characteristics of a military person; if one is a member of the clergy or an oligarch, one is expected to behave like the stereotypical image of these people; if one is a unionist, there are similarly traits (Marxist, Leftist, militant) that one is expected to take on. In the absence of cross-cutting affiliations, one is expected to behave precisely according to one's position and role. This kind of role playing in the absence of multiple group memberships tends to heighten the differences among groups in Spain and Portugal and to make compromise among groups very difficult.

As with so many things Spanish and Portuguese, these conceptions have also begun to change in the last 30 years as associability and multiple group membership have increased. But to the degree that Spain and Portugal still remain countries of limited associability, of few interest groups, without many cross-cutting loyalties, and thus societies of almost stock types, the possibilities for the politics of accommodation—and, hence, for democracy itself—will remain precarious.

FAMILY, CLAN, AND PATRONAGE INTERESTS

Spain and Portugal are countries of extended families, of clans and cliques, and of elaborate patronage networks. Some historians trace the clan system, which is sometimes so intense as to be almost "tribal" in character, to the influence of the Moors; others say it lies in the regional character of the Reconquest; still others trace this "clannishness" back to the early origins of Iberian history. Whatever the exact historical roots, there can be little doubt about the importance of family groups, clans, and patronage networks in Iberian history *and* in current politics.

By "extended family" we mean not just aunts, uncles, grandparents, cousins, and "distant relations," but godparents and godchildren as well. The extended family thus encompasses ritual relations as well as blood relations. The godparents-godchildren relationship in historically Catholic countries like Spain and Portugal is an important one, meaning not just an occasional birthday present as in the United States (if we even have godparents), but implying a *lifetime* of commitment, mutual help, and mutual obligations.

"Political relations" are also important. Political relations are persons connected to one by school ties, friendship, business relations, military comradeship, social connections, or alumni associations. If we put together blood relations, ritual relations, and political relations, these family or clan groups may number in the hundreds. If we are talking about prominent families whose patriarchs may be the godparents of many children, the numbers may reach into the thousands. When several of these extended families and clan groups are banded together in defense of a common interest, it is plain that we may be talking about some very numerous and powerful networks.

These groups are tied together not only by blood and family loyalty but also by mutual obligation—patronage. Historically, this patronage system was based on Seneca's concepts of "the gift" and by the Christian concepts of charity. Just as God gave the ultimate gift in the form of His son crucified on the cross, so the privileged must also take care of those lower than they in the social scale. If one is an upper- or middle-class Spaniard or Portuguese, then one has a Christian obligation to help those less fortunate. Such gifts may take the form of charity, benefices, food, clothing, medicine, or—most important for our purposes—jobs and patronage. In return, the recipient of such gifts also owes an obligation: to provide loyalty and service to his or her benefactor or *patrón*. In feudal times this often meant a certain number of days of labor or perhaps a military obligation. In the modern era, such patronage may take the form of steadfast loyalty or voting support. Moreover, the current basis of the patronage system is secular rather than religious, although the practice and understanding of mutual obligations is the same: favors in return for loyalty and service.

Whole careers and entire lives may be built around such patronage ties. A budding politician may have a network of followers who support his candidacy in return for the promise of jobs or favors if he wins. As he moves up in political importance, his followers also move up with him into better patronage jobs. And, as a politician becomes more prominent, his coteries of followers, hangers-on, loyalists, and job seekers, become larger. Politics often consists of one such extended family network, or usually an alliance of several families, competing against a rival clan group. In these contests, ideologies and issues are often less important than personal connections and patronage.

In Portugal under Salazar, eight such extended families dominated the political and economic landscape. They lost a great deal of their power and wealth in the revolution of the mid-1970s, but now these families are making a comeback and their clan networks are being rebuilt. In Spain, because it is a larger country and has a strong tradition of regional loyalties, the clans are more diverse. Moreover, such clans are no longer based just on land and wealth; these are political clans as well. For example, when Socialist Felipe González was elected prime minister of Spain in 1982, he brought with him into power his whole political clan from his hometown of Seville—a move that remained very controversial in Spain all during González's rule.

These family or clan groups are not usually formally organized, so it is very hard to find out accurate information about them. Nor do they advertise their positions the way an interest group or a political party would. They have no membership lists, and they do not talk to strangers about their activities. Hence, one would almost have to be a Spaniard or a Portuguese, to be born into this family or clan group network, or to spend a lifetime in the country to understand fully how this system operates. Certainly U.S. embassy officials do not usually have that kind of knowledge, nor—because the data and exact family relationships are so difficult to get—have scholars much studied these extended families.

Nonetheless, anyone who spends any amount of time in Spain and Portugal cannot help but be impressed by the strength and staying power of these vast patronage networks. Frequently they have now reorganized themselves formally as interest groups or political parties. That is because in the modern era the family alone cannot mobilize sufficient power; instead, a party or an interest group has to be put together. As outside observers, we may look at them and call them interest groups or political parties. But behind the facade, the formal structure, and the ideology or platform that outsiders sometimes take at face value, there may be an extended family network or group of families still protecting its private interests. In this way the family structure has "modernized" and taken on the form of a full-fledged interest group system, but lurking behind may still be some ancient family rivalries and the patronage interests already described. The family network thus existed prior to the emergence of a modern interest group and party system, and even now continues to coexist and even flourish alongside it.

THE HISTORIC TRIUMVIRATE OF POWER: ARMY, CHURCH, ECONOMIC ELITES

Historically (which means through the nineteenth century), Spain and Portugal were dominated by three major *intereses:* the Church, the army, and the nobility. Recall that these three are not "mere" interest groups in the American sense, but something more fundamental than that: integral parts of Spanish and Portuguese society and politics, parts of the organic body of these two countries, integrated into the culture and very backbone of the Iberian regimes.

These three powers formed the pinnacle of Spanish and Portuguese political society from medieval times until the present century—some would say even today. Not only was each of these powers strong in its own right, but they were also closely related. Those who led the Church, the army, the oligarchy, and the government almost all came from the same families, the same class, the same ranks in the social hierarchy. The leadership of these sectors was intimately interrelated—often literally so. Under Spanish laws of primogeniture, it was the first son that inherited all the family land, so the second son of elite families usually went into the army and became a general, and the third son went into the Church and became a bishop. In these ways, landed wealth, military strength, and the moral suasion of the official religion came together in the same closely interrelated families—usually not quite so literally as has been portrayed here, but not far from it either.

The Armed Forces

The armed forces of Spain and Portugal trace their origins back to the military orders of medieval times.[5] The military orders were autonomous from the state and, formed during the Reconquest of the peninsula from the Moors, may have antedated it. The military orders were thought of—and thought of themselves—as a separate caste in society, independent from any civil authority. To an extent, the armed forces of Spain and Portugal still think of themselves in that light. The American model of civil-military relations, of a strict separation of the civilian and military spheres and of clear military subordination to civilian authority, has never reflected operating reality in Iberia.

Large preprofessional infantries were formed in the sixteenth century to enhance and defend Spanish interests in Europe, and there has long been a tradition in Iberia of heroic guerrilla struggles. A modern army of a professional sort began to be organized in the nineteenth century as Spain's and Portugal's earliest military academies were organized. However, in the numerous civil wars of that period, much of the fighting was still done by irregular peasant armies. Politics often took the form of one (or a group of) *caciques* (regional chiefs) gathering up their irregular forces to do battle with other *caciques* and their forces. The prize was national power and a share of the spoils, patronage, and national treasury that went with it. Officerships were mainly limited to the sons of the elite families who gained their positions through ascription rather than achievement.

By the twentieth century the military was becoming more professional, and the regional *caciques* were slowly divested of power. Franco and Salazar centralized control even more and demanded the absolute loyalty of the officer corps to themselves and to their authoritarian, corporatist, and traditionalist principles. They further professionalized the military, gave it a bigger budget and better equipment, and greatly increased its size. The military was both an institution of national defense *and* an instrument of political control to help maintain Franco and Salazar in power. However, in both regimes a class change occurred: The older, aristocratic officer corps who identified with the *ancien régime* were moved aside and a more dynamic, middle-class officer corps became dominant. Henceforth, the military could no longer be counted on automatically to side with the traditional status quo and its oligarchic defenders. The traditional triumvirate of power began to break up.

These changes were most obviously apparent in Portugal in the revolution of 1974, when the senior officers backed a democratic opening while the junior officers opted to go in a more radical direction. But recall that, in keeping with their traditional orientation as an autonomous institution, the Portuguese military (not the political parties or the civilian groups) *led* the revolutionary changes of the mid-1970s and then gave themselves a special position as leaders and guardians of Portuguese socialism. This elevated role was subsequently incorporated in the 1976 Portuguese constitution, where the armed forces constituted almost a fourth branch of government—in some respects more important than the other three.

In Spain, the transition to democracy was under civilian auspices, but that the military allowed it to take place at all—given the nature of the Franco regime and Spain's past history—was nothing short of remarkable. The peaceful transition reflected the change to a predominantly middle class and politically centrist officer corps. Only in 1981, with the invasion of the Cortes (parliament) by a group of estranged officers and the unsuccessful call for a coup, did it appear that the democratic and civilian-led transition might be upset. But there were not enough officers sympathetic to a coup, so the civilian democratic forces prevailed. Both the Spanish government and the NATO allies during this period were clever at enveloping the Spanish armed forces in various NATO exercises and responsibilities, thus giving them important new missions in place of staging coups. The retirements (some of them forced) of many senior officers also helped reduce the military threat to democracy.

Both the Spanish and the Portuguese armed forces remain divided, but these divisions are less deep than they used to be. The divisions are both political and professional. First, there are divisions between the services, though in both countries the army is by far the most important branch. Second, there are sometimes divisions and jealousies between the armed forces and the national police force or special paramilitary units such as the *guardia*. Third, there are generational differences, with the senior officers often more conservative and the junior officers both more liberal *and* wanting to inherit the cushier positions and opportunities available to senior officers. Fourth, there are professional differences regarding the role of the military, including what its constitutional position should be and whether or not it should continue to play a balancing and "moderating" role. And fifth, there are political differences between left- and right-wing officers, and with various factions of the officer corps associated with the major political parties. Fortunately for Spanish and Portuguese democracy, the largest group within the military now seems to have accepted its nonpolitical and professional role, its subservience to civilian authority, and the requirement of not interfering in national political life—except in a situation of national emergency.

Many problems exist, however, within the military institution. In both countries there are rival factions and ambitions within the military institution, often overlapping with rival civilian factions, that might still upset the applecart of Spanish and Portuguese democracy. Moreover, in both countries the armed forces are among the institutions *least* altered by the democratizing changes since the mid-1970s. Third and related, the armed forces, even while currently out of power, continue to operate close to the surface of power and are still the ultimate arbiters of national affairs. Fourth, in neither country is the line between the professional and institutional interests and autonomy of the military, and its political involvements quite as clear-cut as we would like them to be. And finally we should say that although there is a civilian government presently in power in both countries, that fact should not be interpreted as a renunciation of military autonomy. In many ways the relations of the Spanish and Portuguese armed forces to the state are still like those of the military orders in the Middle Ages: often jealous and prickly, two separate sovereignties and even societies existing side by side, with neither able to dominate the other completely, two separate pillars of power coexisting sometimes uncomfortably within the same political system with neither able to totally subordinate the other or to function without it.

The Church

The position of the Roman Catholic church in Spain and Portugal is in many ways analogous to that of the armed forces. Here we have, historically, one of the most powerful institutions in the country. Moreover, because Spain and Portugal have traditionally been Catholic societies and cultures, and with their political systems also based on Catholic precepts, the Church is more than a mere interest group in the American sense. Rather, the Church is part of the fiber of the regime, one of the essential pillars undergirding the entire national system, and inseparable from it.[6]

Now, however, as Spain and Portugal have become more materialistic and secular, the influence of the Church has waned. Like the army, it is still an important and, in many ways, special institution, but both countries are now in a new era in which the traditional institutions are but one among several main influences and no longer so predominant.

The Church, by any objective criteria, is not as all-pervasive as it used to be. In terms of the percent of the population that is active, practicing Catholic (maybe 12 to 15 percent), the number of priests per capita (one for every 7000 to 8000 Catholics) and the number of Catholic schools, hospitals, and so on, the figures are all down. Under the constitution of 1977, Spain is no longer designated as a Catholic country, and other religions are guaranteed freedom to practice their beliefs. Protestantism is growing, and during the 1980s the first synagogue and the first mosque in 500 years, since the expulsions in 1492, were reopened. Even on those issues that it feels fall within its moral domain—divorce and abortion—the Church in Spain has been unable to prevent new and liberalizing legislation from being enacted. Catholicism in Portugal, however, remains considerably stronger than it is in Spain.

The Church itself has changed over time but not, as in some parts of Latin America, to the extent of embracing liberation theology. Like the army officer corps, the Church hierarchy, and especially parish priests, have come increasingly from middle-class backgrounds and are no longer to be identified closely with the elites or the traditional status quo. Vocations are down in both Spain and Portugal, so the Church has had trouble filling its ranks and serving its flock. The Church has had to adapt to the liberalizing currents emanating from the Vatican (though not without protest— conservatives among the Spanish clergy have sometimes threatened to establish their own national church that would be independent from Rome). And it has had to adjust, which it is doing slowly and with great uncertainty, to the realities of a more materialistic and irreligious population. It should be said that the problem for the Church in this regard is indifference toward religion and no longer anticlericalism as in the 1930s.

Like the military, the Church has its factions. The older clergy, which includes the hierarchy, tends to be conservative, whereas the younger priests are more liberal. The Jesuits and *Opus Dei*, a secretive Catholic lay organization that at times has wielded considerable influence, tend still to defend the old values of hierarchy and discipline. Other orders, however, are less politically committed, and even the Jesuits now have a radical and worker-priest movement within their ranks. But it is probably fair to say that most of the clergy have gravitated toward the center, toward more middle-of-the-road politics, and toward a position that eschews involvement in partisan politics—again a far step from the politically heated days of the 1920s and 1930s.

The Catholic church respects the majesty of facts, and the facts are that Spain and Portugal are quite different societies—more urban, middle-class, literate, and secular—than they were during the upheavals of 50 or 60 years ago. The Church has slowly adjusted to these changes, albeit not always easily. It is still struggling to find its place in this new and rapidly changing context. The Church has weathered these storms, but it has lost influence in the process. As a main power contender, it has fallen from one of the top three (along with the army and the historic nobility or oligarchy)—a position it occupied historically in a more traditional Spain and Portugal—to a position now of maybe seventh or eighth—behind not only the army but also the bureaucracy, the parties, industrialists, bankers, commercial elements, the EEC, maybe the labor unions, and the middle class. On most issues, therefore, the Church has withdrawn from partisan politics, and it may be that the Church is no longer the "backbone" or "pillar" of the system as it once was.

Economic Elites

The Spanish and Portuguese economic elites have long been powerful in the two nations' political affairs—to the extent of almost being able to dictate policy at various times in ways that mainly served their own interests. These groups remain powerful today; however, their power has been considerably attenuated to the point that now they must *compete* in the political arena, one group among several.

Because of the long reconquest of the peninsula from the Moors, Iberian feudalism was always different from that of other areas of Europe. Iberian feudalism was closely related to territorial conquest. As the Iberians militarily pushed the Moors farther south, they also occupied the lands formerly controlled by the Moors. Hence, in Iberia military prowess and might were closely related to economic wealth. Out of this process of conquest and land consolidation emerged the Spanish and Portuguese oligarchy. For centuries economic power, military power, as well as the power of the Church were closely intertwined.

Most of the land was concentrated in the hands of this elite. A true oligarchy began forming when the elite acquired the right also to the labor of the peasants working on the land and when the land titles became hereditary and passed on from generation to generation. Over time the landed elite also acquired titles of nobility—prince, duke, lord—which gave it added luster and prestige.

The pattern of enoblement and of the emergence of an oligarchy was not uniform. In Portugal, for example, the north was dominated by small landholdings whereas the south was the center of large estates and absentee landlords—a situation that would later produce marked geographical differences in voting preferences, as we will see in the next chapter. In Spain, a country chopped up by mountain ranges and geographic irregularities, each region had its own economic elites, production patterns, and class system—with little overall national system.

The power of the nobility and the oligarchy ebbed and flowed, corresponding to the large currents of Iberian history. During the late Middle Ages, before the emergence of a national monarchy, this elite consolidated its power and ruled largely unfettered in its regional enclaves. Then, Ferdinand and Isabella, in their efforts to centralize Spain, stripped the nobility of its independent political power, although the elite still often retained its economic influence. As the strength of the monarchy later waned, the power of the elites increased once again. The chaotic, on-again off-again liberalism of the nineteenth century also had the effect of further weakening central authority and giving more power to the local or regional elites and the *caudillos* (men on horseback) or *caciques* (chiefs, bosses) who served their interests. Hence, although the independent political strength of the elite class has sometimes fluctuated, it has consistently remained influential socially and economically, and usually politically as well.

Toward the end of the nineteenth century and extending into the twentieth, some new elites began to emerge alongside the traditional landed ones. These included business and commercial elites, banking elites, import-export elites, and eventually an industrial elite. Often these new elites came from the same families as the old landed elites, or else the new people of wealth succeeded in marrying off their sons and daughters to the children of the landed and titled elites, expanding and thus reconsolidating elite control. But in many cases, too, the newer people of wealth did not come from the old titled families; rather, they represented a new, ambitious, entrepreneurial class. Some married into the old elite, but others did not. Thus, at this point the elite structure of Spain and Portugal became somewhat more diverse, even pluralistic, than had been the case earlier.

SOCIAL CHANGE

Both Spain and Portugal, from the middle of the nineteenth century on, had begun a process of economic growth and development. The economic historian W. W. Rostow has referred to this as the "take-off" stage leading to sustained growth.[7] Spain's and Portugal's development was not so impressive as that of Great Britain, France, or Germany—the other "early developers"—but it was present nonetheless. The discussion in this section deals with the social changes in Iberia from the late nineteenth century until the 1930s.

One of the results of this economic growth was the emergence of the new business class already referred to. A second result was the growth of a new middle class and a variety of new middle-class associations, interest groups, and political parties. These include civic associations, intellectual groups, a lawyers' association, a doctors' association, and so forth. The organization of these groups helped to fill the associational void—the *falta de civilización,* or organizational infrastructure—that had long been the bane of Spanish and Portuguese political life, and a key underlying reason for both nations' lack of stability.

A third facet of social change during this period was the organization of trade unions. The industrialization and urbanization that Spain and Portugal experienced in the late nineteenth and early twentieth centuries gave rise to an urban, industrial proletariat that became unionized. Partly because of the poverty of Iberian workers compared with others in Europe, the rigid class system, the influence of Italian trade unionism, the presence of Russian anarchists in Spain, and partly because the Iberian political systems repressed the early unions, Spanish and Portuguese trade unionism was quite radical in these early decades.

In Portugal the main labor groups were the Socialists and the Communists—and that remains true today. In Spain trade unions were both more advanced and more complex. There were Socialist and Communist trade union groups—both quite radical. In addition there was a Trotskyite labor group, a strong anarcho-syndicalist labor group that was especially strong in Barcelona, as well as a labor sector associated with the Falange that was, in many ways, modeled after Mussolini's Fascist state in Italy.

The unions were strongly politicized, as distinct from constituting basic bread-and-butter unions. Each major labor federation was considered a branch of one of the major political parties. They were known for their *political* positions more than for the benefits they brought to the rank and file. In addition, they employed a political bargaining model rather than a collective bargaining one. That is, they sought to influence the state and the political system through demonstrations, politically motivated strikes, marches, and political action, rather than dealing directly with employers. They tried to get the government to put pressure on management to grant their demands—or perhaps sought to topple the government itself—rather than using collective bargaining. Such political action implies a political model of trade unionism rather than the more limited, nuts-and-bolts bargaining over salaries and benefits with which Americans are more familiar. To a considerable extent this political bargaining model of trade unionism remains present today, although now collective bargaining also exists alongside the more political tactics.[8]

The Spanish and Portuguese trade union movements faced many problems that for a long time kept them from becoming major interest groups. To begin, only a small percentage (less than 5 percent) of the workers were organized, so the unions lacked the numbers to be a powerful lobby. Second, Spain and Portugal had a large labor supply of unorganized workers that employers could utilize if and when their own workers got "too uppity." Third, employers were often able to use the repressive apparatus of the state (police, national guard, army) to keep workers in line. Fourth, the labor organizations—divided along ideological lines—were fighting as often with each other as with their more natural adversaries: employers and management. There was intense competition among the rival union federations and sometimes even pitched gun battles. Hence, although in the pre-Franco and pre-Salazar periods the trade unions had emerged as significant and particularly vocal actors in the political arena, they were still weakly organized, often suppressed, easy prey for employers or the police to utilize divide-and-rule tactics, and, therefore, not yet a legitimated or effective player in the emerging, more pluralist, political order that was then coming into existence.

LIMITED PLURALISM UNDER AUTHORITARIANISM

By the 1910s and 1920s in Spain and Portugal, and on into the 1931–36 period of the republic in Spain, a considerable degree of social and political pluralism had emerged. New business and commercial groups had grown up, a larger middle class was becoming organized, and diverse trade union groups were politically active. But that was precisely the problem from the point of view of the "other Spain" and the "other Portugal"—the more traditionalist groups that had long been dominant. They viewed this new pluralism as chaotic, disorganized, and potentially disruptive, even subversive of the traditional order. The newer groups, particularly the trade unions, had organized around principles (Marxism, Leninism, anarchism) not considered legitimate by the traditional wielders of power; moreover, in the strikes, the street action, and the formation of armed popular militias the old elites saw the possibilities for a repeat of the Bolshevik revolution.

Hence, under Franco and Salazar the radical labor groups, and many others besides, were illegalized or snuffed out. In their place, the Franco and Salazar regimes created docile official unions and other groups that would be subordinate to the authority of the state.

The matter was complicated by the facts that the corporative regime permitted *some* of the old interest groups to continue functioning and that in the 1960s it negotiated with some of the underground labor groups. But the basic fact is that the freewheeling and rather chaotic interest group pluralism of earlier years now gave way to a system of authoritarian controls over most interest group activity and to a system not of unfettered but of restrictive pluralism.[9]

What, then, was the interest group structure under Franco and Salazar? Remember, first of all, that these were dictatorships, tightly controlled, with top-down decision making, so basically there wasn't a lot of interest group activity. Second, both Franco and Salazar, like George Washington and, later, de Gaulle, were opposed to "factions"—they often didn't listen to the interest groups at all and thought of them as detracting from the unity and glory of the state. Third, under the system of limited pluralism, the number of interest groups was kept small, their activities were closely monitored, and most of them had little influence on policy.

The army was the most important group and the ultimate arbiter of national affairs. At times the military high command became impatient, especially with Salazar, and launched a number of coup attempts that were quickly put down. But Franco and Salazar were careful to watch out for the army, lavish favors upon it, and at the same time keep rotating the high command to prevent any one officer from achieving a position of personal power from which he might challenge the regime itself. The military served as a "moderative power" that lurked behind the regime, keeping it "honest," and was prepared to step in or moderate should the regime fall or if stability were to be upset.

The economic elites were powerful on an everyday basis, probably more so than the military. Because Franco and Salazar wanted to continue economic growth that only the entrepreneurs could provide, they did not clamp down on the business groups and force them to reorganize under corporative auspices as they had with the trade unions. The economic elites filled cabinet positions and, thus, held direct political power, they held indirect power through the regimes' dependence on them for expanding prosperity, and they held financial power through the banking/insurance networks that they owned and via the money they loaned to the government, thus keeping it in their debt. The economic elites became the most powerful group in Spain and Portugal—more powerful than the army, because, whereas the army only reacted to change—the elites actively initiated it. The fact that it was an interlocking elite, well organized and closely interrelated, gave it added power.

The Church slipped in influence under Franco and Salazar. That is paradoxical because these were *very Catholic* regimes that paraded their religiosity on their sleeves. However, as an institution the Church lost power from the 1930s to the 1970s, and its capacity to influence politics declined. Secularism had set in; in addition, neither Franco nor Salazar consulted the Church on political matters on a regular basis. The Church lent legitimacy to these two regimes, but public opinion surveys showed that the Church had slipped to seventh or eighth in the ranking of the power of the major interest groups.[10]

Opus Dei, the secretive Catholic lay organization, surged in importance for a time in Spain, and in the mid-1960s was ranked fourth in influence among Spanish interest groups. But that was just about the time Franco began shuffling the *Opus Dei* members out of his cabinet, again demonstrating that it was Franco that really ruled and not *Opus Dei*.

The major emerging new groups during this period were the banks and the bureaucracy. Because banking wealth, commercial wealth, and industrial and other kinds of wealth were so closely integrated in the Spanish and Portuguese systems, we do not here consider the banking elite as separate from the economic elites. But it is the case that the opinion surveys that showed the Church dropping in influence and *Opus Dei* rising for a time also showed the banks rising to third or fourth place in terms of the public's perception of their influence.

The civil service or bureaucracy was also perceived by the public as rising in power. As the Spanish and Portuguese economies grew, as Franco and Salazar introduced central planning, and as the state's responsibilities in social and economic affairs increased, the public bureaucracy grew by leaps and bounds. The state became the largest employer in the country, particularly of educated persons, with perhaps 20 to 30 percent of the gainfully employed work force working for the state. Their critical positions as regulators, overseers, and patronage dispensers gave these state bureaucrats added power. Opinion surveys showed the state bureaucracy occupying the fifth or sixth most important position in the hierarchy of influence.

The power of the trade unions had waxed and waned, and then waxed again. In the pre-Franco and pre-Salazar period the unions seemed to be increasing in numbers and influence; then they were suppressed and tightly controlled by the regime. Later in the 1960s and early 1970s their strength as interest groups and underground organizations began to increase again. The surveys showed them ranked seventh in terms of influence.

Other groups were weaker. The middle-class professional associations grew in numbers under Franco and Salazar, but they largely avoided taking political stands and were not paid much serious attention when they did. The student groups followed the same general trajectory as the unions. They were activist, highly politicized, and very vocal in the pre-Franco and pre-Salazar period, but then they were suppressed, silenced, and reorganized as apolitical, state-run organizations under the dictatorship. Occasionally they would rally or stage a demonstration, but few listened. The phenomenon that we find in some countries where the students, in alliance with workers and peasants, constituted a powerful force was not present under Franco and Salazar. The students ranked eighth or ninth in influence.

Numerically the largest group, but politically the weakest, in both Spain and Portugal were the peasants. Peasants are inherently hard to organize; in addition, the Franco and Salazar regimes kept them illiterate, immobilized, and without significant political influence. As with urban labor, the regimes created officially run organizations for the peasants, but, fearful of upheaval and revolution, they kept the countryside de-politicized as much as possible and did not force them even into the regimes' own peasant associations. Hence, the peasantry remained poor and without significant political influence. Meanwhile, heavy emigration from the countryside (just about all able-bodied males) to the cities and abroad fundamentally changed the nature of rural society and rendered the few political organizations that did exist for the peasants completely powerless.[11] The peasantry ranked at or near the bottom of Spanish and Portuguese interest groups.

As we have seen the number of interest groups in Spain and Portugal was kept small: only about 10 major groups, as compared to the hundreds or even thousands of groups in the United States and other genuinely pluralist systems. Moreover, among the 10, only a half dozen or so had any influence, and even that was usually subordinated to the power of an authoritarian regime. This is what we mean by "limited pluralism." Remember, this is not totalitarianism, with *no* independent interest organizations, but authoritarianism with at least a few. The limited and controlled nature of the interest group system under Franco and Salazar helped keep these two regimes in power for so long, but gave them the ability to tap at least some segments of public opinion when they wished.

But now, in the post-Franco and post-Salazar periods, we would see an explosion in the number of interest groups, and also a considerable reordering in their relative power.

DEMOCRACY AND THE PROLIFERATION OF INTEREST GROUPS

Since the death of Franco and the ouster of the Salazar/Caetano regime, Spain and Portugal have become far more pluralistic. The greater freedom and diversity of interest groups reflected the openings toward democracy that occurred in both countries. Democratization meant greater freedom to organize new interest groups and to engage in political activities. Moreover under democracy, the balance of power among the various groups began to shift.

While there was undoubtedly greater pluralism and more interest group activity in the post-Franco and post-Salazar/Caetano era, it was not yet completely unrestrained and unfettered interest group pluralism. The number of interest groups, although greater than before, was still not like the myriad and frenetic interest group activity of the United States (Washington, D.C., alone has over 50,000 registered interest groups; Madrid and Lisbon have less than one one-hundredth of that number.) Furthermore, although it was now easier to organize an interest group, and there was much greater tolerance of activities such as strikes and street demonstrations, considerable restraints on the organization of interest groups still existed. In most cases the group still had to petition the state for recognition, have a certain minimum number of members, adopt a charter or constitution that had to be approved by the state, and fulfill other requirements before it could carry on its activities legally. In both countries, some of the corporative controls that had been in effect under the old dictatorship remained operative, or they were reformulated. Hence, even though there was now greater freedom for interest groups to organize and play an active political role, these were not yet political systems of complete liberty of association because even the new democratic governments wished to retain some degree of control to protect themselves and the nation from the possibility of complete interest group anarchism and political breakdown.

Among the interest groups, a considerable reordering of their relative power also took place under democracy. For example, it is probably accurate to say at this stage that the armed forces is one of the groups that has lost power. The military was the backbone of the old dictatorships, but now its power has been decreased *relative to other important groups*. It is still the ultimate arbiter of national affairs and capable of intervention, but that seems less likely to occur now.

In Spain, some elements within the *military* attempted a coup in 1981, but it was unsuccessful. Since then there has been a decade of rule by a Socialist government whose ascension to power the armed forces did not try to block. The Portuguese revolution of 1974, which deposed the old regime, was carried out by the military—an action that for several years vaulted it into the forefront of political power and influence. But during the 1980s the armed forces were slowly de-politicized, returned to the barracks, and played a less overt role in national politics. The armed forces in both countries continue to stand as sentries and guardians of the political order, but they have not been directly running either country, and behind the scenes their political influence is being further eroded.

The declining influence of the military in Spain and Portugal is owing to several factors. The first is increased education and professionalism on the part of the officer corps: The armed forces now know better their own professional roles, which do not include constant meddling in the political process. Second, civilian institutions are stronger than before, which gives the military less reason to intervene. Third, the civilian governments since the 1970s have been very careful in pampering the armed forces, giving them promotions and benefits as well as perquisites, providing adequate military budgets, consulting them and not interfering in internal military affairs, which is always resented by the proud armed forces. Fourth, with U.S. and European help, the Spanish and Portuguese officer corps have been incorporated into NATO affairs, put on committees, given opportunities to travel, awarded postings in

Brussels, and in general kept so busy that they don't have the time or opportunity to get involved in political activities. Moreover, both militaries have been reduced in size.

But the main reason for the military's current, rather nonpolitical stance is that since the 1970s Spain and Portugal have been stable, functioning democracies. There has been no reason for the armed forces to get involved in politics. Should a real economic, social, or political crisis occur, and the population begin to clamor for the military to save the country, then we will see if all the change factors mentioned are sufficient to keep the military out of politics or if it will feel obliged to intervene.

The *Church* is another declining influence, but its long-term political prospects look even more dismal than those of the armed forces. The Church in Spain and Portugal is facing a severe shortage of personnel; Church institutions (hospitals, schools, charitable organizations) face drastic shortages of funds and are in crisis; and, as both countries have become more secular, the number of communicants is way down. Since Franco and Salazar/Caetano the Church has largely eschewed politics, not gotten deeply involved, and mainly refrained from trying to tell voters how to vote—instructions to which few Spaniards or Portuguese would listen anyhow. However, in the mid-1970s the Church in the north of Portugal did have some influence in steering voters away from the far-Left parties and toward the Center.

Spanish and Portuguese political culture is also changing, and one would be hard-pressed now to make the case that it is the same Catholic political culture of the sixteenth century that still undergirds the polity. The Church is so politically weak that it could not even block the legislation providing for divorce and family planning—issues that the Church feels fall within its moral domain. Spain does not have a Christian-Democratic party or trade union organization of major significance, although in Portugal the Christian-Democrats are still a significant party and electoral bloc. The difference reflects the fact that although both countries have experienced major secularization in recent years, Portugal is still a more Catholic country than Spain.

The *business community* in Spain and Portugal is in a somewhat uncertain position. But first, some distinctions. In the new democratic era in both countries, the old nobility has faded in importance. Their exploits are often still chronicled in the popular tabloids, but as a political influence the historic, titled elite have little remaining power. At the same time, as Spain and Portugal have modernized and industrialized, the power of the old landed elites has also declined markedly. Spain and Portugal are no longer "banana republics" where a handful of wealthy landowners can dominate the political process. That leaves the business/commercial/banking/industrial/entrepreneurial elite(s) as the main element with which we are here concerned.

In Portugal, with its "Socialist" revolution in 1974, the business community lost a great deal of influence. The main *grupos* connected with the Salazar regime were nationalized, many firms were taken over by their employees, some of the most prominent among the business elite were sent abroad, the banks and their extensive holdings were nationalized, and for a time the business community lost all influence in the government. The years since the upheavals of the mid-1970s have seen a gradual recovery in business influence, but many of the Socialist constitutional provisions and restrictive laws of that period remain in effect. Some of the state-owned enterprises are now being privatized, almost all of the business exiles have returned, Portugal's entry into the EEC has given an enormous boost to the business community, and the government is no longer hostile to business. Still, because of the legacy of the revolution and the Communist and left-wing influence in the trade unions, both employer-employee relations and relations between business and some offices of the government are still often tense and prickly.

Spain experienced a more peaceful transition after Franco, and, therefore, its business community has not gone through the same traumas of nationalization, seizures of private property, and so on, as has Portugal's. In addition, the Spanish economy has been booming, so the business elites have not had many reasons to complain. The business groups did not play an active part in the transition to democracy, and their attitudes toward the transitional government of Adolfo Suárez were ambivalent. Business was apprehensive of Felipe González and the PSOE, but even under Socialist rule business interests have been free to carry out their activities. Business is regulated—often irregularly—but it has not been nationalized or even strongly interfered with.

The main Spanish business group is the *Confederación Española de Organizaciones Empresariales* (Spanish Confederation of Entrepreneurial Organizations—CEOE). The CEOE is an umbrella group that tries to speak for the entire business community. But there are also separate, more specialized, associations for the several main sectors of the economy—banking, industry, and so on. In addition, there are two national confederations of small and medium-sized businesses, as well as local and regional business organizations in the main industrial centers of Spain: Madrid, Catalonia, the Basque country, Valencia, Sevilla, and others.

The older corporative system of Franco and Salazar, under which both business and labor were incorporated into an official system of associations or "syndicates" controlled by the regime, has now been abolished. And yet many features of that old system remain in place. At one level, through the structure of official licenses and permits, the state still seeks to control and regulate business groups to serve the national interest; its ability to do this in the new era of greater pluralism is often problematic. But at another level the old system also operates: Business is still often not very entrepreneurial or risk-taking and depends heavily on the government for contracts, special access, and monopolies. So there is both cooperation as well as a built-in tension between the state and the business community.

In both countries big business is now in a key and influential position. That is so because Spain and Portugal are heavily dependent on business to provide the jobs, economic growth, and prosperity that all governments need to survive and remain politically popular. This dependency has given business enormous clout over government policy—as demonstrated by the unwillingness of even a Socialist government in Spain to tamper with business. Businesspeople and bankers now regularly command cabinet and other high positions in whatever government comes to power in Spain and Portugal, and the business voice is heard at the highest levels of government. It could be said that in the present era big business has become the most important interest group in Spain and Portugal—more important, particularly on the crucial everyday issues of management of the economy, than even the army.

Organized labor has also emerged from the shadow of the Franco and Salazar dictatorships. Forced to operate clandestinely or with only quasi-official status under the old regimes, the trade union movement since the mid-1970s has evolved as one of the major influences in the new pluralist order.

In both countries the union movement is highly political and strongly politicized. The two main labor organizations in Spain are the *Confederación Sindical de Comisiones Obreras* (CCOO), which is closely associated with the Communist party, and the *Unión General de Trabajadores* (UGT), which is closely associated with the Socialist party. In addition, there are some smaller labor confederations, some independents, and some regional and local unions that often go their way independent of the larger national organizations.

At the time of Franco's death the CCOO was considered the largest labor organization, and there was some fear that the Communist party might use the strong labor confederation associated with it to seize control. But, aided by the United States and some Western European countries, the Socialist labor movement grew in strength; also, Spanish voters proved to be quite moderate, opting for middle-of-the-road candidates and Socialists—but not Communists. What is interesting is that although the electoral strength of the Spanish Communist party has declined steadily since the 1970s, the influence of the Communist trade unions has remained largely constant. That means the militant Communist workers have remained generally loyal to their union but not necessarily to the party; at the same time, the Communist party has not been able to attract voters who are not already Communist militants.

In Portugal the labor situation is now remarkably parallel to Spain's, but it was not always that way. In the revolutionary upheavals of the mid-1970s, the strong, formerly underground Communist *Intersindical* not only rose to the surface and was legalized, but it also made a bold bid for full power. It sought not a pluralism of labor organizations but control over *all* the trade union movements. Under the leadership of the strong Portuguese Communist party, it sought in 1974–75 to create a revolutionary situation in which it could seize power.

The Communist Intersindical was opposed by the Socialist labor organization, the *União Geral dos Trabalhadores* (UGT). Things looked bad for the Socialists for a time but, again, with U.S. and European help, as well as the good sense of the Portuguese voters, the tide was turned. Today, although Communists remain strong and militant in many labor sectors, the Socialists have pulled up to a position of parity and, in terms of actual numbers, may now have a larger organization. In addition to these two major labor organizations, there is a small Christian-democratic trade union movement, several independents, and some regional and local unions.

Several interesting features stand out about the Spanish and Portuguese trade unions: (1) how political they are; (2) their close associations with political parties; (3) their efforts to influence (or capture) the government rather than employers; (4) their dependence on the state for favors and salary increases; and (5) the intense rivalries between the several labor organizations along political lines. In addition, the Portuguese and Spanish labor movements still exist in a quasi- or neocorporative arrangement with the state and with employers. Neocorporatism is most clearly seen in the series of pacts between labor, employers, and the state that have ensured labor peace while also giving the workers some increased benefits. This is different from the ideological corporatism of Salazar and of Franco's advisors, but it is a form of corporatism nonetheless about which more will be said later on.

In terms of their relative power, the labor organizations were weak under the old dictatorships, strong in the late 1970s, and growing weaker in the 1980s. In Portugal in its revolutionary years, the unions and their allies could paralyze and even bring down a government; in Spain a Socialist government in power during most of the 1980s nonetheless followed a quite conservative economic policy. In both countries, the political demands of providing steady economic growth as well as stability and prosperity meant increasingly that strikes had to be avoided and that business interests predominated over labor interests.

<u>*Peasants* in Spain and Portugal are still not well organized</u> politically. In contrast to the years of dictatorship, now they are *free* to organize but few are actually members of political interest groups. Peasants can vote, of course, in the new era of democracy, and many have joined or associated themselves with the political parties. But interest groups in the countryside remain few and far between.

In Portugal in the revolutionary mid-1970s there were many peasant seizures of private landholdings and strenuous efforts by the Communists and other militant groups to organize revolutionary peasant movements. Although there was little revolutionary upheaval in Spain following Franco's death, some peasant efforts to seize privately owned estates were attempted there as well.

But since the 1970s the countryside has once again become more docile, under the pressures for stability, productivity, mechanization (mainly in Spain), and economic growth. Those who object to the agrarian system or to life in the countryside now do so mainly with their feet, by emigrating to the cities or abroad rather than by militant action. This kind of movement has recently become massive, meaning that the possibilities of organizing and mobilizing the countryside are even less than before since most of the able-bodied people are leaving.

Nor have the *students* emerged as a major political force. For a time in the mid- to late 1970s, with the revolution occurring in Portugal, Franco's death, and militancy in the air, the student groups were highly politicized (and also associated with the major parties), militant, and activist. But since then, with a more conservative climate prevailing in both countries, the extent and degree of student activism have declined. For one thing, the economy demands growth and stability and not student militancy. For another, the students themselves, for the most part, are caught up in an ethic that demands study, graduation, and the acquiring of a good job—none of which are advanced by continued political activism. Students may organize and demonstrate over specific issues but they do not have the power or potential to destabilize the political system.

Two other groups, meanwhile have continued to grow—albeit quietly. The first is the *middle class*, which we have seen is far larger now in both countries than 30 years ago. With that growth has come a multiplying of middle-class associations: community groups, professional associations, neighborhood associations, groups of all sorts. The proliferation of these predominantly middle-class intermediary organizations has added new dimensions to Spanish and Portuguese pluralism; it has also helped fill the "vacuum of associability," which has long been lamented in both countries. But so far, other than in these general ways, the new middle-class associations have not had a great deal of political impact. For one thing, their memberships often remain small and the organizations themselves quite weak; for another, it has mainly been the political parties that have articulated and championed various policy positions, and not the middle-class associations, many of whose charters—approved by the government—require that they be "nonpolitical." So far we have not seen in either Spain or Portugal the development of an interest group lobbying system as in the United States; however, the very presence of a sizable and growing middle class may signal a more solid base for democracy and moderation than in the past.

The *bureaucracy* is another "quiet" interest that merits attention. The bureaucracy had been growing for quite some time, even under Franco and Salazar, particularly as they launched their economic modernization plans in the 1950s. As the government played a greater and greater role in the economy and launched new social programs, the size of the civil service continued to increase. The growth of the bureaucracy continued in Spain in the post-Franco period; it took a quantum leap upward in size in Portugal when the nationalizations of the mid-1970s' revolutionary period occurred.

The bureaucracy has grown, in part, because the government has been called upon to do more in the way of housing, health care, education, and so on. In addition, there is in both Spain and Portugal a tradition of looking to the state to solve problems rather than to the private sector. Third, the state has taken on a greater regulatory role as the economies of these two countries have modernized and become more complex. Finally, in the new era of democracy, government leaders have been more obligated to reward their friends and supporters with government patronage positions. The patronage situation is not so bad as it is in some Latin American countries, but at the same time the civil service in Spain and Portugal is not so modern and efficient as it is in most Western European countries.

Everyone agrees that the Spanish and Portuguese bureaucracies are bloated and inefficient, but that is hard to change because political loyalties require patronage opportunities in return. Most everyone also agrees on the need to privatize some inefficient Spanish and Portuguese state-owned firms, but that is also hard to do politically if it means a loss of jobs for party loyalists. In both countries the bureaucracy is now organized into civil service unions or organizations, and these also make it difficult to reform and streamline the public service. But the main problem is the continuing political and patronage functions that public employment serves. In other words, it is difficult for any government, which needs the loyalty of the bureaucracy in order for its programs to be carried out successfully and is also expected to reward its friends, to effect a wholesale restructuring of the bureaucratic system.

LIBERALISM, PLURALISM, AND THE CONTRACT STATE

Neither Spain nor Portugal has had an abundance of interest groups historically.[12] They are not like the United States, which, as early as the 1830s, impressed Alexis de Tocqueville with its vast web of intermediary associations standing between the citizen and the state.[13] Tocqueville and most analysts since have thought of such a web of associability as the best defense of democracy and against dictatorship. Lacking such strong associations, it is small wonder that Spain and Portugal historically have alternated between dictatorship and chaos. The Iberian countries have been dominated traditionally by extended family networks and rival clans that often fought with one another, not by a strong system of interest associations.

When, finally, interest group pluralism began to grow in twentieth century Spain and Portugal, it was opposed by conservative groups who wanted to retain an organic order, and then largely snuffed out under the traditionalist regimes of Franco and Salazar. In the place of an interest group system of free and independent associations, Franco and Salazar created a corporative system in which most major groups were subordinated to state control and direction.

Since the mid-1970s a new and more pluralist interest group system has emerged. Moreover, the balance between the interest groups has changed over time. Our analysis has shown that the economic elites, the middle class, the bureaucracy, and the trade unions have gained in power. The big loser in the Spanish and Portuguese interest group system has been the Church. Since Franco and Salazar, the army has also lost some degree of power, although not as much as the Church. The peasantry has not gained much power in either country, but then its ranks are being heavily depleted through emigration. Another striking feature of change within the economic elites is how the old agricultural landholding class has been supplanted by newer business, commercial, banking, and industrial elites.

In both countries, however, the interest group system when viewed as a whole tends to be nascent and weak. It is still, after all, only about 20 years old and it takes considerable time for these interests to become established. Family, patronage, and clan connections and considerations are still often more important and influential than the formal interest groups. The system is more competitive and freewheeling than before, but it is still a system of somewhat limited pluralism and of generally weak organizations. Memberships in the associations are often small, the political parties tend to preempt the articulation and aggregation functions that interest groups perform in more developed countries, and the state—even in the new democratic era—still tends often to make decisions by decree-law, in a top-down manner, without consulting the interest groups.

The Spanish and Portuguese states are thus still bureaucratic states and only partially pluralistic. The interest groups tend to deal with each other not directly but indirectly, through the state system. It is the state that is still the leading voice in settling labor disputes, for example, not so much organized trade unions and employer groups dealing directly with each other. The Spanish and Portuguese states are still a directing influence over the interest associations and require the interest groups to fulfill various requirements before they can be recognized as legitimate and can, therefore, legally bargain in the political process. These features—a strong directing state, its leading role in interest group disputes, its power to grant or withhold recognition—have led many analysts to conclude that Spain and Portugal are still *corporative systems.* They are no longer corporative in the old, Franco and Salazar, exclusionary sense, but in the newer, more modern and inclusionary sense of trying still to tie all the groups together under the guidance of the state for integral national development.

Spain and Portugal, therefore, remain somewhere in between: not fully pluralist but no longer authoritarian either. In fact what we are seeing since Franco and Salazar is an effort to redefine and renegotiate the relations between the state and the various societal interests. These include the relations of the military to the state, the Church to the state, labor and business to the state, as well as (in Spain) the several regions to the central authority. These relations were defined one way under the old dictatorships, but those regimes are no longer in power, we are now in a freer and more democratic era, and, hence, the relations of the state to these various groups all need to be reformulated to reflect the new realities. This suggests that we pay particular attention both to the informal political processes of Spain and Portugal (public opinion, electoral competition, street demonstrations, and so on) *and* to the formal-legal redefinition of state-group relations as reflected in the organic laws that spell out the powers of the state vis-à-vis the armed forces, vis-à-vis the Church, and so forth.

Because these laws often take the form of formal compacts, I have chosen to call this a "contract system."[14] These contracts between the state and the various interest groups represent an understudied but important political arena—as important, I suggest, as the political party arena and others as well. If we wish to understand Spain and Portugal, this contract system, the world of compacts and organic laws defining the relative power and responsibilities of the state and the several *intereses*, is essential to our comprehension.

NOTES

1. Theodore Lowi, "The Public Philosophy: Interest Group Liberalism," *American Political Science Review*, 61 (March 1967): 5–24.
2. For an elaboration of the contract state idea see Howard J. Wiarda, "State-Society Relations in Latin America: Toward a Theory of the Contract State," in Howard J. Wiarda, *From Reagan to Bush: Issues and Controversies in U.S. Latin America Policy*, Chapter 8 (New York: New York University Press, 1992); for Spain, Amando de Miguel, *Manual de Estructura Social de España* (Madrid: Ed. Tecnos, 1974); and de Miguel and Jaime Martín Moreno, *La Piramide Social Española* (Madrid: Fundación Juan, March 1977).
3. The data comes from the World Bank, *World Bank Development Report 1990* (New York: Oxford University Press, 1990).
4. For a comparative perspective on these differences see Louis Hartz (ed.), *The Founding of New Societies* (New York: Harcourt Brace Jovanovich, 1964).
5. Stanley Payne, *Politics and the Military in Modern Spain* (Stanford, Calif.: Stanford University Press, 1967).
6. Stanley, Payne, *Spanish Catholicism: An Historical Overview* (Madison, Wis.: University of Wisconsin Press, 1984).
7. W. W. Rostow, *The Stages of Economic Growth* (Cambridge, England: Cambridge University Press, 1960).

8. For the general model and a case study see James L. Payne, *Labor and Politics in Peru: The System of Political Bargaining* (New Haven, Conn.: Yale University Press, 1965).
9. Howard J. Wiarda, *Corporatism and Development: The Portuguese Experience* (Amherst, Mass.: University of Massachusetts Press, 1977).
10. Amando de Miguel, *40 Milliones de Españoles 40 Años Después* (Barcelona: Ed. Girjalbo, 1976). See also the many related surveys of Spanish public opinion carried out by de Miguel's polling agency, FOESSA.
11. José Cutileiro, *A Portuguese Rural Society* (Oxford, England: Clarendon Press, 1971).
12. Juan Linz, "A Century of Politics and Interests in Spain," in Suzanne Berger (ed.), *Organizing Interests in Western Europe* (New York: Cambridge University Press, 1981), pp. 367–415.
13. Alexis de Tocqueville, *Democracy in America* (New York: Mentor Books, 1956).
14. Wiarda, Howard J., "State-Society Relations"; we return to this theme in the conclusion.

Chapter 7

Political Parties and the Party System

*P*olitical parties and a functioning party system are relatively new in Spain and Portugal.[1] Early in the twentieth century a nascent party system began to form in both countries, but it was snuffed out by the 40-year dictatorships of Franco and Salazar/Caetano. Both Franco and Salazar then created a single, official party to serve as a further apparatus of control in their authoritarian systems, but the regimes provided no choice among candidates, no regular and competitive elections, and very limited pluralism. It was only in 1974–75, with the Portuguese revolution and the death of Franco, that a modern, competitive, democratic party system came into existence for the first time.[2]

The parties and a functioning party system, therefore, like the interest group system, have only been in operation for about 20 years. That is too short a time for the parties and the party system to have been fully consolidated and institutionalized as *the* means of presenting candidates, aggregating interests, and determining political outcomes. On the other hand, within this relatively short period, the parties have been well established, a full party spectrum has come into existence, and elections and democracy in which the parties play crucial roles have been strongly legitimated. Hence, in this chapter we look at both the emergence of the political parties and their strengths, as well as their continued weaknesses—for to the degree the parties are strong and functioning, democracy in Spain and Portugal is strengthened, but to the degree they are weak and disorganized, democracy can also be in trouble.

HISTORY OF THE POLITICAL PARTIES

Spain and Portugal have long had "factions" that can be seen as precursors of political parties. During the late Middle Ages, as Spain and Portugal emerged as centralized kingdoms, these factions debated vigorously the degree of centralization versus the degree of local or regional autonomy, the extent of popular participation in government, and the degree of group or corporate "rights" (*fueros* in Spanish, *foros* in Portuguese) as opposed to the absolutist tendencies of the crown. These debates, and the wars and struggles over the different issues involved, serve to indicate that Spain and Portugal were not always monolithically authoritarian, that there were rival factions and positions, and that there was a real political process even in premodern times.

It was not until the eighteenth century, however, that the factions that would serve as the forerunners of the modern political debate emerged. The issue was the reforms carried out by the new Bourbon monarchy in Spain and by the reformer Pombal in Portugal. The debate divided Spain and Portugal each into two rival "families," two rival "countries." On the one side were urban Spain and urban Portugal, the new middle class, commercial elements, the modernizing elements in both countries who favored the new reforms, favored the enlightenment, and were European-oriented. On the other side were rural Spain and rural Portugal, the landed class, the Church, and the peasantry who were conservative, Catholic, traditionalist, and inward-looking. This split in the Spanish and Portuguese soul deeply divided the two countries and persisted into modern times.

In the nineteenth century these divisions became deeper. On the one side was an emerging liberalism that sometimes verged on libertinage (chaotic, almost anarchic); on the other was traditionalism that hardened into reaction. The immediate issue was the liberalizing Spanish constitution of 1812, but the underlying question was the future direction and destiny of the Spanish and Portuguese nations. One group favored constitutionalism and its progressive notions such as limited monarchy and representative government, and it aligned itself with one faction, mainly Isabella II, in the Spanish royal family. The other group opposed all change and sided with the Spanish pretender Don Carlos, who vowed to abolish the restrictions on the Church and on royal authority. Portugal in the 1820s and

1830s had similarly divisive conflicts about whether the Catholic church should enjoy official status, the role of the Jesuits, and the extent of royal authority. These conflicts produced numerous battles in the nineteenth century and repeated civil wars, and severely retarded Spanish and Portuguese political progress.

In the last quarter of the nineteenth century and the first decades of the twentieth, some real political parties began to emerge out of the earlier factions. Portugal remained a monarchy until 1910 and Spain until 1931, but even under the monarchy parties began to grow. In the early years the main parties in opposition to the monarchy were the Republicans, but at different times and clandestinely Socialist and Anarchist parties also began to emerge. The establishment of the republic in Portugal in 1910 meant also the triumph of the Democratic party which dominated for the next 16 years; but other, more radical parties also grew up and the conservatives likewise began to compete in the party arena through the establishment of a Monarchist party. The founding of the Spanish republic in 1931 similarly led to a flowering of political parties, including the Falange, Socialists, Anarchists, Communists, and moderates. But the coming to power of the military and then of Salazar in Portugal and Franco in Spain meant the end of the parties and the emerging party system. All the parties associated with radicalism and republicanism were now snuffed out.

POLITICAL PARTIES UNDER AUTHORITARIANISM

With the coming to power of the Salazar regime in Portugal and Franco in Spain, political parties and anything resembling a party "system" were eclipsed. The parties that had been prominent during the republic were illegalized. Many of their leaders were jailed, forced underground, or sent abroad; persecution and execution also sometimes occurred, especially in Spain during the civil war and on into the dark days of World War II.

The most severe actions were taken against the parties on the Left (Socialists, Communists, Anarchists); there clearly was an ideological dimension to the suppression of the parties. But in addition it must be said that Franco and Salazar were against *all* parties. They took steps against the right-wing and centrist parties as well as those of the Left. They viewed political parties as divisive agencies, factions, that detracted from the unity, integrity, and grandeur of the state. Their attitudes toward political parties were parallel to their attitudes toward interest groups: Both were seen as agencies of discord and fragmentation that had torn Spain and Portugal into warring factions and which needed to be exorcised. And if one recalls the fractious history of the Portuguese republic, 1910–26, and the at least equally divisive Spanish republic, 1931–36, there are ample justifications for such negativism directed at the political parties.

To replace the old, largely discredited, and now illegal parties, Salazar and Franco created, or gave their blessing to, parties of their own. Salazar created the *União Nacional* (or National Union—UN), and Franco gave his support to the Falange, a largely right-wing and quasi-Fascist party that had been active during the preceding republic. Note that neither of these were called "parties," reflecting the two dictators' distaste for the political party phenomenon. Rather, they were called a "union" or a "phalanx" to demonstrate unity and progress as distinct from the incessant party quarreling of the past. The two parties were supposed to be rallying organizations, civic agencies of unity, movements rather than "parties."[3]

Immediately after the National Union was founded in Portugal and Franco gave his blessing to the Falange, it was thought that these would develop into full-fledged Fascist parties as in Nazi Germany and Mussolini's Italy. But that never happened. The parties never developed a complete ideology of fascism. Even more important was the fact that neither Franco nor Salazar ever devolved much power upon their two party creations. It was *they* who effectively ruled, not their parties. Spain and Portugal were never monolithic "party states" in the Fascist sense, nor were these two organizations ever at the core of national decision making. Rather, these two regimes were basically personal dictatorships that Franco and Salazar effectively governed and in which the parties were just one instrument of domination among several.

If the parties were not at the heart of these two regimes, what then were their functions? Actually, there were several activities that the UN and the Falange carried out, only a few of which are familiar to students of more competitive and pluralist political systems. First, the parties stood for and symbolized unity, in contrast with the divisiveness of the past. They extolled unity, talked *ad nauseam* of national rejuvenation, and sought to propagate themes of nationalism and the distinctiveness of Spain and Portugal.

Second, they functioned as agencies of propaganda. They published exhortations to love of duty and country, distributed the speeches of Franco and Salazar, answered the regimes' critics, issued books and studies of the regimes' accomplishments, and distributed the regimes' version of "correct thinking" on almost all subjects.

Third, along with the secret police, the parties helped keep tabs on the population. They kept files on politically active persons, sought to root out dissent and dissenters, and maintained core groups of persons loyal to the two Iberian regimes.

Fourth, the parties served as a recruiting agency for upwardly rising politicians and as a resting place for falling ones. Loyalty and service to the party were ways by which young *políticos* could move upward in the otherwise socially rigid Spanish and Portuguese systems. At the same time, old or out-of-favor politicians could be "retired" or put out to pasture by being given a position in the vast party apparatus.

The party was also, fifth, a means to keep the loyalty of the population. For any government and many private jobs, membership in the party was a requirement. One could not get a bureaucratic position, qualify for public welfare, travel abroad, or do virtually anything without a party membership card. If so many basics of life depended on loyalty to the party, one was careful to maintain one's membership in good standing; dissent was thereby also strongly discouraged.

Sixth, the two parties served patronage functions. The party machinery provided many jobs. Jobs elsewhere in the government likewise depended on being able to demonstrate party loyalty. In addition, these two political machines provided toys to children at Christmas time, a little relief to people in need, sewing machines for widows, artificial limbs to incapacitated military veterans, and so on. The party functioned as a gigantic patronage machine, dispensing goods and services in return for loyalty and service. If one understands Mayor Daley's Chicago or other big-city machines in the United States and can envision such machine politics taking place on a national scale, then one will have a good idea of how the Portuguese UN and the Spanish Falange (renamed "The Movement") functioned.

Only incidentally, seventh, and almost as an afterthought, did these two "parties" do what we think of political parties doing: articulate a platform and run candidates in elections. Elections were held more or less regularly in both countries, but all the other parties had been banned and, with only a couple of exceptions, competition was not allowed. So the two official parties put up candidates who always echoed the regimes' line, who "ran" in a desultory fashion (why campaign if there is no competition?), and who were almost always reelected unanimously. These were reaffirming elections designed to ratify the regime in power and its programs, not to provide for any real choice. Such "elections" provided some limited popular legitimacy to the Franco and Salazar regimes, but they were by no means democratic.

Toward the end, both these long-term authoritarian regimes began to open up somewhat. Within the Falange, Left, Center, Right, and Christian-democratic groups began more openly to compete for control; and outside the Falange new political associations and "study groups" began to be formed. In Portugal, Salazar's successor Marcello Caetano changed the *União Nacional* to the *Aliança Nacional Popular* (ANP) as part of his efforts to liberalize somewhat the old regime; and there were also "study groups" that *de facto* began to function as political parties. But it took the Portuguese revolution in 1974 and the death of Franco in 1975 before a functioning, democratic party system began to come into existence.

THE EMERGENCE OF A NEW PARTY SYSTEM

The new and more democratic political parties and party systems that now began to emerge in Spain and Portugal had their origins under the old dictatorships, but it required the end of these regimes before the new party system could fully develop. At least four forces were at work.

The first was the increasing factionalism already alluded to *within* the official party apparatus of the two dictatorships. In Spain, as indicated, there were right-wing Falangists, left-wing Falangists, Christian-democratic Falangists, as well as several centrist groups. In Portugal, Caetano's ANP had a "liberal" wing as well as an "old guard" of loyalists to Salazar's principles. These factions gave the Spanish and Portuguese authoritarian regimes somewhat greater pluralism in their later years than in their earlier ones; a number of these factions within the old regimes and in the regimes' official parties also served as the nuclei for the new and broader-based parties that formed after the dictatorships were dissolved.

A second source of new parties was the "tolerated opposition" that existed under Salazar/Caetano and Franco. By the early 1970s these regimes had become *dictablandas* rather than *dictaduras*—"soft" dictatorships and no longer "hard" dictatorships. Thus, they provided more room for opposition activities than they had before. There were opposition newspapers that published with only a minimum of censorship, opposition "study groups" that met regularly, opposition student groups, and so on. These groups were monitored by the authoritarian regimes still in power, but seldom were they persecuted or repressed. Such toleration on the part of Franco and Salazar/Caetano was still limited to the moderate opposition—liberals and Social-Democrats, Christian Democrats, some Socialists; it did not extend to the more radical Socialists and Communists. Eventually, once the dictatorships were removed and their controls relaxed, these study groups and opposition elements helped form the several centrist and social-democratic political parties that were organized.

A third source of future political party cadres was the underground. In both Spain and Portugal during the 1960s, the Socialist and Communist parties were active in the underground movement, recruiting and organizing students and intellectuals and especially workers. They organized labor movements called in both countries the *Intersindical* ("United Workers") and pressed the government for higher wages, better benefits, and improved working conditions within the workplace. They often challenged the official unions or corporate organizations. Surprisingly, given the dictatorial practices of the Franco and Salazar regimes, the government frequently tolerated these radical movements, negotiated (irregularly) with them, and acceded to some of their demands. These underground movements would later surface, once Caetano had been overthrown and Franco had died, and form the mass base for the strong Socialist and Communist parties that would emerge in both countries.

The fourth element important in the formation of a new party system was the exiled opposition. This included mainly the leadership of the Socialist and Communist parties who had lived many years, respectively, in the Western European and Eastern European capitals, as well as a number of liberals, independent Marxists, and others who had fallen out with Franco and Salazar for various reasons. The Socialist and Communist cadres were already organizing clandestinely *within* Spain and Portugal, but the leadership was still mainly outside Iberia. However, when Caetano was ousted and Franco passed away, these persons hurried back to Lisbon and Madrid to assume the leadership of the formerly underground organizations that were now springing quickly to the surface.

This portrait of the later Franco and Salazar/Caetano regimes shows them to be considerably more porous than the usual picture we have of them as rigid dictatorships. In fact, toward the end of the old regimes and with everyone sensing that the end was near, all kinds of political and organizational activities were going on that would not have been tolerated before. These strenuous activities by a variety of groups even before Franco died and Caetano was sent into exile help explain why a full-fledged political party system sprang up so quickly, almost instantaneously, once the old regimes did, finally, come to an end. In fact the nucleus of the party systems that would emerge full-blown under democracy were *already in existence* while the old dictatorships were still in power. All that was required now was for the dictatorships to end, the controls to be relaxed, and the party leaders to return from exile. When that happened, the parties and a party system quickly sprang full-fledged to life.

THE PARTY SPECTRUMS

The political party spectrums in both Spain and Portugal are wide and remarkably parallel. In part, this is due to the common culture and history of the two countries, to the fact that they both rid themselves of authoritarian regimes in the same time period (mid-1970s), and to their both watching and learning from each other. However, even within this picture of two polities whose party systems are parallel in many respects are subtle differences and nuances that make each regime unique.

The political party spectrum in the two countries may be graphically displayed as shown in Table 7.1. Out on the far left in both countries are a variety of radical, often Marxist, sometimes revolutionary groups. These groups tend to be small in number but capable of getting attention out of proportion to their voter support.

Table 7.1. THE PARTY SYSTEMS OF SPAIN AND PORTUGAL

Spain					
Left		Center		Right	
Radical left groups	Communist party (PCE)	Socialist party (PSOE)	Union of Democratic Center (UDC)	Popular Alliance (AP)	Other right-wing factions
			Regional/Provincial Parties		

Portugal					
Left		Center			Right
Radical left groups	Communist party (PCP)	Socialist party (PS)	Social Democratic party (PSD)	Social Democratic Center (Christian Democrats—CDS)	Monarchist party; other right-wing parties

These groups are often centered in the universities and among intellectuals, with some modest support among workers. They often call themselves "independent Marxists" and take pride in being, according to their own slogans, "to the left of the Communist party" or "more to the left than anyone."

In Portugal immediately after the 1974 revolution, the far-left groups, mainly the Popular Democratic Movement or MDP, had considerable influence. Their ranks were augmented by revolutionaries from all over the world (Germany, Japan, the United States, Western Europe) who flocked to Portugal to be a part of the revolution. They often engaged in guerrilla tactics, industry and land takeovers, and street demonstrations. Alone they could mount major demonstrations; in alliance with the Communist party they made the Left look quite powerful. But since the heady revolutionary days of the mid-1970s, these groups have been mainly absorbed into the larger parties, and the *Internacionalistas* have gone on to other causes. The far-left groups still exist in the universities and elsewhere, but they are now viewed as on the fringe and are without the significant disruptive capacity of earlier years.

The Spanish far-left groups have gone through the opposite trajectory. They were weak after Franco's death, and their capacity to play a leading role in a revolutionary transformation as in Portugal was given little credence. However, the moderation and gradual decline of the Spanish Communist party, coupled with the conservative social and economic policies of Felipe González's governing Socialists, have given a boost to the more radical elements. They cannot overthrow the prevailing system or even cause much disruption, but they can and do launch protests, and their criticisms of "the system" have sometimes been telling.

The main group on the far left in both countries is the Communist party. Both the Spanish and the Portuguese Communist parties have long histories of defiance and martyrdom forged during the years of resistance to the Franco and Salazar dictatorships. The leaderships of both parties spent long years in jail or exile or both; they had reputations for being tough and able. The party leaders lived in Moscow and Prague and other European capitals; however, some of their cadres continued to function underground in Spain and Portugal where they formed peasant associations and organized the labor *Intersindical*. Both the Spanish and Portuguese Communist parties were long considered orthodox, Moscow-oriented, Marxist-Leninist parties in the Stalinist mold.

But after the fall of the old regime in Portugal and Franco's death in Spain, the two parties diverged. In both countries, the long-exiled leaders returned and the underground organizations now emerged to function in the open, but the directions taken by the two parties were quite different. In Spain the Communist party (PCE) had a fairly moderate leader, Santiago Carillo. Shaped as much by the Western European model of democratic socialism as by the Eastern European kind, the Spanish party took a "Eurocommunist" position. It said that it believed in elections and would respect the democratic process. Self-serving motives were also involved in the PCE's choice because, unlike Portugal, Spain was not in a revolutionary situation in the mid-1970s and, therefore, the party's only hope was through the electoral route.

The Spanish Communist party won 9 percent of the vote in the 1977 elections; thereafter its electoral popularity gradually faded. Spain was already sufficiently affluent that the Communist appeal no longer had so much attractiveness; in addition, the governments of the centrist Suárez and then the Socialist González proved to be fairly effective and able to provide the goods, services, and democracy that most Spaniards desired, thus undermining the Communists' more radical appeal. As the PCE's fortunes declined, the party was also torn by personal squabbles among its leaders and ideological differences over whether it should continue following the Eurocommunist or the harder Marxist-Leninist line. The unraveling of the Soviet Union in the late 1980s and the revelation of Marxist-Leninist economic and political incompetence there and in Eastern Europe caused the party's attractiveness to fall even further.

In Portugal, in contrast, the Communist party (PCP) leaders returning from exile and resurfacing from the underground found in 1974–75 a genuinely revolutionary situation. Hence, they moved to try to seize power by means of a *putsch*, allying themselves with revolutionary elements in the Armed Forces Movement (MFA). This more forceful revolutionary activity was also in keeping with the desires of the party's hard-line Stalinist leadership led by Alvaro Cunhal. The PCP came within a whisker of succeeding in taking power in the fall of 1975, but ultimately it was turned back by more moderate elements within the armed forces, the democratic political parties, and the international community.

The PCP, along with its far-left allies, got 17 percent of the vote in the first democratic elections in Portugal in 1975, and for several elections after that it held its position at approximately 12 to 15 percent of the vote. But during the 1980s, as Portugal began to recover from the political upheavals of the mid-1970s and then eventually to prosper economically, the PCP's popularity began to decline to 5 to 8 percent of the vote. It remains strong in some of the trade unions, but by now there are challenges to the old-generation leadership and persistent questioning of the party's hard-line positions. It is striking that, once the initial trauma of the post-Franco and post–*Estado Novo* transition had been surmounted, in Iberia, neither the Eurocommunist position of the PCE nor the hard-line position of the PCP could gain much electoral support; and that as both Spain and Portugal grew more prosperous in the 1980s, the Communist appeal declined still further.

Moving next to the Socialist parties of Spain and Portugal, we again find striking similarities as well as differences. Both Socialist parties have a long history, both were forced underground or into exile by Franco and Salazar, and both reemerged following the end of the authoritarianism, building on the nuclei (less persecuted than the Communists) that existed in the two countries. Both parties have their more militant (Marxist and even Marxist-Leninist) as well as more moderate (social-democratic) wings, and both have come to power electorally (unlike the Communists) in the post-authoritarian period when their programs were moderated still more.

During the revolutionary situation in Portugal in 1974–75, the Socialist party (PSP) was looked on as the most viable, *moderate* alternative to the Communist party. It, therefore, received considerable foreign support and domestic votes that it might not otherwise have had. Led by the articulate and politically shrewd Mario Soares, the party was in power from 1976 to 1978 and in a number of governing coalition arrangements thereafter. It followed a moderate, centrist program, but as the Portuguese electorate became more conservative again in the 1980s, the Socialists gradually lost support. A new, younger leadership has taken over in the party and the disputes between the moderate and Marxist factions have been renewed. The party currently functions as the main opposition to the Social-Democratic government.

In Spain, where there was a real center for a time (Suárez) and no serious Communist threat, the Socialists (PSOE—Socialist Party of Spanish Workers) formed the main, left-wing opposition. After Suárez resigned as prime minister and his supporting movement disintegrated in the early 1980s, the Socialists won the election of 1982, and then again in 1987. The Spanish Socialists had long been considered a true Socialist and even Marxist party—more to the left at times than the Communists—but before it won its electoral victories, it became politically "acceptable" by tempering its views. Under Felipe González's leadership in the late 1970s, the party formally abandoned its Marxist slogans ("class struggle," "dictatorship of the proletariat") and adopted more centrist positions. In power it proved moderate and nonthreatening, refused to nationalize various industries as its earlier program called for, and even came out in favor of NATO membership for Spain. González followed essentially a social-democratic course, though there were rumblings from the party's left wing that the Socialist government was "selling out" to capitalism and imperialism. People asked, what was socialist about the Socialist party; and the answer was "not much." But such moderation is what enabled the party to come to power in the first place and made it acceptable to a majority of Spaniards, enabling it to stay in power for a decade and more.

Thus, the left of the political spectrum—occupied by the radical groups, Communists, and the socialists—looks strikingly parallel in Spain and Portugal, although with interesting differences. But as we move toward the center and right of the political spectrum, the similarities fade and the differences between the two countries become more pronounced.

In Spain, the middle of the political spectrum was *formerly* occupied by the Union of the Democratic Center (UDC). The UDC was put together hastily after Franco's death by then prime minister Suárez in order to give him a mechanism for mobilizing electoral support. In the aftermath of Franco's death, with free elections scheduled and a well-organized Socialist party challenging on the left, Suárez found himself with the need to create an electoral mechanism in a hurry in order to stay in power. The UDC was really not a party at all but a loose coalition of fourteen groups—bureaucrats, technocrats, Christians, moderates, independents, government workers, former Franco supporters, and friends of the prime minister—that had no real program or ideology except for opposition to socialism and the desire to see the prime minister (and themselves) stay in office.

But after that first electoral victory in 1977, when the UDC got 34 percent of the vote and the Socialists got 28 percent, the disunity of the groups making up the "party" reasserted itself, the several leaders fell to bickering, Suárez resigned as prime minister, and the "Union" completely fell apart. The UDC suffered an inglorious defeat by the Socialists in 1982 and then largely disintegrated. Suárez, meanwhile, had put together a new organization, the *Centro Democrático y Social* (Social and Democratic Central—CDS), but it remains to be seen whether he can put a broad-based centrist coalition back together. So far Spain lacks a broad centrist party, and the center is probably where the bulk of the electorate in the country lies.

Nor does Spain have a moderate Christian-Democratic party with a popular base or a genuinely social-democratic party to help fill these holes in the political spectrum. Given that Spain has historically been a Catholic country, and given also that the older traditional and reactionary Church associated with Francoism had been discredited, one would expect that a moderate Christian-Democratic movement, like the Christian Democratic Union of Germany, for example, would have strong possibilities in Spain. But that has not happened as yet and, although there is now a Christian Democratic party, it has not had much success electorally. Nor has anyone organized a serious and mass-based Social Democratic party that might be able to challenge the Socialists electorally. Therefore, we can conclude that there is a huge chasm in the Spanish political spectrum stretching all the way from the Socialists on the left, through the broad center and moderate right. Anyone who could put together a party encompassing that range and with a broad popular appeal would have a formidable electoral apparatus and would probably be the next prime minister. But so far such a coalition has been far easier to envision in the mind than in actual fact, and to this point no one has been able to put it together.

There is in Spain a party on the right called the Popular Alliance (AP). The Alliance was long headed by Manuel Fraga, who was considered a liberal when he occupied a cabinet slot under Franco but is thought of as belonging to the far right in the new democratic Spain. The AP suffered two successive defeats at the hands of the Socialists, even though they steadily increased in strength to about 25 percent. Seeking to become the principal opposition (and to fill the organizational space in the center-right of the political spectrum), the party has gotten rid of Fraga, brought in newer and younger leaders, moderated its positions, and sought to become the broad-based conservative opposition to the Socialists. But at this stage we do not know whether the AP will be able to fill that niche or whether it will remain a far-right party, with some other organization eventually filling the space in the center-right.

Portugal has both the popular and broad-based Social Democratic and Christian Democratic parties that Spain lacks. The Portuguese Social Democratic party (PSD) emerged as the more-or-less open and tolerated opposition under Caetano. It had its own weekly newspaper, *Expresso*, that published the most critical analyses the regime then permitted. But when the revolution came in 1974–75, the PSD was considered too weak and conservative to serve as a viable counterweight to the Communists, and hence the Socialists stepped into that role. In the early postrevolutionary elections, the PSD scored well in the conservative north of Portugal but not in the rest of the country. However, under dynamic Franciso Sá

Carneiro the PSD's electoral support grew, the PSD began to occupy the broad center of the political spectrum, and it formed a larger electoral bloc with other centrist and right parties (called the AD or Democratic Alliance) that actually brought it into power in 1980. But when Sá Carneiro was killed in a plane crash while campaigning for reelection, his successor, *Expresso* editor Francisco Pinto Balsemão, lacked Sá Carneiro's charisma and political skills, and the party suffered several reversals. By the mid-1980s it had recovered its momentum, and in 1987 new PSD leader Anibal Cavaco Silva was returned as prime minister and the PSD became the first democratic party in Portugal to win an absolute majority of votes. The PSD was the chief beneficiary of the gradual return to a more conservative Portuguese electorate following the upheavals of the mid-1970s.

The Portuguese Christian Democrats (Social Democratic Center, or CDS) have also emerged as a significant party on the more conservative side. Given Portugal's long tradition of Catholicism, the existence of such a party should not be surprising; what is surprising is that Spain does *not* have a comparable party. Portugal's Christian Democrats are not a radical or Liberation Theology party; rather they represent the more centrist-to-conservative wing of Portuguese Catholicism, which is the dominant wing. The Christian Democrats are led by Diogo Freitas do Amaral and they have been slowly increasing in electoral support. They have also benefitted from the swing back toward conservatism in Portugal, although they have not benefitted as much as the PSD. The Christian Democrats can probably count on 20 to 25 percent of the electorate—not enough to be a governing party but sufficient to be a significant voice. The Christian Democrats, thus, are looked to by both the Socialists and the PSD as a possible coalition partner (which implies a certain number of cabinet positions) should either of these come within range of a majority but in need of the Christian Democrats to push them over the top.

Portugal does not have a strong right-wing party comparable to the AP in Spain. Unlike Spain, most of those associated with the ousted Salazar/Caetano regime were driven into exile, and parties of the right were illegalized by the MFA in the white heat of the 1974–75 revolution. For a time in the 1970s, being on the right meant one was ostracized and one's political rights were taken away. Some of these prohibitions against right-wing political activities remain on the books, although in recent years many of those associated with the former regime have been coming back into the country and a couple of them have even been elected to parliament. When they do reenter politics, conservatives and supporters of the old regime are most likely to do so through the PSD or the Christian Democrats.

Portugal *does* have a monarchist party (Popular Monarchist party, or PPM), which is also quite conservative. After all, Spain has a monarchy that in fact has been a rock of democracy; why should Portugal not also have a monarchy? The Portuguese Monarchists wish to restore the Braganza pretenders to the throne. It should be said that the Monarchist party is not a throwback to the "Hapsburgian Model" of the sixteenth century, but stands for a limited and constitutional monarchy like the British or the Spanish. The monarch would be chiefly the ceremonial head of state, not a ruling head of government. The Monarchist party can command upwards of 5 percent of the vote, which means its support in Portugal is not insignificant.

Both Spain and Portugal have other, largely personalistic parties. These are parties that rally around a single leading personality rather than an issue or program. Most of these are small parties, they frequently come and go, and they command little strength electorally. They are often organized by persons who have an elevated sense of their own importance, who like the prestige and social *caché* that go with heading one's own party, or who wish to use their personal influence and following as a bargaining chip in the larger political arena. For example, they might trade their personal electoral support for a cabinet or other position in someone else's government.

Although most such personalistic parties are small and quickly fade away, in Portugal the Party of Democratic Renovation (PRD) of General Ramalho Eanes achieved some significance. Eanes was a respected military officer, a moderate, and a rock of stability in the otherwise chaotic Portuguese political system of the late 1970s and early 1980s. His austere demeanor reminded many Portuguese of Salazar which, in a time of great troubles and disorder, was not a bad political attribute. Eanes was seen as a sensible, stable counterweight to the often fractious Portuguese parliament and parties, and on that basis he was twice elected president and his followers even garnered some parliamentary seats. The Portuguese presidency is mainly a ceremonial position symbolizing the unity of the nation (especially important when it is *not* unified), but it also has the power to select and dismiss prime ministers when the electoral mandate is not clear, and to serve as a balance wheel and moderating element when the parliamentary system starts to break down. Since both these things have happened several times in Portugal in the last 15 years, that has given the president considerable influence beyond his ceremonial functions. However, we should not expect the former president's personalistic party to last beyond the career of its leader.

Both countries also have small right-wing movements that we can call Fascist. These are comparable on the right to the fringe groups we saw on the left, and the two often respond to and reflect each other. Recall that both Spain and Portugal in the 1930s had real Fascist movements, which were distinct from the Franco and Salazar regimes (often called "Fascist") and with which they often dealt harshly. Today these extreme right-wing movements represent carryovers from this older fascism, or else remnants of Franco and Salazar authoritarianism who still have not reconciled themselves to democratic and electoral politics. Such elements may still be found in the armed forces and a few other institutions, but they have almost no electoral support and their capacity to stage a coup—as in the attempt in Spain in 1981—is severely circumscribed. One would be very surprised if this fringe came to power in either Spain or Portugal. In both countries the extremes of the political spectrum have been greatly reduced in size and become marginalized.

Finally, both countries have regional parties, but they are far stronger in Spain than in Portugal. Portugal's regional parties are really branches or subdivisions of the main national parties that sometimes go their own way; in this they are not much different from the regional party factions in the United States. For example, in the Portuguese islands of Madeira and the Azores, the PSD tends to be more conservative than its mainland counterpart because the islands themselves are more conservative. The islands' separatist movements are small and insignificant, though to the extent Lisbon ignores the islands or goes off in radical directions of its own (as during the revolution of the mid-1970s), nationalist and separatist sentiment tends to grow.

The regional parties in Spain are far more serious, because regionalist sentiment in Spain is far stronger. Here several distinctions must be made, between the several regions and between their several political parties, because the political situations are quite distinct in each region. For example, in Galicia in Spain's far northwest corner, where the language, landholding pattern, ethnic composition, and culture are somewhat different than the rest of Spain (and comparable to that of northern Portugal), there are regional, autonomous, and sometimes separatist sentiments; but the regional parties are not very powerful, there is limited desire for independence from Spain, and politics reflects more the national political divisions and parties than the local ones. In Catalonia (Barcelona) and the northeast Basque provinces, however, regional and separatist sentiments are far more intense, local and regional issues are often more important than the national ones, and, hence, the regional parties are often more important.

But even in these areas there has been change; two major political trends may be identified. Immediately following Franco's death, sentiment for regional autonomy increased markedly in these provinces, new autonomy statutes were negotiated with the central government that made these provinces virtually self-governing in certain areas of responsibility, and regional politics at times tended to subordinate national politics. But now that the early glow of regional autonomy has faded, first, there is a trend toward more and more attention to and voting for the national issues and parties rather than just the regional ones; and second, within these regions the more reasonable and pragmatic political groups have begun to win out and the more radical and ideological ones have begun to decline. That is, in both Catalonia and the Basque provinces, the parties that stand for limited autonomy and a kind of loose federal arrangement with the central government (*Partido Nacionalista Vasco* and the *Pacte Democràtic per Catalunya*) have become dominant, whereas those that desire complete independence and socialism and are willing to use terror to achieve those goals (*Harri Batasuna* and *Euskadiko Ezkerra*) have begun to lose ground.

BASES OF PARTY CLEAVAGE

Spanish and Portuguese politics are divided not just along partisan and ideological lines but also along class, geographic, and religious lines. These patterns first emerged in the early elections after Franco and Salazar/Caetano and, though attenuated, have remained present ever since.

The patterns are clearest in Portugal. As shown in Table 7.2, in the 1975 election the Portuguese Communist party won a strong showing among rural tenant farmers or peasants in the large estate dominated provinces of the Alentejo (the southern so-called red belt) and in the labor centers and industrial concentrations of the central cities of Setúbal and Lisbon. The more centrist and conservative parties (the PSD and the CDS) were more attractive to rural smallholders (farmers who owned their own land), who dominate in the north of Portugal, to Catholics (Catholicism is also stronger in the north), and to the urban middle class in both the north and the south. The Socialist party also attracted some persons from the urban middle class, many intellectuals, many peasants and workers in the south who did not want to vote Communist, and many smallholders in the north who did not want to vote conservative (see Table 7.2). These patterns prevailed for several elections after the initial one in 1975 and seemed to be permanent; but during the 1980s the Socialists, the CDS, and the PSD began to break into the seemingly solid Communist electoral belt in the south and the urban industrial areas. Eventually, the PSD began taking these votes not just from the Communists but from the Socialists as well.

In Spain, in the first post-Franco election in 1977, the social, religious, and political patterns were not altogether different from those in Portugal, although the geographical distribution was different. First, there was a regional split, although not so clearcut as in Portugal, between the conservative, rural, Catholic, and agricultural provinces of the south and west, and the urban, industrial, less parochial, and more European-oriented provinces of the North and East. Prime Minister Suárez's electoral alliance, the UDC, did well in the rural, conservative, Catholic, and non-industrial provinces and among the urban middle classes and government workers. In contrast, the left did well in the urban, industrial, and more cosmopolitan centers, sweeping such centers as Barcelona, Valencia, Madrid, Sevilla, and the Basque provinces. This recent electoral split corresponds almost exactly to the division of the country into the "two Spains" which has been present since the eighteenth century.

In the elections after 1977, as the Socialist party built up its electoral strength, the urban centers have remained Socialist strongholds. But as the Socialists demonstrated their moderation and capacity to govern, they also picked up votes from rural elements and the urban middle classes. Meanwhile, the center-right

Table 7.2. PORTUGAL: DISTRIBUTION OF VOTES BY REGION, 1975 ELECTION*

	MDP (Far-left)	PCP (Communists)	PS (Socialists)	PSD (Social Democrats)	CDS (Christian Democrats)
Rural north	3.3	4.2	30.1	28.2	11.0
Urban north	3.8	7.2	41.6	27.5	9.7
Rural south	6.8	28.1	41.5	8.6	2.4
Urban south	4.7	22.3	45.1	12.6	4.3
Totals	4.2	13.1	38.6	24.7	7.7

*Source: John H. Hammond, "Das Ruas as Urnas: Electoral Behavior and Noninstitutional Militancy—Portugal, 1975," in L. Graham and H. Makler (eds.), Contemporary Portugal (Austin, Tex.: University of Texas Press, 1979): 257–80.

UDC had broken up. Some UDC members then voted for the Socialists, a larger number gravitated to the AP at least initially, some went back to the CDS (Suárez's new party), but the majority were uncertain for whom to cast their ballots and often stayed home. Once again we are reminded of that big hole out there on the Spanish center-right and the large number of votes that would go to a party that might effectively fill that slot.

WEAKNESSES OF THE POLITICAL PARTIES

The Spanish and Portuguese political party systems, in modern times, have been in existence only since the mid-1970s, and, therefore, we should not expect the parties to be as well institutionalized as in some other countries where they have been around longer. The parties and party systems have come a long way in this time, but they still exhibit many weaknesses that lead us to question whether party politics and the electoral arena are as yet the only legitimate or even main arena for achieving power in these countries.

First, the leadership of most of the parties is quite thin. The best-led parties are the Communists in both countries, the Socialists in both countries, the PSD and CDS in Portugal, and the AP in Spain. The other parties have very weak leadership—and even in the parties mentioned as well led, once one drops below the topmost rung, the number of talented, experienced political leaders is very small. It should be said that this problem of thin leadership—probably as a result of such rigid top-down control by Franco and Salazar for so many decades—is present in all Spanish and Portuguese institutions, and the political parties are not an exception in this regard.

Second, party stability has not been great, especially in Portugal; therefore, the loyalty and votes of the parties' followers and voters have not been stable either. The parties have often changed their positions, changed their ideologies, and even changed their place on the party spectrum. Voters have also shifted allegiance rapidly and sporadically; hence, the parties have not yet built up cadres of loyal and predictable followers whose votes can be consistently counted upon. In Portugal the Communist party has a stable albeit shrinking following, but the shifts in political position have been so rapid over the last 15 years that the other parties have volatile and sometimes fleeting followings. Spain, which did not have such a sharp *ruptura* in the mid-1970s as Portugal, has also had stabler parties and programs, with the result that stable electoral blocs have begun to build up.

A third problem is the poor reputation of the parties and the parliament. In both Spain and Portugal, although among the public there is widespread acceptance of the principles of representative, democratic rule, there is far less acceptance of democracy's essential accompanying institutions: parties and parliament. In Portugal, where democracy is supported, according to opinion surveys, by 85 to 90 percent of the population, only about 30 percent have a favorable impression of the parties—any party!—or the parliament. The low figures reflect what is widely seen by the public as cynical opportunism on the part of the parties and a "circus" atmosphere sometimes reigning in the parliament. Spain's parties and parliament, which have been stabler and less chaotic than Portugal's, also have a better reputation, but it is not so high that one should stop worrying about the stability and future of democratic institutions in both countries.

A fourth problem is the still weak links between the parties and socioeconomic groups: labor, business, farmers, middle-class professionals, and other societal actors. In most other European countries the ties between parties, socioeconomic groups, and the state are quite close—and may be described as representing an updated form of corporatism. But in Spain and Portugal, which are still trying to live down the old-fashioned authoritarian state–corporatism of Franco and Salazar, there are strong reactions against *any* form of corporatism. Such attitudes, as well as the relative newness of the Spanish and Portuguese parties, have served further to retard the parties' links with societal groups. Spain and Portugal have rejected one form of corporatism but they have not so far accommodated themselves to a newer European form.[4] Without those corporative ties the parties have continued to exist in relative isolation without close associations with socioeconomic groups and as yet are not well integrated into the society.

Finally, there are patronage problems. These have several dimensions. At one level, as new democracies, Spain and Portugal have sought to avoid the vast patronage and sinecure activities associated with various regimes and parties in their pasts, thinking that such patronage is unseemly and probably corrupting. At another level, however, party officials and their followers, deprived from office for so long under Franco and Salazar, are now clamoring for the jobs, sinecures, and opportunities for private advancement that they believe their support for the parties now in power are due them. A third level involves going from such old-fashioned patronage to a newer, "corporatized" form in which it is socioeconomic groups that are tied into the state apparatus and derive program benefits (social programs and the like) from such ties, and no longer just individual party loyalists who want jobs or a cushy deal.

These are all major problems. They indicate that although the Spanish and Portuguese parties have accomplished quite a bit in 15 years, they are not as well established as the supporters of Iberian democracy would like to see.

OTHER "PARTIES" WITHIN THE SYSTEM

Although parties, elections, and parliament have by now been quite well established in Spain and Portugal, they are not the only actors operating and may not even now be the most important or most legitimate ones. Other arenas and other actors, sometimes even called "parties," are also operating, frequently with more force or authority than the parties themselves. These comments were most apropos in the early phases of the transition to democracy in the 1970s; whether they are still applicable today is a question that not only needs answering but also goes a long way toward answering the question of how well consolidated Spanish and Portuguese democracy is.

In Spain in the immediate post-Franco period, the most important actors and political arenas included the king and his efforts to build support for the monarchy; the king's relations with the armed forces; the internal politics of the several military institutions as they sought to grapple with fast-moving political changes and whether even to permit such changes (for example, the legalization of the Communist party); the conflict between Communists and Socialists for control of the trade union movement and their relations to the new regime; the maneuvering of various elite families and their extended family connections; the political maneuvering in and around the prime minister's office; the relations of the central state to the regions clamoring for greater autonomy; the election of a constituent assembly and the writing of a new constitution; the relations of the government to the Cortes or parliament; Spain's relations with the EEC, NATO, Europe, and the United States; and so on. All these were critical arenas of politics and conflict in the 1970s, yet only a few of them had anything to do initially with political parties and the electoral arena.

Similarly in Portugal: the principal arenas were also the internal politics of the armed forces and the Armed Forces Movement (MFA); the relations of the MFA to the Communist party; the activities of various foreign actors (the United States, Germany); the internal conflicts within businesses, families, and offices; the politics of the elite families and the mass mobilizations against them; again the all-important anvil of labor relations; the popular mobilizations and the struggle for control of the streets, factories, or land. None of these arenas were party arenas directly, and several of them were at least as important as what happened in the party and electoral arena.

One could say, therefore, that although the party struggle in both countries was important and the electoral arena was also critical, other arenas were at least equally important. Particularly in Portugal, the action in the streets, the popular mobilizations, and the machinations of the armed forces and the Communist party were at least as important as what happened electorally. In other words, there were several routes to power and not just the democratic formula; moreover, in the Spanish and Portuguese contexts these other routes also had a certain legitimacy, or at least the potential for acquiring some. For example, the Portuguese MFA came to power in 1974 through a *coup d'état*, not by electoral or constitutional means, and yet for a period the MFA enjoyed considerable legitimacy. At least initially, then, there were multiple arenas of politics and many different legitimized routes to power. Since the mid-1970s, the party/electoral route has come to have greater, even overwhelming, legitimacy, whereas these other arenas have declined in importance somewhat; but the earlier experience should give us pause before concluding that in times of national crises these other routes to power might not be used again.

These practices in Spain and Portugal are so common, in fact, that there is a whole separate nomenclature used to describe them. When the military is particularly active, such as the MFA, it is not at all unusual for Spanish or Portuguese journalists to refer to it as the *Partido Militar* ("Military party"). An activist Church, labor union, or business group may similarly take on the "party" label. Moreover, we will need to distinguish between rumors of generalized *descontento* (discontent) within the military, a more specific military *pronunciamiento* (a statement on political matters issued by one or more officers), a *cuartelazo* (an actual barracks revolt), a *golpe de estado* (a full-fledged military takeover), and a military-led *revolución* (as in Portugal in 1974–75). These terms indicate a separate set of categories and language largely unfamiliar to Americans to describe what are actually common political practices of the Spanish and Portuguese armed forces and other institutions. They also may serve to warn us that, to the extent these other avenues to power still exist, the Spanish and Portuguese party systems—and democracy itself—are not quite so well established as we would prefer.

CONCLUSIONS

Political parties, a party system, and party government are relatively new phenomena in Spain and Portugal. With the exception of the chaotic and short-lived republics in both countries of two or three generations ago, neither country, up until recently, had ever had a functioning party system. Some observers, however, would go so far as to say the parties and party systems are mainly concessions to foreign demands, contrived and synthetic organizations created to satisfy European insistence on "democracy" and the requirements of U.S. foreign aid. In this view the parties serve, expediently, to show that Spain and Portugal are as "modern" and "democratic" as their European neighbors, when in fact a scratching of the surface of political life reveals the parties to be ephemeral and not central to the functioning of the political system. As the Spanish writer José Iglesias has said:

> In Spain there has been a tendency to think of politics much more as aesthetics than as an attempt at the practical manipulation of reality in a positive determined sense. There has been no effort to fit political formulations to the exigencies of reality in its rambling process of change, but to adapt that reality to an *a priori* scheme of ideas totally conceived outside its conditions.[5]

The analysis here bears out these conclusions, but only in part. In both countries the parties are still weak and not well institutionalized. To a certain extent they *are* rather artificial creations, derived from *a priori* and often foreign criteria. With some exceptions, they are not well organized, their leadership is thin, membership is small and party identification "soft," voter loyalties are fleeting, the parties are often splintered and fragmented, and party government is still in its infant stage. At the same time the real foci of power in both countries often lie outside the party arena, lodged in the armed forces, the government and bureaucracy, powerful vested interests, the system of labor relations, street demonstrations, and so on. Elections, similarly, provide one route to power but perhaps not the only one.

And yet parties and a party system have emerged, they do perform critical functions, and a system of party government is evolving. These are real political parties that have developed, with real programs and ideologies, and a genuine mass base—and no longer just patronage agencies or political fronts (as often in the nineteenth century) for family and clan-based rivalries. Nor should one discount the impressive turnouts at the polls (consistently over 80 percent), the enormous expansion of popular participation since the mid-1970s, the refreshing climate of liberty and freedom, and the sheer joy and outpouring in favor of democratic rule. The parties have been established, they articulate programs, they present candidates for elections, and the winners then form governments. Respect for the results of the ballot box has gained new legitimacy—perhaps by now it is the only source of legitimacy. Support for democracy is sufficiently well established that no military or civil-military factions, seeking to employ other means to achieve power, could afford to ignore or ride roughshod over the widespread sentiment in favor of democratic legitimacy.

Spain and Portugal thus have a dual power structure; this has been characteristic for three centuries. The important question now is how far the relative balance between them has shifted in this new democratic era. On the one side is the structure and paraphernalia of democracy: parties, campaigns, elections, parliament, cabinet, party government, and so on. But on the other there are some elements of the military, the traditional and vested *intereses*, the strong state structure and powerful corporatist elements, and unreconstructed authoritarian elements of various sorts left over from the past. The political system usually rests on an often uneasy, frequently renegotiated balance and compromise between these two rival power structures. The issue at present is whether that balance has now tipped toward the democratic side, perhaps even irreversibly so.

Although there are always unforeseen contingencies, it is the conclusion of this analysis that the balance has so tipped. Spanish and Portuguese democracy is probably stronger now than ever before in Iberian history. The institutions of democracy—parties, public opinion, elections, Cortes—have become firmer and more consolidated. Overwhelmingly, Spaniards and Portuguese prefer democracy to any other alternative. Moreover, while the social base of democracy—a larger middle class, rising affluence, higher literacy, a political culture of greater pragmatism, integration into Europe—has been steadily growing, the base and support for authoritarianism has been shrinking. This venerated authoritarian-traditionalist "other Spain" and "other Portugal," could conceivably still make a comeback; but it is becoming harder and harder to envision that happening while democratic Spain and democratic Portugal continue over the years to be strengthened. We return to these themes in the book's conclusion.

NOTES

1. For some earlier discussions of political parties in Iberia by the author see "Spain and Portugal," a chapter in Peter Merkl (ed.), *Western European Party Systems* (New York: The Free Press, 1980), pp. 298–328; and "Portugal" in Myron Weiner and Ergun Özbudun (eds.), *Competitive Elections in Developing Countries* (Durham, N.C.: Duke University Press, 1987), pp. 283–327.
2. Good discussions may be found in Tom Bruneau and Alex MacLeod, *Politics in Contemporary Portugal: Parties and the Consolidation of Democracy* (Boulder, Colo.: Lynne Rienner Publishers, 1986); Richard Gunther *et al.*, *Spain after Franco: The Making of a Competitive Party System* (Berkeley, Calif.: University of California Press, 1986); and Howard Penniman (ed.), *Spain at the Polls* (Durham, N.C.: Duke University Press, 1987).
3. For further discussion see Juan Linz, "From Falange to Movimiento-Organización: The Spanish Single Party and the Franco Regime," in Samuel P. Huntington and Clement Moore (eds.), *Authoritarian Politics in Modern Society* (New York: Basic Books, 1970); and Howard J. Wiarda, *Corporatism and Development: The Portuguese Experience* (Amherst, Mass.: University of Massachusetts Press, 1977).
4. See Martin O. Heisler, *Politics in Europe: The Corporatist Polity Model* (New York: McKay, 1974).
5. José Iglesias, *The Franco Years* (Indianapolis, Ind.: Bobbs Merrill, 1977).

Chapter 8

Government and the Role of the State

Since the mid-1970s, Spain and Portugal have made remarkable strides toward democracy. Having replaced the authoritarian and highly centralized regimes of Franco and Salazar, Spain and Portugal appear to have successfully bridged the transition to democracy. This is not to say these countries are without continuing political and governmental problems or that democracy is now fully consolidated; but democracy has been established, it is functioning, it enjoys widespread legitimacy, and there is no other likely alternative. The successful transitions to democracy in Iberia may be thought of as one of the most significant political transformations of the late twentieth century, comparable in importance to the toppling of the Berlin Wall and the reunification of Germany, the transformations in Eastern Europe and the Soviet Union, and the similar democratic transitions in East Asia and Latin America.

In this chapter, we look at government institutions and the role of the state. The purpose is both to show how governmental institutions work in Spain and Portugal and to understand the larger, changing patterns of state-society relations. That is, is it the strong state that has been dominant in Spain and Portugal over time, or is it strong societal groups (the military, the Church, the landed class), or perhaps some alternation throughout history between these two? And, ultimately, do these patterns add up to something we could call a distinct model of Iberian state-society relations?

HISTORICAL PATTERNS

The United States is a country with strong interest groups and a comparatively weak central state. By contrast, the Soviet Union, both before and after the 1917 revolution, is a country with a strong central government (until recently) and very weak interest groups. Spain and Portugal present a third model: a strong state historically, at least in aspiration if not always in actual fact, *and* strong societal or corporate groups.

Throughout Spanish and Portuguese history these two, the state and the society, have vied mightily for domination and control. At some times the societal groups have seemed dominant, at others the state has been all-powerful. Spain and Portugal are usually thought to have been governed "constitutionally" and "democratically" when the relations between the state and the societal groups are in balance and have been defined by compacts or charters that prescribe the powers of each. That is, there may be a compact or an "organic law" between the state and the military orders, between the state and the Catholic church, or between the central state and the municipalities or regional entities.

These organic laws are like contracts or constitutions in that they prescribe the powers, responsibilities, and rights of each party to the agreement. Each group within the system may thus have its own organic law, as distinct from a single, all-encompassing constitution governing the entire political system. Or, the organic laws may be combined with a formal constitution—as at present. Note also that such compacts will put an emphasis on group rights (of the armed forces, of the clergy, of the towns, and so on) over individual rights—which remained a problem in terms of human rights and civil liberties in Spain and Portugal right up to recent times.

Much of Spanish and Portuguese history can be read in terms of the complex relations between the central state and these component societal groups. The state has been trying for nearly a thousand years to expand and consolidate its power, while societal groups have sought to retain autonomy and to hang on to their rights and privileges. This arena of a constantly expanding state and a resistant society may well have been historically the most important arena in politics—more important than the electoral arena. Now the electoral arena is acquiring greater importance in the new democratic era, but the state-society one may still be as important.

In Spain and Portugal, strong societal groups often predated the organization of the central state, and thus, have often staked out a claim to legitimacy greater than that of the state. For example, the military orders (Templars, Hospitalers, and so on) were organized to fight the Moors long before there was a central state in Spain and Portugal, a fact that in part explains why the military, intensely proud of this long history, remains reluctant to subordinate its authority to "mere" civilian government. The Catholic church in Iberia also predates the formation of the state, and it has similarly been reluctant to subordinate itself to political authority. In Spain an organization called the *Mesta*, the sheepowners' guild, also predated the state and for a long time was considered the country's most powerful interest group. In parallel fashion, long before there was a central state, various town and regional governments had been organized during the period of the Reconquest, and they proved—even to this day—extremely reluctant to give up their rights and charters to what they often viewed as an encroaching and arbitrary central state.

As the Reconquest went forward, however, more and more power came to be concentrated in an emerging central state. Portugal was the first to be consolidated (and became the first centralized nation-state in Western Europe) under King Alfonso Henriques by the year 1143. In Spain, a bigger and more diverse territory, the process was longer. The earliest Spanish kingdoms were in León in the northwest of the peninsula and in the Basque country in the northeast. But there were also separate kingdoms in the provinces of Castile, Aragon, Catalonia, and others. The Spanish situation was not only one of complex relations between the emerging state and powerful societal groups but also of rival regional kingdoms seeking to become dominant in the peninsula as a whole.

The issue was not resolved until the reign of Ferdinand and Isabella, 1479–1516. By their marriage, first of all, these sovereigns united the two most important Spanish kingdoms, Castile and Aragon. Second, they drove out all dissenting minority voices and religions in the country: Jews, Muslims, Protestants, freethinkers. And third, they suppressed the societal forces that had long vied with the emerging monarchies for power and control. Isabella stripped the nobility of its power, revoked the independent power of the military orders, abolished the historic *fueros* (rights) of the towns and individual citizens, and ruled with absolute power. The state had now triumphed completely. This was the beginning of what we had earlier termed the "Hapsburgian Model" of absolute, centralized authority.

The centralized authoritarian model dominated for the next three centuries. Two of these were under the Hapsburg monarchy—which remained highly centralized even though its later kings were less and less competent—and one was under the Bourbons. The Bourbons were reformers, but their *system* of rule was as centralized and authoritarian as that of the early Hapsburgs. Societal forces remained subservient.

Beginning in the early nineteenth century, following the Napoleonic occupation of the peninsula, this imbalance in state-society relations began to change. On the one hand, in both Spain and Portugal, monarchical authority, *the* symbol of strong, centralized statism, began increasingly to be challenged and gradually weakened. The Spanish constitution of 1812 called for limits on royal absolutism, a constitutional monarchy; and in both Spain and Portugal throughout the nineteenth century, pitched battles and full-scale civil wars were fought over the question of absolutism versus limited government. On the other hand, during this same period, societal forces became stronger as new business groups, a middle class, political parties, trade unions, and other groups began to be organized.

These developments reached culmination in the Portuguese republic of 1910–26 and the Spanish republic of 1931–36. The monarchy had fallen and the central state was crippled. Both countries wrote republican constitutions that severely limited government authority and lodged power in a weak, partisan, and deeply fissured parliament. In Spain, not only was the power of the central state limited by checks and balances, but the Republican government also decentralized authority by granting a great deal of autonomy to regional entities. Under republicanism, therefore, "society" had reemerged as triumphant—for the first time since Ferdinand and Isabella—but that is not to say the now-weakened governmental system was able to function effectively or well.

That was precisely the argument put forth by Franco and Salazar, who then carried the logic to ridiculous extremes. First, they called for a restrengthening of the central state in the face of the disorganization and seeming unraveling tendencies of the republics. Second, they moved to put restrictions on "societal" activities (political parties, interest groups, and the like) whose untrammeled liberalism, they argued, was leading to chaos, anarchy, and national breakdown. To control societal activities such as trade unions and others was one key reason for the creation of the corporative system. Third, they sought to correct what they perceived as an imbalance in the societal structure by increasing the power of such traditional groups as the armed forces and the Church, decreasing the power of such newer entities as unions and radical political movements, and restoring "harmony" in the area of labor-employer relations. In Spain, fourth, Franco also stripped away the autonomous power of the regions granted by the Republican government and imposed a suffocating centralization that in long-range terms proved as unworkable as the earlier radical decentralization.

POWER AND AUTHORITY UNDER FRANCO AND SALAZAR

Franco in Spain and Salazar in Portugal instituted highly centralized, authoritarian regimes. These were not pluralist regimes with power draining off in various directions. Rather, they were rigid, authoritarian, top-down systems in which virtually all power was concentrated in the hands of Franco and Salazar. That is, after all, why these regimes are called dictatorships.

It must be emphasized that Franco and Salazar were the real locus of power, the real decision makers, in these systems. They were not "fronts" for anyone or any groups, as is sometimes alleged. It was not the Catholic church or *Opus Dei* that ruled Spain or Portugal during this period, nor was it the armed forces or big business. These groups were often influential, but when the chips were really down or when there was conflict between them and the government, it was clear to all that it was Franco and Salazar who effectively ruled their countries, not some behind-the-scenes force.

Nevertheless there was a hierarchy, a pecking order of influence, within the system. Next to Franco and Salazar in power and influence were the armed forces, the backbone of their regimes and the ultimate arbiters of national politics. Because the armed forces were so influential, they were often referred to as the *poder militar* (the "military power"), as if they were a full-fledged second branch of government. Financial, banking, and economic groups were also influential, sometimes also referred to almost as a branch of government: the *poder financiera* or "financial power." The Catholic church was similarly influential and was sometimes referred to as the *poder legitimador* or the "legitimating power," because for a long time it gave its blessing to the authoritarian regime.

Other groups and influences—what we would think of as the more democratic forces—had very little power within the Spanish and Portuguese systems. For example, public opinion was not accorded great respect now was it often listened to by Franco and Salazar. Elections were thought of as ways for Spaniards and Portuguese to express approval of the Franco and Salazar regimes, not to provide any real choices among alternative candidates. Nor was there much real competition among rival interest groups, and certainly not in any way resembling the American interest group struggle. Recall that in Spain and Portugal most interest groups were tightly controlled by the regime; in addition, unlike politicians in democratic systems, Franco and Salazar gave no legitimacy to and refused often to listen to the voices of the interest groups. These traits also marked the regimes as authoritarian dictatorships and not as liberal democracies.

The centralization and authoritarianism of the Franco and Salazar regimes meant the near-complete subordination of civil society. Society was submerged to the needs of the state. In terms of the state-society arena of conflict that has been so powerfully a part of Spanish and Portuguese history, under Franco and Salazar the central state emerged as overwhelmingly dominant whereas civil society was all but snuffed out. Essentially what Franco and Salazar did was to restore the sixteenth century, centralized and authoritarian Hapsburgian Model of Ferdinand and Isabella and to eliminate the liberalizing and democratizing forces that had emerged since that time. The greater balance in state-society relations that had begun to emerge in the nineteenth and early twentieth centuries in both Spain and Portugal was now completely reversed.

Toward the end of both regimes, civil society began to reassert itself. During the 1960s and early 1970s, as the end began to draw near for Franco and Salazar, political parties (or "study groups"), interest groups, neighborhood and community associations, and other organizations began once again to reemerge. There were strict controls and often repression practiced against these groups. But both among the underground and among those groups operating legally, there was a growing sense that change was in the air and that greater "societal" activities would be tolerated. Society did not yet achieve equivalence with the state, let alone surpass it in power—that would happen only after Franco and Salazar were gone and democracy was reestablished—but at least in the last years of dictatorship societal forces had begun to stage a comeback.

Not only was power highly concentrated and centralized under Franco and Salazar, but the functions and authority of the state were greatly expanded as well. First, in the political sphere, these two regimes created extensive single-party systems, they created and expanded the secret police, they modernized and enlarged the armed forces, and they created new national police forces and paramilitary units. In short, there was a vast expansion of the coercive apparatus of the state. But more than that, these two regimes also created new civilian ministries (corporations, labor, social welfare) and considerably expanded the size of the traditional ministries. In both regimes there was sizable growth in the extent and functions of the public bureaucracy.

Second, in the economic sphere, there was also a vast expansion of state functions. Two distinct phases may be noted. The first phase—in the 1930s in Portugal and during the 1940s in Spain—saw an immense enlargement of the state's regulatory functions. The state now regulated areas of economic activity—prices, wages, production, working conditions—that had never been regulated before. In addition, the state now used the regulatory offices and agencies that it created as instruments to further its domination over previously unregulated socioeconomic groups. Both labor and business (the latter less so) were now subject to extensive regulations, controls, licensing requirements, and so on that effectively served as political checks on their activities and, thus, further increased the power of the central state.

The second phase of state expansionism in the economy came in the 1960s, after both countries had determined to modernize their economies and that the state would play a primary role in development. There was in Spain and Portugal an increase in central planning; the state began to play a stronger role in promoting infrastructure development and industrial growth (roads, bridges, port facilities, ship building, steel, petrochemicals), and the state entered into various cooperative arrangements with private banks, both domestic and foreign, as well as with large industrial *grupos* or consortia. The state became, for the first time, a partner in economic development, both helping to stimulate the miracle economic growth rates that both countries experienced in the 1960s and early 1970s, *and* leading to the vast proliferation of state power.

The third area in which state power expanded under Franco and Salazar was in terms of social programs. This area has often been overlooked, particularly by critics of these two regimes who would prefer not to say anything positive about Franco and Salazar. But the fact is that beginning in the 1950s and expanding considerably in the 1960s, both regimes initiated a vast range of new social programs. What previously had been left to families or to the Church, in the form of charity and benefices, now became public functions. The state initiated new programs in social security, unemployment insurance, medical care, welfare, public assistance, and a variety of other areas. The entire structure of a modern welfare state was put in place. Now, we know that many of these programs did not function very well and had extremely limited funds and personnel, and some of them existed more on paper than in reality. Nevertheless, at least the structure was put in place, parts of it functioned, and the expectation was created that the state had responsibilities in all these areas. In many cases the agencies charged with carrying out these new social programs were the same corporative agencies that had been moribund for many years and were now, finally, given something to do.[1] The expansion of state activities into these social program areas also increased the size of the state bureaucracy and the power of the central government.

The Franco and Salazar regimes, therefore, not only saw a complete reversal of the state-society equation back toward a sixteenth century (Hapsburgian) model in which the state was all-powerful and society was completely subjugated, but they also resulted in a vast expansion of state authority. By the end of the Franco and Salazar regimes the state had become politically more powerful, economically more activist, and socially more involved. These were no longer traditional *laissez-faire* economies but ones in which the state and its modern regulatory mechanisms were playing a much larger role. Of course, the state's greater economic power also gave it greater political power and more levers of control.

By the mid-1970s, hence, with the immense expansion of state power, these were no longer simply private enterprise economic systems but, increasingly, systems of state capitalism or updated, modern mercantilism.

We saw that in the last days both the Franco and Salazar regimes opened up somewhat, liberalized, and allowed a measure of openness for civil society. But while Franco and Salazar were still alive these openings were closely restrained; now, however, with the collapse of these regimes, the floodgates opened and civil society reasserted itself. The balance in state-society relations would turn back the other way.

POST-FRANCO, POST-SALAZAR

When the Salazar/Caetano regime collapsed in Portugal in the spring and summer of 1974, its institutional structure collapsed along with it. One after another during this revolutionary period the basic institutional supports of the old regime were torn away by decree law. The secret police were abolished, the official party was abolished, the Salazar constitution of 1933 was declared null and void, the Republican Guard (a paramilitary organization) was abolished, the Salazar labor laws and regulations were also nullified. In successive weeks the entire structure of the corporative state—*sindicatos, gremios,* corporations, corporations ministry, and so on—was abolished. By the fall of 1974 the old Salazar structure had ceased to exist. Nothing permanent had yet been created to replace it, however, and power drained off in various directions: the streets and street demonstrations, private takeovers of lands and buildings, revolutionary actions and ad hoc organizations. A definite *ruptura* (rupture, break) with the old regime had taken place.

Spain watched the events in next-door Portugal with rapt attention and considerable foreboding. Recall that Franco did not die and the Spanish transition did not begin until 19 months after the Portuguese revolution began. Spain did not wish to experience the chaos and economic, social, and political breakdown that Portugal had, nor did it want to run the risk of a Communist takeover which seemed quite possible for a time in Portugal. To the extent, therefore, that the Portuguese revolution resulted in chaotic breakdown or seemed to be leading to civil war (which Spain had experienced in the 1930s and now wanted, above all else, to avoid), Spain sought to prevent a Portuguese-like *ruptura*. It opted instead for a slower *reforma*, which, though more gradual than the Portuguese revolution, produced over the long term results that were just as dramatic.

In a sense, Spain had an easier course to achieve change because the basic institutions of Franco's regime had never been so rigid as those in Portugal. Unlike Salazar, Franco had never adopted a constitution—let alone one so rigid and ideological—and had preferred to govern through a series of fundamental laws that were now changed and liberalized. Nor had Franco ever been so committed to the corporatist ideology as had Salazar, so it was relatively easy to change those structures. Spain changed its basic institutions through a process of consultation and compromise, not through revolution. Franco's fundamental laws were reformed to allow for greater freedom, the political process was gradually opened up, elections for a new constituent assembly were held, a new constitution was adopted and then ratified by an overwhelmingly positive popular vote, and a move toward democracy and greater freedom was made slowly and incrementally. All this was done without upheaval or bloodshed.

Constitutional Structure

The Portuguese constitution of 1976 was the product of a particular time and set of circumstances.[2] The constitution was written in the white heat of the Portuguese revolution. It was written by a Constituent Assembly, elected in 1975 on the first anniversary of the revolution, comprised of the two dominant parties (with 60 percent of the seats): the Socialists (PS—116 seats) and the Communists (PCP—35 seats). In that period the country was still dominated by revolutionary sentiment, the assembly was subject to the blandishment of revolutionary groups, and a great deal of talk about establishing a new Socialist and revolutionary regime was in the air.

The Constituent Assembly eventually adopted a constitution that provided for a democratic, parliamentary system (political parties, elections, parliament, prime minister); a number of its special features command our attention. First, the Portuguese constitution is among the longest in the world with elaborate and detailed sections on desired social and economic goals. Second, the constitution is a highly ideological document with numerous references to socialism, the rights of workers, and the desirability of a Socialist economy. It also put severe restrictions on private investment and business activity. Third, the constitution created a special agency for the armed forces, called the Council of the Revolution, and gave the military extraordinary constitutional powers. Recall that it had been the military, in the form of the Armed Forces Movement (MFA), that had led and initially guided the revolution. The Council of the Revolution was supposed to be an advisory body for the president, a kind of court to decide whether parliamentary laws were in accord with the MFA's desires, and a decision-making body for the armed forces themselves. Thus, the MFA became almost a fourth branch of government with veto power over parliamentary legislation. The council was also a means by which the Left parties, through the MFA, sought to ensure their dominance of the legislative process even though they were only a minority in the parliament.

The other interesting feature of the Portuguese constitution was the enhanced power it gave to the president. Portugal has long maintained a dual executive structure—president and prime minister—in which the prime minister effectively governed and the president, usually a military person, was mainly a ceremonial head of state except in times of crisis. But in the 1976 constitution the president was given enhanced powers—both as a way of providing for a stronger, unifying executive and because the Left saw this as a way to get an officer from the MFA in the slot who would thus be in a position to stand against any rightward drift. Actually, the president elected in 1976 and reelected in 1980, General Ramalho Eanes, proved to be something of a moderate, although a populist.

Even before the constitution was officially promulgated in 1976, there was talk of amending it. The constitution made so many ideological arguments and was so restrictive in terms of economic activity that the country could barely function. In addition, in the 1979 and 1980 elections the country moved rightward in a coalition dominated by the PSD and the CDS—parties that had been critical of the constitution from the beginning. Amendments enacted two years later in 1982 centered on four areas. First, the Council of the Revolution was replaced by a Council of State, a similarly consultative body but one that was more broadly representative. Thus, the armed forces were removed from playing such a central role in government. Second, the powers of the president were reduced, which, therefore, gave greater power to the more conservative parliament and prime minister. Third, many of the hortatory ideological slogans calling for socialism, which had never been implemented, were removed. And fourth, many of the restrictions on private investment and business activity were also removed, making Portugal a more attractive country for investment and serving as a major incentive for renewed economic growth, which had been at a virtual standstill since the revolution.

There is still dissatisfaction with the Portuguese constitution, mainly from centrists and conservatives who think it remains too ideological and restrictive. But at least now the Portuguese can live with it, and the country and economy can function within its constraints. Additional changes will probably be forthcoming.

The Spanish constitution of 1978 was the product of a quite different history and context than the Portuguese constitution.[3] First, there was no revolutionary process underway in Spain as there was in Portugal. Second, the constitution was the product of a moderate and centrist government and Cortes (parliament), not a revolutionary one. Third, the constitution reflected a series of compromises between the major political groups; it was not an ideological document reflecting only one viewpoint. The 1978 constitution thus succeeded in abrogating the Franco political system and establishing Spain as a democratic state under law, but it accomplished this through a long negotiating process that made the constitution acceptable to all major political groups.

The constitution was written by the Committee on Constitutional Affairs of the Cortes elected in 1977. Within both the Cortes and the committee, Prime Minister Adolfo Suárez's centrist UCD was the dominant party. The most difficult issues dealt with by the drafting committee concerned the role of the Church, education, labor lockouts, and the question of regional autonomy. On at least two occasions the Socialist (PSOE) delegates walked out in protest, but the prime minister worked out compromises that brought them back in. At the end only the Basque Nationalist party failed to support the constitution in the Cortes because of what it felt were inadequate provisions for regional autonomy. In October 1978 both houses of the Cortes overwhelmingly approved the new constitution, and in December 1978 the constitution was overwhelmingly approved (87.8 percent) in a popular plebiscite.

The constitution defines Spain as a parliamentary monarchy. The king is head of state with some extraordinary powers in times of crisis—roughly comparable to the Portuguese president. The parliament, or Cortes, is bicameral, and there is an independent judiciary. Although the Spanish constitution contains few of the hortatory and ideological expressions of the Portuguese constitution, it does declare Spain to be a social and democratic state and says that liberty, justice, equality, and political pluralism (this phrase is missing from the Portuguese constitution) are the country's essential values. Sovereignty is said to reside in the people from whom all state power derives.

The constitution achieved compromise on many of the issues that have torn Spain apart in the past. For example, Catholicism no longer enjoys the status of being the official state religion, but the constitution is not stridently anti-Catholic as the 1931 constitution was, and urges public authorities to take Spanish religious beliefs into account. The role of the armed forces is also reduced in the new constitution: Although the military is still assigned the role of preserving the sovereignty and independence of Spain and defending its constitutional order, ultimate responsibility rests with the popularly elected government and not with the armed forces. On the regional issues, the constitution affirms the indissoluble unity of the nation, but it also provides for substantial regional autonomy as compared with Franco's strict centralism.

The Spanish constitution of 1978, in contrast to the Portuguese constitution, is a consensus document. It does not just represent one faction of public opinion but a broad spectrum of public views. Less ideological and less rigid than the Portuguese constitution, it has not been subject to the same pressures for sweeping amendments either. The Spanish constitution is thus a functioning, working constitution, not the ideological document that the Portuguese one was, at least initially.

Government Institutions

Both Spain and Portugal since Franco and Salazar are essentially European, democratic, parliamentary regimes. Let us see how the main institutions in each country have functioned.

Portugal The *president* of Portugal is more than a symbolic head of state. He does more than kiss babies and snip ribbons opening bridges and highways. He is a symbol of national unity; he has considerable veto power over legislation; in times of national paralysis he can make or unmake a government, and even in more "normal" times (when the government is weak and no party has a majority, for example), he can exercise considerable influence behind the scenes.

Portugal so far has had only two presidents since the revolution of 1974–75. General Ramalho Eanes was elected in 1976 and reelected to a second term in 1980. In 1986, longtime Socialist party leader Mario Soares was elected to the presidency and then reelected in 1991 for a second five-year term. In none of these four presidential elections was a runoff necessary, even though in all of them there were several candidates (to avoid a runoff a candidate must get at least 50 percent of the vote in the first election). That means that the two presidents since 1976 have been genuinely popular candidates; they are chosen because of their national prestige and statesmanlike qualities, above partisan politics. General Eanes was widely thought of as the man who helped guide Portugal back to its senses after the tumult of the revolution—a moderate and a conciliator unassociated with any of the main contending political forces of that time. And Soares, even though a partisan, was thought of as a heroic figure who helped save the country from communism and guided it to democracy. Soares is also the first nonmilitary person to hold the position in over 60 years.

Eanes chafed sometimes at the limits on his power, which were limited still more after the constitutional revision of 1982. But he was effective in the presidency and helped to keep Portugal on an even keel despite frequent changes of government. There were times when he flirted with the idea of launching an independent political career, and even gave his blessing to a political party that rallied his supporters. Soares also proved to be a popular president, increasing his margin of victory from 51.3 percent in 1986 to 70.4 percent in 1991. His avuncular manner and smooth cooperation with the center-right Social Democratic government won him support in 1991 from across the political system.

The *prime minister* of Portugal is the effective head of state and governs the country on an everyday basis. He is not elected on a direct, popular basis as is the president but, as in other parliamentary systems, is chosen because he is the leader of the largest party in the parliament, or of a coalition of parties. The prime minister's term may be up to five years—although if he senses an advantage he may call elections before that time, or he may be ousted by a vote of nonconfidence in the parliament or through a leadership change in his own party.

Portugal has had many short-lived prime ministers since 1975; only three have achieved some prominence. Mario Soares (the current president) was the first democratically elected prime minister after the overthrow of the old dictatorship; in the mid-1970s he helped launch Portugal on a democratic course. In the late 1970s and early 1980s, the dynamic Francisco Sá Carneiro put together the center-right coalition that replaced the Socialists in power, but he was tragically killed in a plane crash before he could put much of his program into effect. The in the late 1980s Anibal Cavaco Silva of the PSD became prime minister, the first to win an absolute majority of the votes; he put in place an economic plan of more open markets that helped revive the Portuguese economy.

The *cabinet* or *Council of Ministries* in Portugal is not an effective decision-making body. It consists of members of the prime minister's own party who are chosen to help him administer some 15 to 18 ministries. Members of the council must also be elected members of the parliament, which is part of the problem because the Portuguese parliament lacks prestigious standing in the country. Moreover, few of these cabinet officials are effective administrators; and as a collective group of advisors to the prime minister or as a collective decision-making body, their influence has been negligible.

The *parliament* or *Assembly of the Republic* (Portugal has only a single legislative house) similarly lacks prestige. The parliament meets in an ancient monastery and is a victim of the fact that seldom in Portuguese history has any parliament enjoyed respect or much legitimacy. The functioning of the parliament is further plagued by the absence of adequate resources and staff, abysmally low salaries for members, and the lack of a well-functioning infrastructure of committees and subcommittees.

It is on the parliament that the Portuguese frequently vent their political frustrations regarding the country's lack of progress and efficiency. To the public, parliament personifies all that is wrong with democracy: inefficient, quarrelsome, splintered, patronage-dominated. The members are perceived as putting their own interests ahead of that of the nation and of sometimes using their parliamentary positions to enhance their own private careers and fortunes. In newspaper editorials and cartoons, parliament is often portrayed as buffoonish, silly, and irrelevant. With the parliament viewed and portrayed in such lights, it is small wonder that democracy in Portugal at times appears wobbly as well.

If we ask the Portuguese public who or what institution really governs the country, the parliament comes out at or near the bottom of the list. The survey results shown in Table 8.1 also provide a measure of popular attitudes toward other key government institutions and provide a good way to conclude this section.

Spain Spain is a parliamentary monarchy. The *king* is a hereditary and constitutional monarch. Like the Portuguese president, the king serves as head of state, but unlike the Portuguese president he is not an elected official. The Spanish constitution makes it clear, however, that the king is not sovereign; rather, sovereignty rests with the people as represented in their parliament.

The monarchy had been restored by Franco, and the decision to retain it after democracy was reinstated represented a compromise. The Left wanted to do away with the monarchy entirely

Table 8.1. WHO OR WHAT INSTITUTION REALLY GOVERNS PORTUGAL?

	1978	1984
President of the Republic	39%	31%
Prime Minister	26	25
Cabinet	20	23
Assembly of the Republic (parliament)	14	19
Council of the Revolution	11	—
Council of the State	—	4
No one	2	6
Don't know	30	19
No response	3	2

Note: Multiple answers possible.
Source: Thomas C. Bruneau and Alex MacLeod, *Politics in Contemporary Portugal* (Boulder, Colo.: Lynne Rienner Publishers, 1986), p. 129.

whereas the Right wanted to retain a strong monarchy as a way of preserving Francoism. A limited monarchy in which republican institutions were clearly dominant was the compromise.

King Juan Carlos and his family (his wife Sofia, from the Greek royal family and their three children: one son and two daughters) have proved to be remarkably popular. At first the king was referred to as "Juan the Brief" for the presumed shortness of his rule; but now almost all sectors of Spanish public opinion support the monarchy. That is because King Juan Carlos has adjusted well and gracefully to his new, more limited rule; he has represented Spain well abroad; the family has proved personable and not ostentatious; Juan Carlos is widely credited with helping his friend Adolfo Suárez usher in the new democratic era; and in the widely publicized shootout of the Cortes in 1981 Juan Carlos played an instrumental and perhaps even heroic role in saving Spanish democracy.

The king's functions are largely ceremonial. But he also formally convenes and dissolves the Cortes, calls for elections and referenda, ratifies civil and military appointments, signs decrees promulgated by the cabinet, appoints the prime minister after consultation with the Cortes, and serves as supreme commander of the armed forces. Most of these are symbolic and largely *pro forma* functions; but one could envision circumstances in which the Cortes was deadlocked with no party having a majority where the king's authority to appoint the prime minister would take on added importance.

As in Portugal, the *prime minister* is the actual head of government in Spain. He is the leader of the dominant political party in the Cortes, he directs the government's program in both domestic and foreign affairs, he chooses the cabinet ministers with the king's approval, he is responsible for the actions of the government, he governs the country on an everyday basis, and he is in control of the armed forces (even though the king remains the supreme commander). The prime minister may ask for a vote of confidence from the Congress of Deputies, he may propose the dissolution of the parliament, and he may call for new national elections to strengthen his legislative position. Elections for the Cortes *must* be held in Spain every five years, but they can be held before then if the prime minister loses a vote of confidence in the Cortes or if he thinks he can gain electoral advantage by having an earlier vote. There is also a deputy prime minister.

There have been only four prime ministers in Spain since Franco, thus reflecting the relative tranquility of the Spanish transition as compared with the Portuguese: Carlos Arías, who was appointed by Franco and presided over the early post-Franco transition; the centrist Adolfo Suárez, who ushered in Spanish democracy; Leopoldo Calvo-Sotelo, who served briefly after Suárez resigned; and the Socialist Felipe González, who became prime minister in 1982.

The *cabinet* or *Council of Ministers* in Spain is the state's highest executive institution. It consists of the prime minister, the deputy prime minister, and the other ministers of state—all of whom, in a parliamentary system, are also members of the Cortes. The Council of Ministers has both administrative and policymaking functions; it is responsible for national security and defense affairs and is in charge of the implementation of government policy. Ultimately the council must answer to the Cortes.

Each council member, as in Portugal, is responsible for the administration of a particular ministry. The ministers have considerable discretion in the running of these departments but are also responsible to their prime minister and to the council as a whole. Thus, within the council there is both individual and collective responsibility. And although there have been several cabinet ministers who have proved to be poor administrators of their individual departments or who got out of step with the prime minister, in general the Spanish cabinet has enjoyed greater prestige than the Portuguese cabinet.

The *Cortes* or *parliament* is, by constitution, the highest governmental institution in Spain. It is here where sovereignty ultimately resides. Spain has a two-house parliament (which differs from Portugal), consisting of a Congress of Deputies and a Senate. The congress is the most powerful and democratic of the two houses and has 350 deputies. Its members are elected by proportional representation.

The Congress of Deputies may ratify or reject decree laws promulgated by the government. A vote of support from the congress is also necessary before a prime minister may be sworn in. A majority in the congress must approve all legislation proposed by the prime minister (largely *pro forma* in a parliamentary system because both the prime minister and the majority must be from the same majority party or coalition), and the congress has the authority to vote a censure or an expression of nonconfidence in the government, in which case new elections must be held.

The Senate is mainly an institution to ensure territorial representation from Spain's sometimes separatist-leaning regions. It consists of 208 members elected on a provincial basis, plus 49 regional representatives. Although either the congress or the Senate may initiate legislation, the congress may override a senate veto by a simple majority vote, thus nullifying the Senate's action. The two chambers may also meet jointly as the General Cortes (*Corteses Generales*); when that happens it is the president of the congress who presides, again attesting to the superior power of that house.

Like Portugal, Spain has a Council of State that functions in an advisory capacity. The members are appointed by the Council of Ministers and are representative of the country's main corporate groups: the armed forces, civil service, Catholic church, universities, professions, farmers, business and industrial groups, and the autonomous regions. The council is a broadly consultative group, a kind of throwback to an earlier Spanish and Portuguese concept of corporative or functional representation; but it has no executive functions or powers and in recent times has been called into advisory capacity only rarely—that is, in Portugal when Salazar was incapacitated in 1968 and in Spain when Franco passed away in 1975.

A DEMOCRATIC AND BUREAUCRATIC STATE?

Shortly after the 1974 revolution in Portugal, the left-leaning government of the Armed Forces Movement (MFA) moved to nationalize large sectors of the economy that had previously been in private hands. Its primary targets were the banks and *grupos*, which consisted of eight or ten of Portugal's leading families who were now referred to derisively as "the oligarchy." But when the Portuguese government nationalized the banks, it found out that they were really vast holding companies that dominated not only the banking industry but also construction, transportation, insurance, tourism and hotels, minerals, land (including large holdings in Portuguese Africa), automobiles, and publishing. Almost literally overnight, the Portuguese discovered that they had nationalized a huge share of what had been the private sector. The percentage of gross national product (GNP) generated by the state shot up from about 30 percent, where it had been under Salazar/Caetano, to about 75 percent. Almost instantaneously Portugal's had become a predominantly Socialist economy with a suddenly immense public sector.

Following a policy of *reforma* rather than Portuguese-style *ruptura*, Spain largely avoided nationalizations. Its government did not want to disrupt the economy, nor did it wish to antagonize the private business community or discourage private investment. Even the Socialist government of Felipe González, for these same reasons, steadfastly resisted nationalizations, to the consternation of its more militant followers.

Nevertheless the Spanish government and bureaucracy, even without nationalizations, did continue to grow. The change was, in fact, quite dramatic, even though it represented a form of "creeping bureaucratization" as contrasted with the highly visible and sudden Portuguese transformation. In Spain the share of the GNP generated by the public sector went from about 20 percent, where it had been under Franco, to about 40 percent in 1990. That is a far cry from Portugal's 75 percent, but it still represents close to a 100 percent increase in the size of the state sector in about a quarter century. The question then becomes: Are Spain and Portugal really democratic states or, with their vast public sectors and state employment, have they become essentially bureaucratic states—impersonal, with vast and bloated public sectors, and with bureaucracies grown so large and powerful that democratic responsibility has been lost in the process?

The reasons for this considerable expansion in the public sector (besides the nationalizations in Portugal) are several. For one thing, democracy means rewarding your friends and supporters; therefore, in both countries since the mid-1970s there has been a large increase in the number of patronage and patronage-related positions as politicians, party hacks, and voter loyalists have insisted on being rewarded with new government positions from which they were deprived during the long years of dictatorship. For another, these democratic regimes have inaugurated vast new public programs in the areas of health, housing, education, public works, and so on, and these have also brought forth large new bureaucracies to administer the programs. A third change is particularly applicable to Spain: Although Spain has not nationalized large industries as has Portugal, it *has* vastly increased the regulatory responsibilities of the state. A host of new offices, bureaus, commissions, directorates, and so on has been created in Spain to regulate and control the economy even while avoiding nationalizations.

The overall result in both countries is the emergence of a dual structure. On the one hand, these are undoubtedly democracies whose transitions to same have been publicly acclaimed and widely touted. At the same time (and far more quietly), we have also witnessed a tremendous growth in the size of the public bureaucracy. This bureaucratic growth is not necessarily incompatible with democracy, but it has the potential to become so if the public sector grows too large, becomes a state almost to itself, becomes corrupt and self-serving, and loses all sense of democratic responsibility. In addition, there is the worry about whether a country that champions democracy and freedom politically should also allow considerable economic freedom; if the latter is sacrificed, the former can easily be curtailed as well.

The governments of both Spain and Portugal have recognized this dilemma. Hence, the Spanish government has taken significant steps to ensure that its regulatory mechanisms function fairly and well, that its bureaucracy does not become dominated by sinecures and corruption, and that the state system remain responsible to the electorate. Although there is growing public corruption in Spain, so far that has not gotten out of hand and Spain's still-young bureaucratic institutions have not been discredited. Spain has even taken steps to reduce the size of its public sector by selling some national industries back into private hands, but so far these efforts have been very limited.

In Portugal the problem is much more acute. First, the public sector is proportionately much larger; second, Portugal, unlike Spain, has relatively few alternative sources of employment besides government for its population. Third, the Portuguese revolution of the mid-1970s carried such strong ideological overtones of socialism that it has remained politically difficult to return the nationalized patrimony to private hands. And fourth, the principles of socialism and state ownership are embedded in the constitution of 1976 and are, therefore, as part of the basic laws, difficult to change.

Nevertheless, the Portuguese government under the Social Democrats has begun to confront this problem, has reopened the country to both private initiative and foreign investment, has made the bureaucracy somewhat less cumbersome, and has begun the process of de-nationalizing some of the nationalized industries. Where the government could not change or amend the laws and constitution, it has sought to work around them so as to provide new economic opportunities. But the government also has a dilemma on its hands: Whereas it wants and needs to privatize large parts of its vast public sector if it is to achieve greater efficiency and economic growth, it also has patronage obligations that it must fulfill (jobs for its supporters) if it wishes to maintain political support. Hence, what is rational economically may not be rational politically—and vice versa.

REGIONAL AUTONOMY

The issue of regional autonomy is a longstanding one in Iberia and one that is intensely felt. Historically fragmented and decentralized, the peninsula has gone through oscillations of centralization-decentralization from Roman times to the present. Isabella, Ferdinand, and the Hapsburgs sought to snuff out regional sentiment—which ultimately reasserted itself; and Franco tried also through strict centralization to repress Spanish regionalism. But the regionalist flame was not extinguished by the dictatorship, and now it has reasserted itself in the form of various independence and autonomous movements. The question is: Has Spain now finally achieved a happy balance between its centralizing and decentralizing tendencies?

The issue has long been sensitive and divisive, and it continues so, for Spanish society is unique in Western Europe in the depth and extent of regionalist sentiment. The country includes ethnic/regional groups—most particularly the Basques, Catalans, and Galicians—that are culturally and linguistically different from the rest of Spain and from each other. Many people within these regions are intensely proud of their distinctiveness and wish to preserve it. Loyalty often goes primarily to their region and only secondarily to the nation. Even Portugal is sometimes referred to by Spaniards not as a separate and sovereign country but as a "lost province" that somehow went astray. Someday—presumably with its own autonomy statute—Portugal should return to its rightful fold: Spain.

The issue is not just regional, ethnic, and linguistic, however; it is also profoundly political. Historically, successful efforts at regional autonomy have been associated with liberal governments; if one recognizes the *fueros* (rights) of the several regions, then usually other *fueros* (for labor or other groups) have also been recognized. Conservatives in contrast, recognizing the "invertebrate"[4] and disintegrative forces that have long been active in Spain, have feared that abandoning strict centralization would lead to the unraveling and possible dismemberment of the state. Moderates and centrists have often tried to work out a balance in the form of a federal-type system, but they have usually been few in number and squeezed between the two extremes.

The 1978 constitution reached a compromise on the regional issue: It says that the nation is indissoluble, but it also guarantees the right of regional autonomy. Castilian Spanish is declared the official language of Spain, but other languages are recognized as co-official in their respective regions. Flags and emblems of the regions may now also be displayed alongside the Spanish flag. None of these provisions were permitted in Franco's day.

There are two procedures by which a region may achieve autonomy: one fast, the other slow. The fast route was applied to those regions—Galicia, the Basque provinces, and Catalonia—that had sought autonomy during the 1930s republic; these were also the areas where the regional pressures were coming to a head in the 1970s. Once approved by the Constitutional Committee of the Congress of Deputies, all that was required for autonomy was a vote for approval in a regional referendum. The slow procedure, by contrast, required an initiative on the part of municipal and provincial governments as well as final approval by the Cortes; the *degree* of autonomy was also less for those employing this route. In 1981 a new organic law or charter was approved by the Cortes governing these procedures in detail, and in 1983 the process was essentially completed when elections were held in 13 new autonomous communities. Andalusia received its autonomy under a compromise procedure that represented a mixture of these two routes, thus making a total of 17 autonomous communities in Spain with varying degrees of autonomy.

Each regional entity has its own capital and a unicameral legislative assembly whose members are elected by popular vote. The assembly selects a president from among its members who then represents the community; there is also a regional Council of Government headed by the president and responsible to the assembly. The regions may also have their own courts, although they are ultimately subject to the Supreme Court sitting in Madrid.

The national government retains exclusive jurisdiction in areas such as defense, foreign affairs, civil aviation, finances, public safety, foreign trade, economic planning, justice, and criminal, commercial, or labor legislation. The regional communities may be responsible for their own municipal boundaries, town planning, housing, forestry, public works, sports, tourism, social welfare, and so on. The regions receive subsidies for these programs from the central government, but they may now, in addition, levy their own taxes and conduct their own financial affairs. Hence, since Franco, the regions have enjoyed a remarkable degree of autonomy. Although many problems in the system remain to be worked out, it may be that Spain has finally achieved a workable balance between its centralist and its autonomous tendencies.

Both Spain and Portugal have island possessions that exist in relationship to the mainland much as the regional entities of Spain do to the central government. In Spain, the Balearic Islands in the western Mediterranean and the Canary Islands in the Atlantic have the same right to form autonomous communities as do other regions in Spain. In Portugal, the Azores Islands and Madeira, both in the Atlantic, similarly have a degree of autonomy from the central government in Lisbon and a measure of self-government.

STATE-SOCIETY RELATIONS: A NEW BALANCE AND A NEW MODEL?

The balance in Spanish and Portuguese state-society relations has indeed been altered since the mid-1970s. What was once a strictly, even rigidly, centralized state and polity under Franco and Salazar has now been considerably decentralized and made more pluralistic. The authoritarian-autocratic Hapsburgian Model has now been replaced by a genuinely democratic one. With the rebirth of civil and associational life (parties, interest groups, regional organizations, and the like), coupled with the system of limited government and checks and balances found in the constitution, the societal component of the state-society equation has been enormously strengthened and the state component constrained. That is, after all, what democracy is all about; its firm establishment in Spain and Portugal in so short a time is nothing short of breathtaking.

Although Spain and Portugal are now democracies, they may still represent a unique form of democracy. The subject area is worthy of further research. It is striking how many of Spain's and Portugal's state-society arenas are dominated by special charters or organic laws that have the power of nearly constitutional basic laws. These compacts provide for a polity that is not completely unfettered or *laissez-faire* as in the United States, but one still dominated by provisions of mutual rights and obligations that owe a great deal to earlier Spanish and Portuguese history.

Such compacts between the state and its component societal units have their roots in medieval Spain and Portugal and in the efforts to strike a balance between the emerging central government and the autonomy of local and corporate units. Now, as then, there are organic laws governing the relationship between the Catholic church and the state, the armed forces and the state, the autonomous regions and the state, the universities and the state, and so on. In the modern era, of course, there must also be a charter governing the relations between political parties and the state, another for labor and the state, and so on. For virtually every group there is a separate organic law spelling out the rights and obligations of that group with regard to the state.

In this way Spain and Portugal have sought to blend their ancient traditions of group and regional *fueros* ("rights"; *foros* in Portuguese) with the modern constitutional provisions of parliamentary democracy. It is a fascinating blend and combination—one that may make Spanish and Portuguese democracy unique, for what Spain and Portugal appear to have done successfully (and this is very unusual in the world) is to blend their own historic traditions and meanings of democracy with a modern European parliamentary form in ways that are distinctively Iberian. For want of a better name, we can call this a "compact" or a "contract" state.

If Spain and Portugal have, in fact, succeeded in blending European democracy with their own indigenous tradition of rights in a satisfactory, working relationship, then that is not only a major accomplishment worthy of far greater study than it has so far received, but it may have significant implications, as a new and innovative model, for the field of study known as comparative politics. On both a theoretical and a practical level, it may also have major implications for Latin America and other countries, cast in the Hispanic mold, that are similarly searching for ways to blend Western democracy with their own indigenous traditions and institutions.

NOTES

1. For elaboration on these developments see Howard J. Wiarda, *Corporatism and Development: The Portuguese Experience* (Amherst, Mass.: University of Massachusetts Press, 1977).
2. The materials in this section derive from Thomas C. Bruneau and Alex MacLeod, *Politics in Contemporary Portugal* (Boulder, Colo.: Lynne Rienner Publishers, 1986).
3. For some of the technical details in this section I have relied on the Library of Congress, Legislative Reference Service, *Spain: A Country Study* (Washington, D.C.: Government Printing Office, 1991).
4. After the title of the book by José Ortega y Gasett, *Invertebrate Spain* (New York: Norton, 1937).

Chapter

9

Public Policy: Domestic and Foreign

Foreign policy and domestic policy represent mirror images in Spain and Portugal. For long decades and even centuries Spain and Portugal were extremely isolated internationally. They were also very poor countries, underdeveloped, closer to the Third World than to the First World of prosperous nations; and their social programs also lagged behind the rest of Europe. Spain and Portugal were so poor, isolated, and underdeveloped that they could not afford a more aggressive and involved foreign policy; at the same time their very isolation from Europe and the world's mainstreams helped keep them poor and underdeveloped. Poverty meant a concentration on the basics, on eking out a meager subsistence, on surviving; there was little time or inclination to participate in the "luxury" of a strong, long-term involvement in foreign affairs. These twin problems, the vicious circles of poverty and lack of international standing or importance, served to retard Iberia's development and to keep this area locked in—geographically *a part of* Europe, but hemmed in by the Pyrenees as well as by poverty and distance, psychologically, politically, culturally, and economically *apart from* Europe.

In recent years this has all changed. Not only have Spain and Portugal come out of their historic isolation, but their greater prosperity enables them to play a more active role in international affairs. Foreign policy and domestic policy are thus still interrelated, but in ways that are the reverse of only a few decades ago. Now the two countries are both economically more affluent, *and* they are more closely integrated into European and global currents, in the realms of politics, economics, psychology, and culture. Given their historic isolation and proximity to Africa, it used to be said of the two Iberian nations that "Europe stops at the Pyrenees." But now not only are Spain and Portugal becoming fully integrated into Europe; they are also, in terms of their economic and social development, beginning domestically to approximate the other countries of Western Europe.

Hence, in this chapter we treat domestic and foreign policy as closely interrelated, and as tied to developmentalist progress. The approach is to use the basic outline of the systems model. As compared with what earlier in the book were considered "input functions" (history, background, political culture, interest groups, political parties—those factors that go *into* the political system) and, in the previous chapter, the "process variables" (the state, bureaucracy, governmental institutions), we here consider the "output functions": the public policies and programs that come *out of* the political system and in turn have their impact on it. We begin with a discussion of domestic economic and social policy in each country, and then move to an analysis of each country's foreign relations.

DOMESTIC POLICY

The economies of Spain and Portugal had long been closed and autarchic. The dominant economic philosophy in both countries, historically, was mercantilism. Mercantilism was a system of political economy that developed in Europe upon the decay of feudalism; under mercantilism a strong state sought to secure a favorable balance of trade, did so by establishing foreign trading monopolies, centralized power in the hands of the state, and tried to build up its bullion reserves. This centralized, monopolistic system clearly fits Spain and Portugal during their three centuries of colonial conquest from the late fifteenth through the eighteenth centuries, but what is surprising is that an updated, somewhat modernized mercantilist system survived into the nineteenth century and even into the regimes of Franco and Salazar in their earlier stages—at a time when other developing, industrializing nations of Europe were already moving toward a system of more open markets and toward capitalism. Economists are agreed that Spain's and Portugal's practice of mercantilism way beyond the time when such a system was beneficial served to retard Iberia's development and to consign these nations to a less developed category.

Paradoxically, while under mercantilism the state was supposed to be strong, directing, and forceful; in Spain and Portugal the state's actual role in the economy was often weak and indecisive. A strong state in Iberia represented an aspiration to achieve rather than actual operating reality. In fact, the Spanish and Portuguese states from the early nineteenth century on provided confused, indecisive, and incompetent direction to the economy rather than real leadership. Moreover, in the social as well as the economic spheres, Spain and Portugal lagged way behind. The state systems in both countries failed to provide the modernizing education, health, housing, and other social programs that these countries sorely needed or that their populations came to expect.

In recent decades this has all turned around. It began under Franco and Salazar when both dictators finally, tardily, abandoned mercantilism in favor of a more open market system. This change triggered a tremendous boom, more evident in Spain than in Portugal but present in both countries, that helped raise prosperity and living standards in the 1960s and 1970s. The economic takeoff also enabled Spain and Portugal to expand social programs in ways they could not afford before. Recently Spain's and Portugal's entry into Europe and the EEC has provided a further stimulus to economic and social development that is lifting these countries out of their historic doldrums. Spain and Portugal are no longer to be identified with the poverty and hopelessness of much of the Third World but with the much greater prosperity and affluence of the First World. Many problems remain, but it may now be that Iberia has not only turned a political corner (democracy) but an economic one as well.

Spain

Spain's economic decline began as early as the sixteenth century. Then, in order to raise money for its European wars, the Hapsburg monarchy began the sale of public offices on a large scale, cut off trade with the more productive parts of Europe, drove out its entrepreneurial class, and taxed agriculture and commerce so heavily that these sectors were ruined. Even at the height of Spain's imperial glory under Philip II, 1556–98, the seeds of economic devastation had already been planted.

When at last Spain began to industrialize in the late nineteenth century, it did so slowly and very unevenly. The lateness of Spain's industrialization helps account for the extreme poverty of its urban workers—and their attraction to such radical political philosophies as Marxism, anarchism, and syndicalism. When industrialization finally came, moreover, it was concentrated in a very few areas: the Basque provinces, Catalonia, and Madrid. The relative economic prosperity, especially of the first two of these compared with the rest of Spain, helps account for the rise of separatist sentiment in these provinces. The Basques and Catalans have long thought that they were contributing more to the national treasury in the form of taxes than they were getting in return by way of programs.

Social programs in Spain also lagged behind the rest of Europe. Spain, after all, remained a poor country and could not afford the advanced social programs that other European countries and the United States began to implement in the 1930s. In addition, neither the monarchy nor, later, the Franco regime had much interest in implementing programs that they saw as "Socialist." A third reason for the lag in social programs was that many Spaniards, including the government, thought of these activities as the province of the Catholic church or of individual families. The Church, through its benefices and charity, was presumed to have responsibility in the areas of welfare, assistance to the poor, care of orphans and the indigent, even health care and education. Families were similarly expected to take in and help out those members who were sick or fell on hard times.

These were not such bad arrangements as long as Spain remained rural, strongly Catholic, and with large extended families who shared a sense of community and responsibility. But as the country became increasingly urban, secularized, and impersonal in the early decades of the twentieth century, these traditional services began to break down. Families separated as some members moved to the cities, population growth called for more and more schools and other public services, and in the mushrooming cities the Church was unable to provide for the large numbers of unemployed and the poor. Spain had the worst of all possible worlds: Its traditional system of family- and Church-sponsored charity and social programs was breaking down, and still the government had not yet stepped in to fill the void.

Economic growth and industrialization nevertheless continued, albeit slowly, during the first half of the twentieth century. Despite the frequent political ups and downs—monarchy, the republic, the civil war, then Franco—the economy continued to move forward. The civil war and World War II marked interruptions in this process, but the general trend of the growth curve was upward. The rates of growth were often only 1 or 2 percent per year, but there was some slight improvement. These rates, however, lagged way behind the rest of Europe, which had begun a real boom in the 1950s, and, when measured against population growth, began to look quite unimpressive. At mid-century the Spanish economy was thought of as stagnant. More and more Spaniards, especially young males, began leaving the country for better job opportunities in the more prosperous countries of Europe.

For a long time Franco had pursued the same autarkic, quasi-mercantilist policies as his predecessors. The breakthrough for Spain in terms of economic policy came in 1957 when Franco brought into his cabinet a new group of technocrats (associated with the Catholic lay organization *Opus Dei*) committed to economic liberalization. Franco had long avoided such a program because he feared—correctly as it turned out—that economic liberalization would inevitably be related to political liberalization, and that would mean the end of his regime. But in 1957 Franco had little opposition, was at the height of his power, and felt secure enough that he could go ahead with economic liberalization. The program included opening up the Spanish economy to outside investment, encouraging trade, and removing many restrictions on economic activity. In effect the regime gambled that it could introduce economic liberalization while holding its usual political concomitants (a desire for freedom and democracy) in check.[1]

The Spanish economy responded magnificently. All during the 1960s and early 1970s the economy boomed ahead at growth rates of 5 to 6 percent per year. Some years it reached 7 to 8 percent and became known as the "Spanish miracle." Most people during this period were aware of the impressive Japanese and West German economic miracles but were less familiar with the Spanish one. In fact, for about 15 years (1960–1974), the growth rates of the Spanish economy were second or third in the world, behind only Japan and about even with West Germany, and ahead of the United States and the rest of Europe. The Spanish GNP doubled in a decade—and then it doubled again.

These phenomenal growth rates were owing to a variety of factors besides Franco's policies. During the 1960s, lured by the winter sun and Spain's magnificent Mediterranean beaches, tourism became the country's second leading industry, attracting upwards of 40 million tourists annually—mostly Europeans—and bringing in vast amounts of sorely needed foreign exchange. Further, all those Spanish men who had earlier emigrated to Europe in search of work and higher salaries were sending vast remittances to their families back in Spain, which also swelled Spain's foreign exchange reserves and added to the prosperity. In addition, Spain benefitted from close proximity to the booming European economies and from the general prosperity of the 1950s and 1960s—the period before the two great oil price increases, or "shocks," of the 1970s. These factors in the Spanish boom were largely independent of Franco's policies; on the other hand, his government did not stand in the way of any of these changes, and the government's liberalizing of the economy did quite a bit to assist them.

Inevitably, despite Franco's efforts to head them off, such miracle economic growth as that experienced by Spain had its social and political effects. Socially, the growth of the period stimulated urbanization, the emergence of a far larger middle class, the growth of a far larger working class, and the decline of agriculture and of the countryside. Politically, these changes resulted in the widespread adoption of European ideas having to do with lifestyles, changed morals, tastes, and a desire for democracy. The changes were so vast that the post-Franco era, in terms of a changed political culture, had already begun even while Franco was still alive. Increasingly, Franco was seen as a political anachronism, still in place, but with the society and political ideas now so altered that there was little connection between his rule and what people believed. In short, democratization in Spain was led by the changed views that the people had already formed; the party leaders after Franco's death in 1975 largely ratified the changes that had already taken place in the culture and the society.[2]

The economic prosperity of the 1960s had also enabled the Franco regime to implement new social programs that had long been neglected. These included programs in social welfare, unemployment insurance, health care, child labor, maternity care, paid vacations, limits on hours worked, working conditions in the plant, and a variety of others. Over time, these programs were extended to rural workers as well as urban workers, to women as well as men. Some of these programs existed more on paper than in actual fact; others were only incompletely or irregularly implemented. Nevertheless, vast new social programs were put in place, which subsequent governments were able to build on and expand.

The post-Franco era was marked by fewer changes in the economic sphere than in the political. Politically the country made a quite remarkable about-face from authoritarianism to democracy, but economically there was far more continuity than change. The basic liberalizing and expansionist policies of the late-Franco period were kept in place. Nevertheless, there were several "surprises" in the post-Franco era that help explain this continuity.

The first had to do with the smoothness of the political transition. Spain had no revolution following Franco's death, almost no upheaval, and no repeat of the 1930s civil war—as many had feared. The result was that investor confidence remained high, Spanish capital did not flee to Geneva or other safe havens, economic policy remained largely continuous from one government to the next, and the economy kept chugging along. Because of the vast hikes in oil prices in 1973 and then again in 1979, the Spanish economy slowed down in the late 1970s from its earlier miracle growth rates. But growth rates of 4 to 5 percent per year are not bad, and the Spanish performance was still better than most other economies during this period. Political stability also meant stability and growth economically.

The second "surprise" was the continuity in economic policy even after a Socialist (PSOE) government was elected in 1982. The Spanish Socialists were quite militant in some areas, and many expected a wave of nationalizations and programs hostile to business after they came to power. But prime minister Felipe González met with leaders of the business community to assure them of policy continuity; he refused to pursue nationalizations despite the urging of many in his own party; he saw the value of continued prosperity for Spain as well as for his own political future; and he pursued basically the same policy course as his predecessors. He worked out social pacts between employers and workers to ensure both higher wages and maximum productivity and to keep the economy booming without interruption. Over the objections of his own constituency, the unions, he urged workers to forego some wage increases; he enforced an austerity program; and he also began a program of privatization by returning some state-owned enterprises to private hands. These policies, coming from a Socialist government, did not always sit well with González's party followers, but they kept the economy in an expansionist projectory.

The third "surprise" was the strong performance of the Spanish economy during the global economic downturn of the early 1980s. While the United States and the rest of Europe were mired in recession, Spain continued to expand. Tourism, the remittances of Spanish workers abroad, continued foreign investment even in the midst of recession, and the early benefits accruing from becoming a part of the European Economic Community (EEC) were all factors in maintaining Spanish economic growth. Almost alone among the larger economies of the world (Spain now ranked tenth), Spain continued to prosper, with growth rates of 3 to 4 percent, even during the early 1980s recession.

With Spain's formal ascension to full membership in the EEC in 1986, the economy took off once again. Initially there were problems of adjustment, and several clashes occurred at the border between French farmers and Spanish truckers carrying agricultural products. But these events, though dramatic and highly publicized at the time, proved insignificant compared to the benefits that flowed into Spain as a result of joining the EEC. Still, as one of the EEC's poorer members, Spain qualified for a variety of EEC assistance programs and subsidies; it also benefitted from a rapid and large influx of European as well as American investment capital. New factories sprang up everywhere, no longer just in the big cities but in regional cities as well; the prosperity, historically confined to urban areas, began to spread to the countryside; and the labor force (and hence greater affluence) vastly expanded as women as well as men found regular employment. Middle- and upper-class Spaniards soon complained about a shortage of maids; they were all working in the Sony factories! To this side effect of modernization were added some others: inflation and price increases that made habitually "bargain-basement" Spain about as expensive as other European countries.

The boom years lasted from 1986 to 1990; then a slowdown occurred—modest and of short duration. The slowdown brought to the fore other problems that had been simmering for some time: the need for a better national transportation system, the need to modernize and expand energy sources, the persistent unevenness of Spanish development (the western provinces had been left far behind), and the pockets of extreme poverty that still existed in the country. But note the reference here to "pockets of poverty" as compared with an entire, national "culture of poverty" as anthropologists described it in the 1950s. Spain, indeed, has problems, but these are the problems associated with modernization and no longer sheer underdevelopment.

Spain has, in fact, now taken its place with the major economies of the world. It is no longer "transitional" or "developing" but, according to the World Bank's authoritative listing, "an industrial market" economy. One would have to say that Spain's accomplishments in both the political and economic spheres are nothing short of miraculous; Spain has to be considered one of the world's greatest success stories of the last third of the twentieth century. Spain's achievements in these regards are not always acknowledged or even known by the rest of the world, and, actually, Spain rather resents the fact that it is still excluded from the "Group of Seven" when economic summits are held. Spain feels its accomplishments merit its being included in this select group of representatives from other advanced, industrial nations; but unlike the Spain of the past, it is content to wait its turn rather than feel insulted about the matter. Such attitudes may tell us as much as anything about how far Spain has come.

Meanwhile the country has begun to work on its still vast social problems. In these areas Spain lags farther behind the rest of Europe than it does economically. The problems include a rate of illiteracy that is still quite high (15 to 20 percent), but that is now largely limited to a rural older generation that never had a chance to go to school. It includes a vast housing problem in the cities where adequate housing is woefully lacking and the "superblocks" of apartments that have been built are crumbling and lack many amenities. It includes a welfare system that provides inadequate assistance to the jobless and a health care system that is itself sickly. It also includes an educational system that has made great progress in recent years but that needs to expand far more, from top to bottom, to take care of the rising demand.[3]

These are all long-standing problems for Spain. To them has been added recently a host of new problems associated with Spain's modernity. Probably because of Spain's continued emphasis on the family and the historical continuity of certain traditional values—or perhaps because Spain is still less "modern" than the rest of Europe—these problems are not as acute as in some other countries, but they are rising nonetheless and are beginning to attract more public attention. A modern or modernizing society, after all, implies modern problems. These problems include divorce and rising family conflict, drug and alcohol abuse, AIDS, rising crime and lawlessness, the environment especially of the cities, product reliability and consumer protection, ecology and pollution, and so on. None of these are of epidemic proportions yet in Spain, but they are increasing in importance and they will probably get worse before they get better. In this way the problems of a rapidly modernizing society have been superimposed on a society that has not yet solved its traditional ones, but at least Spain now has the economic resources to begin moving on most of them.

Portugal

Portugal's economic and social trajectory has been roughly parallel to that of Spain historically—except that it started at a far lower level and today is still only half as affluent on a per capita basis.

Like Spain, Portugal reached the height of its power and influence in the sixteenth century when Portuguese ships explored vast and heretofore unknown areas of the globe and the Portuguese empire encompassed immense colonies in Africa, Asia, and Latin America. But after that it seemed to be all downhill for the Portuguese. Isolated and distant, Portugal was for centuries the poorest country in Western Europe.

When Portugal—like Spain, belatedly—began its industrialization in the late nineteenth century, the process was very slow, for Portugal lacked the natural resources that Spain had, the internal markets, and the capital for development. Hence, industrialization remained incipient, it was small scale, and it was dominated by miniscule family-owned firms. Nor did the economic quickening that occurred in Portugal around the turn of the century give rise to vast social changes such as in Spain, although during the First Republic, 1910–26, a larger middle class, a nascent trade union movement, and a new entrepreneurial class had come into existence.

Under Salazar, the country remained dominated by mercantilist and autarkic policies—as had Spain under Franco until the big change came in 1957. Salazar was a traditionalist economist who had actually trained in law; he was a penny-pincher who not only believed in balanced budgets but in budget surpluses! He wanted nothing to do with Keynesian economics, budget deficits, or printing paper money to cover extra expenses. Under Salazar, and exploiting the resources and a closed trading system imposed upon its African colonies, Portugal built up some of the largest bullion reserves of any country in the world. To accomplish these goals Salazar put in a strict system of price and wage controls that were largely administered through the corporative system.

The country remained exceedingly backward economically, however, as compared with its neighbors. The world depression of the 1930s, the era of World War II, and the period immediately after the war were particularly hard years for Portugal. Poverty, malnutrition, malnutrition-related diseases, and even mass starvation during the war were widespread. There was almost no foreign investment, and the country could not afford much in the way of social programs. What the Church or a supportive family could not provide, the state was also unable to provide. The figures are not entirely accurate but they show little if any real economic growth in Portugal from the 1930s through the 1940s. Far more than Spain, Portugal closely resembled a poor, Third World country rather than a European one.

The breakthrough for Portugal, comparable to Spain's reforms in 1957, occurred in 1953 when Salazar adopted his first five-year plan. Furthermore, unlike Spain, whose regime was hated by the international community far more than was Salazar's, Portugal received Marshall Plan assistance. Portugal also benefitted from the economic assistance provided through the agreement by which the United States secured an air base in the Azores, and from Europe's growing prosperity, some of which trickled down to Portugal. But as with so many things Portuguese, Salazar's economic reforms of the 1950s were far more tepid than Spain's, and they produced far less dramatic results.

The economy, however, did begin to grow. During the late 1950s and early 1960s the rate of increase was about 3 to 4 percent per year. This was a major breakthrough for Portugal, although the rates were still only half of those for Spain. Portugal's relative prosperity also enabled the Salazar regime to initiate and actually implement during this period a number of social welfare programs. These were quite limited, but at least a beginning was made. The programs were administered through the corporative system.[4]

Portugal's efforts in the 1960s and early 1970s to fight three African counter-insurgency wars simultaneously was undoubtedly a drain on the economy, but perhaps not as great a one as is sometimes thought, for even in the midst of these conflicts, Portugal continued to show budget surpluses and positive economic growth rates.[5] Only at the end, in 1973–74, which corresponded with the first great oil price shock, did Portugal begin to feel a severe economic pinch from its African wars.

Whereas Spain had a relatively smooth transition to democracy and, thus, in the mid-1970s experienced continuity in its economic policies, Portugal's revolution in 1974–75—and beyond—was terribly disruptive of the economy. It was not just the chaos accompanying the revolution that adversely affected economic performance; other factors were also involved. The return of hundreds of thousands of Portuguese citizens from the African colonies after the colonies were granted independence helped push unemployment to approximately 30 percent of the work force. The upheaval and the Communist push for power frightened away both foreign and domestic capital. Then, the nationalizations of perhaps 40 to 50 percent of the productive sector and a new constitution that proclaimed socialism as the national goal and that put severe restraints on private economic activities all but assured that Portugal would remain in the economic doldrums indefinitely. Foreign investment came to a standstill, and there was considerable disinvestment. The second oil shock of 1979 added to Portugal's woes, and a further economic dampener was provided by the world recession of 1981–83.

From 1974 (the year of the revolution) to 1985 Portugal experienced the problems of what are called "stop and go" economic policies. External imbalances and a general downturn in the mid- to late 1970s and early 1980s were followed by austerity programs pushed by the International Monetary Fund (IMF) that led to a depreciation of Portugal's currency (the *escudo*), high inflation (29 percent in 1984), and negative real wage growth rates (−6 percent) between 1982 and 1984. Ironically, it was a Socialist government (that of Mario Soares) that had to carry out these belt-tightening measures and that resulted in Soares's party losing decisively in the next election. An entire decade, from the mid-1970s to the mid-1980s, was thus lost in terms of economic development; indeed, the balance was *negative growth* for this 10-year period.

Since the mid-1980s the picture has brightened considerably, both politically and economically. Politically, Portugal has had remarkable stability since 1985, and in 1987 a single party (the PSD) won an absolute majority in the parliament for the first time since the revolution. Governmental stability, in turn, helped stabilize the economy. In addition, although the unpopular austerity measures carried out by the preceding government caused that government to lose the next election, they undoubtedly helped the economy. Inflation came down from 20 percent in 1985 to about 13 percent, the *escudo* was stabilized, and real growth rates reached 4.5 to 5.5 percent per year.

During the late 1980s this economic momentum gathered further force. In 1986 Portugal, like Spain, joined the Common Market and, as the poorest country in the EEC, immediately qualified for various subsidies that the Market provides. Portugal also benefitted from the strong economic growth of the rest of Europe and the United States during the mid- to late 1980s. In addition, the government's policies of amending the laws and constitution to allow freer economic activities paved the way for a large influx of foreign capital into Portugal, which resulted in the building of scores of new factories and the creation of thousands of new jobs.

Those who remember Portugal from the past as poor, bedraggled, backward, and "quaint" will hardly recognize the country in the 1990s. Portugal was able to all but eliminate unemployment, it has now successfully assimilated and found jobs and places for those hundreds of thousands of refugees from its former colonial possessions (no easy feat for such a small country), and its economic growth is nearing the "miracle" rate. There is a dynamism in Portugal that was absent before and a great deal of construction and *movimento*. Portugal is on the move, its economy is booming, and the whole pace of life is changing. It no longer represents the "proud tower" of a pre-World War I society.[6]

The real strain, however, will come in the later 1990s when the European subsidies will be reduced and Portugal's often inefficient family-based firms have to compete against the European giants. Many of these small firms will likely not be able to survive. Portugal is still far poorer than Spain and has not gone as far on the road to economic development; but it may be that for Portugal, like Spain, we are witnessing the beginning of the end of an entire, societywide "culture of poverty" and henceforth will be able to talk about erasing only "pockets of poverty."

As Portugal has become more affluent, the equity question is again being raised more insistently. Most of the new wealth being generated in Portugal is going into middle-class pockets, some is going to the working class, while the rural peasants have benefitted very little. More and more of the peasants "think with their feet" by migrating, either to the cities where jobs are available or abroad. But left behind in these rural areas, as well as in the urban slums where the recent migrants live, are immense social problems: housing, health care, education, and so on. As Portugal has developed economically and can now afford to do something to begin to solve these problems, more and more calls are going out that the country must also turn its attention to these festering social issues. For Portugal, as for Spain, the question has increasingly become: How can we keep the motor force of economic growth that has recently been so impressive steaming along, and at the same time turn greater national attention to the issue of equity and solutions to the pressing social problems that modernization helps create. It is a daunting task.

FOREIGN AFFAIRS

The remote and isolated location of Spain and Portugal on the southwest periphery of Western Europe, surrounded by sea and ocean on four sides, and inhabiting a peninsula connected to Europe only through the narrow neck of the all but impassable Pyrenees Mountains, has strongly shaped both the psychological attitudes and the foreign policies of Spain and Portugal. The isolation of the peninsula and the natural barrier provided by the Pyrenees have historically kept both foreign armies and influences out, and the Spaniards and Portuguese locked in. The seven centuries–long occupation of the peninsula by the Moors served to further isolate Iberia and cast it as "different"—tainted, in the eyes of most Europeans, by African and Islamic influences. To the natural, geographic isolation of the peninsula were thus added racial, religious, and ethnic prejudices.

In part because of their isolation from the rest of Europe, however, and in part because of the surrounding seas, Spain and Portugal in the early modern era were impelled into becoming major maritime powers, exploring and conquering vast colonies in the Americas, Africa, and Asia. Many Spaniards and Portuguese think of these conquests in the fifteenth and sixteenth centuries as the high points of their histories, a glorious "golden era" that was associated with the Hapsburgian Model of a centralized, authoritarian sociopolitical system. Even today, vast areas of Latin America, Africa, and Asia still speak Spanish or Portuguese. But as Spain and Portugal faded as global powers in the seventeenth and eighteenth centuries, culminating in the loss of their most important Latin American colonies early in the nineteenth century, they also began to pull into themselves, to withdraw and isolate themselves from the main developments in the Western world. Spain and Portugal remained fixed in place, still clinging to their outmoded sixteenth century model. Not only did Spain and Portugal ignore and shut out the Renaissance; the Protestant Reformation; the Enlightenment and the scientific revolution; the movement toward capitalism; industrialism, and limited, representative government; but they also forsook their earlier roles as leading international powers and as global colonial empires.

During the first decade of the nineteenth century, both countries experienced a French occupation led by Napoleon's forces, and then were beset subsequently for most of the rest of the century by almost chronic instability as rising liberalism clashed with rock-hard traditionalism. The fact that they were bypassed by the Industrial Revolution and remained backward and underdeveloped further deepened their sense of isolation. In 1898 Spain suffered another humiliation when it was defeated by that "upstart" nation, the United States of America, and lost the last of its one-time colossal global empire: Cuba, Puerto Rico, and the Philippines. The loss triggered enormous soul-searching in Spain as to why the nation had fallen so low and what its future and destiny would be, but the immediate effects were to increase Spain's sense of inferiority and to force it to withdraw even deeper into itself.

Both Iberian countries remained neutral and nonbelligerent during World Wars I and II. Their corporatist and authoritarian institutions established by Franco and Salazar provided some parallels with the Fascist regimes, but neither Spain nor Portugal were really full-fledged Fascist systems. Their neutrality helped prevent a German occupation army from crossing the border from occupied France; at the same time, the trek across Spain to Lisbon, which both governments facilitated, provided one of the few outlets from Europe by which Jews and other refugees could escape Hitler's gas chambers. Actually one can find in Franco's Spain and Salazar's Portugal during World War II both expressions of admiration for fascism and some institutions that imitated Fascist forms, *and* expressions of admiration for the Allies and their cause. These statements are sufficiently ambiguous that the judgment about which side Spain's and Portugal's loyalties resided during the war must remain uncertain. It is probably fair to say, however, that in the first years of the war when the Axis powers seemed to be winning, Spain and Portugal tilted in that direction; but later when it appeared the Allies were winning the tilts in Iberia were in that direction.

Because of the widespread sense in Europe that Franco's and Salazar's regimes were "Fascist," or at least partly so, Spain and Portugal remained isolated after the war—Spain more so than Portugal. Spain was excluded from participation in the Marshall Plan, NATO, the United Nations (until 1955), and the European Economic Community (EEC); Portugal was incorporated into NATO in 1953, mainly because of the value of its bases, but it was not invited to join the EEC. While Franco and Salazar were in power, therefore, their nations—especially Spain—remained outcasts, pariah states, disdained by the international community. Rejection by Europe, in turn, forced Spain and Portugal into even further isolation and a haughty posture that they would go it alone in the world. In fact this was a familiar pattern in Iberian history: When Spain and Portugal were accepted in Europe as "normal" countries, they then also thought of themselves as European; but when they have been rejected by Europe, they have also tended to withdraw, thumb their noses at Europe, claim they didn't want to be a part of Europe anyway, and pursue an independent, nonaligned, even Third World foreign policy.

Spain

Spain is nearly five times bigger than Portugal in territory, four times more populous, and with a gross national product eight times as large. Spain's voice in international affairs is, therefore, far more important than Portugal's. Spain is also closer to the rest of Europe than Portugal by about two to three days' driving time; is more integrated into European trade, tourism, and mores; and now thinks of itself and wants to be thought of as European. *Europe* writ large is Spain's main foreign policy concern.[7]

The European Community During Franco's rule Spain had sought to have closer ties with Europe, but it was consistently rebuffed. Once Franco died, integration into Europe became Spain's primary foreign policy goal. Spain sought not just political and economic membership in Europe, however; it also sought to have its transition to democracy recognized and legitimated so that it would finally be accepted as a full-fledged, European *democratic* nation.

The negotiations to join the European Economic Community (EEC) were long and complicated. Spain's economy and industry were backward and would require assistance from the EEC, which was already feeling a financial pinch. In addition, there were complications over Spain's far-reaching fishing fleet, which impinged on what other nations considered their fishing areas. The main hindrance was the fear of French farmers who thought that cheaper Spanish agricultural products would undersell their own products. After a decade of negotiations, the treaty admitting Spain (as well as Portugal and Greece) to the EEC was signed in 1985, and on January 1, 1986, Spain was finally and formally admitted. The terms were not entirely favorable to Spain but few people objected because such a major goal of Spanish foreign policy had been accomplished: entry into *Europe*. Over the next five years (after a slow start) membership in Europe proved a tremendous boon to the Spanish economy and to Spaniards' new-found sense of "Europeanness." Spanish polls showed overwhelming favoritism toward remaining in the EEC.

NATO While Spanish public opinion, the political parties, and the government were virtually unanimous in wanting to join the EEC, sentiment with regard to joining the North Atlantic Treaty Organization (NATO) was far more mixed. The center and right parties tended to favor joining, although not without misgivings, whereas the Left (both the Communists and the Socialists) was opposed.

Spain's strategic location overlooking the Mediterranean and the Strait of Gibraltar made it a valuable asset for NATO; Spain also lies astride major air and land communications routes. Advocates of NATO membership argued that because Spain was now a part of Europe politically and economically, it must also shoulder its share of Atlantic Alliance defense responsibilities. They also argued that NATO membership would provide military protection for Spain. An especially compelling argument in terms of Spain's domestic politics was that integration into NATO would mean new equipment for its armed forces, membership on numerous military committees at NATO headquarters in Brussels, and a new mission for the armed forces instead of their meddling in political affairs. Hence Spain joined NATO in 1981 when the centrist UDC government of Leopoldo Calvo-Sotelo was in power.

The Left opposed membership in NATO because it feared that Spain might also be attacked in case of war, and because of general hostility to military matters and to the United States, mainly because of its long support for Franco. Felipe González, the Socialist (PSOE) leader, had earlier opposed membership, but over a period of time he reversed course. González had been frightened by the attempted military coup of 1981, the year before his own party was elected; he also came to see the advantages of having the Spanish armed forces engaged in NATO exercises, rather than in domestic politics where he and his government would likely be the primary target. Thus, in the popular referendum on continuing in NATO held in 1986, the prime minister campaigned vigorously for it. Although polls showed it would fail, the actual vote was 52.6 percent in favor to 39.8 percent opposed.

Spain is *in* NATO, but the referendum reflects continuing uncertainty. Spain has emphasized, furthermore, its *political* commitment to NATO but it has put limits on its military commitments. It requested that a squadron of U.S. fighter planes leave Spain, and there are ongoing negotiations over the U.S. bases in Spain. In 1988, furthermore, in a show of independence, Spain joined the Western European Union (WEU), a European defense grouping from which the United States is excluded. Meanwhile, the collapse of the Communist Warsaw Pact and continuing problems in the Soviet Union reduced the outside threat and, with it, the arguments for NATO.

The Socialist International Spain's international relations are not just between countries or involving groups of countries, but also involve transnational organizations. Of these, the most prominent is the Socialist International (SI).

The SI is an association of Socialist political parties. Spain's PSOE is a prominent member, as are the German Social Democrats, the Scandinavian Socialists and Social Democrats, and various Third World Socialist movements. The SI helped González and the PSOE; he in turn has been active internationally on the SI's behalf.

This caused many early tensions as the SI was widely perceived, for example, to be in favor of the Sandinista revolution in Nicaragua, in favor of the Marxist-Leninist guerrillas in El Salvador, and anti–United States. But over time González became disillusioned with both the Sandinistas and the Salvadoran rebels, made some sharper distinctions between socialism and outright Marxism-Leninism, came to see that these small countries in Central America were not worth angering the United States for, toned down his rhetoric, and pursued a more moderate policy. The PSOE's membership in the SI and González's activities on its behalf are now more constructive than critical.

France France lies right across the Pyrenees border from Spain and there is a long history of rivalries, competition for empires, invasions, occupations, and so on involving the two countries. Spain enjoyed the upper hand in the sixteenth century, but France has been the most powerful since then.

France was often condemnatory of the Franco regime, labeling it "Fascist" and, after World War II, advocated an Allied invasion to remove him. Franco accused France of harboring anti-Franco resistance fighters whom it allowed to use its territory as sanctuary; when some of these fighters were captured and executed by Franco, France vowed not to allow Spain into the UN until the dictator had been removed.

Even after democracy was restored in Spain, France nevertheless led the resistance to Spain's entry into the EEC. With Spain's overwhelming desire to be admitted into *Europe* (the number one foreign policy issue), the French opposition did not endear that country to the Spaniards. The French Basques, who live just across the Pyrenees from the Spanish Basques and sometimes provide a safe haven for Spanish Basque terrorists, are also a source of friction. The relations between Spain and France, therefore, are not amiable, but they are most often cooperative and no longer poisonous.

Germany Germany is further distant from Spain and historically has not been so involved in the peninsula as France. But Germany has growing commercial ties in Iberia, and following Franco's death West German political parties, foundations, labor unions, and the government were instrumental in assisting Spanish democracy. Germany has become a major factor in Spanish foreign policy.

Portugal Spain is more important to Portugal (see following) than Portugal is to Spain. Portugal is small and poor and, therefore, not very attractive commercially to Spain. Spanish stores in the border towns are happy to sell their merchandise to the Portuguese who cross the frontier to get better goods and service, but there is not a lot of Spanish investment in Portugal. Most Spaniards view Portugal as quaint and old-fashioned, a place for tourism and for purchases of inexpensive handmade crafts, a "province" that should rightly belong to Spain but because of now obscure historical reasons does not. In addition, Spain's whole orientation, its main cities, highways, and commerce, are toward the northeast, toward Europe, and not toward the less developed west and Portugal.

There are new cooperative activities between the two countries in the form of highway construction, a high-speed train line, and joint commercial ventures that will help build stronger ties between them. Their prime ministers meet frequently to discuss issues of common concern, replacing the Iberian Pact signed in the 1930s by Franco and Salazar. Overall, there is a new spirit of cooperation between Spain and Portugal based on the facts that both are now democracies and members of the EEC, NATO, and the Western community of nations.

Gibraltar, Ceuta, and Melilla It is hard for foreigners to grasp, as Spain's relations with Europe and other major nations seem so self-evidently preeminent, how important to *Spain* these three small and obscure enclaves are. In fact, they are among the most important elements in Spain's foreign policy.

Gibraltar lies at the southernmost tip of Iberia pointing toward the Mediterranean and North Africa. It is a part of the mainland and had always been considered Spanish territory until the Treaty of Utrecht, signed in 1713, which awarded it to Great Britain. The avowed purpose of every Spanish government since then has been to get it back. The trouble for Spain is that the English-speaking majority on Gibraltar want to remain a part of Great Britain, not be absorbed by Spain, so that raises difficulties for Spain if one believes in self-determination.

"The Rock" has been a major source of tension in Spanish-British relations. Spain has at times closed the border leading to Gibraltar, thus cutting it off from supplies; Britain has retaliated. Negotiations have not solved the problem, although with Spain now a democracy and a member of both NATO and the EC, Gibraltar's opposition to rejoining Spain is decreasing. It may be that some form of regional autonomy structure, similar to others in Spain, may be worked out.

Ceuta and Melilla are located in Morocco, North Africa, across the Mediterranean from mainland Spain. Since Franco's withdrawal from the Spanish Sahara in 1974, these cities and their small offshore islands are the last vestiges of Spain's once glorious and global empire. They have been part of the Spanish crown for centuries and are administered as part of Spain; their populations are also mostly Spanish. Ceuta lies right across the Strait of Gibraltar from Spain, and the atmosphere in that city is predominantly European; Melilla, 300 miles to the east, is more a Moroccan city, and more Islamic.

It is ironic that just the opposite principles apply in Ceuta and Melilla as apply in Gibraltar. Gibraltar is part of the Spanish mainland but speaks English and wants to be English. Ceuta and Melilla are part of the Moroccan mainland and Morocco lays claim to them, but both enclaves are predominantly Spanish-speaking and would rather be Spanish than Moroccan.

If Spain claims Gibraltar for historical and geographic reasons, Morocco can use the same reasons to claim Ceuta and Melilla. Meanwhile, there is increasing tension in these cities between the Spanish and Muslim populations. And at home, some members of Spain's Left parties (Socialists and Communists) have expressed sympathy for the Moroccan claims. No quick or easy solution to this vexing problem appears in sight.

Soviet Union and Eastern Europe Spain and the Soviet Union established formal diplomatic relations only in 1977, after Franco's death. Earlier there had been quite extensive commercial and cultural ties, and Spain had also opened up diplomatic relations with the Communist countries of the Eastern bloc. The slowness in establishing Soviet ties was owing to Franco's anticommunism and his bitterness that the Soviet Union had bolstered the republic in the 1936–39 civil war and had continued to support a Communist underground. Socialists and independent Marxists with long memories also recalled that Stalin had tried to eliminate the noncommunist Left during the civil war.

Spain's relations with the Soviet Union were complicated by other, larger issues stemming from the Cold War. For the Soviet Union, establishing good relations with Spain was important for its larger policy in the Mediterranean and to ensure access through the Strait of Gibraltar to the Atlantic. The United States, in turn, wished to limit the Soviets' Mediterranean activities as much as possible; the United States also had important military bases in Spain. These issues were made even more convoluted by revelations of Soviet espionage activities in Spain and, hence, the expulsion of several Soviet diplomats.

Spain has not shared the United States' Cold War fears of a serious threat emanating from the Soviet Union. Spain is far from the presumed location of such a threat in central Europe; in addition, Franco's anticommunism led many of the new generation Spaniards to look benignly on the Soviet Union as a counter to U.S. influence. In the post-Franco era, Spain's foreign policy has drifted farther toward independence from either superpower, and the winding down of the Cold War accelerated these trends.

The Middle East Spain's relations with the Middle East are strongly shaped by the country's lack of petroleum. In addition, because of its Islamic history during the Middle Ages and its location close to North Africa, Spain has presented itself as a bridge to the Muslim world.

Spain tilted toward the Arab states in most Middle East conflicts and did not recognize Israel until 1986. But it balanced that move the same year by according diplomatic status to the Palestine Liberation Organization (PLO) in Madrid. Spain had carefully cultivated the Arab states for years and had extensive trade and cultural ties there. When Iraq occupied Kuwait in 1990, Spain sent warships to the Persian Gulf area as a way of showing support for the U.S.-led Alliance, but the step was widely criticized in Spain, and so the government talked about it as little as possible. Spain's role in the anti-Iraq Alliance was thus quite ambivalent.

United States Spain's relations with the United States are generally good, although there are many undercurrents of resentment. First, the United States is sometimes resented for being crass, materialistic, and pushy—an upstart nation without a long history, which Spain has. These values are then contrasted with the supposed humanism, idealism, and spiritualism of Spain. Second, the United States is often resented for its political values of liberalism and almost anarchic individualism, as compared with Spain's emphasis on the family, community, and organic unity. Third, the United States is still resented for having defeated Spain in 1898, depriving her of the last of her colonies, and delivering the *coup de grace* to Spain's dreams of grandeur.

Under Franco, a military pact was signed with the United States in 1953, but the Spanish regime resented the meager military assistance proffered. At the same time the Spanish Left resented any assistance to Franco at all, the U.S. efforts to prop up his regime at various times, and the various well-publicized pictures in Spain showing Franco and U.S. leaders locked in a bearhug. The Left also resented the U.S. military bases in Spain, tended to blame the United States for any exacerbations of the Cold War, and was opposed to Spain's participation in NATO. Particularly in earlier years, the Left was convinced that the U.S. embassy or perhaps the CIA were manipulating internal Spanish politics.

Anti-Americanism in Spain thus comes from both the Left and the Right, it is pervasive, and it is widespread. Most often this takes the form of simmering resentments rather than any overt hostility directed at Americans. As Spain has also democratized, however, become more mature and confident of itself as a nation, and put aside some of its historic complexes, these resentments have also begun to fade.

Spain's relations with the United States are now more or less normal and regularized. The United States no longer treats Spain as a Third World country subject to U.S. embassy manipulations, which the Spaniards resent, and has put the relationship on the same mature basis that it maintains with the rest of Western Europe. And as the Spanish resentments have begun to fade and the country become more affluent, a new era has begun to open up based on trade, two-way tourism, expanded student exchanges, commerce, and the normal relations of two nations associated on a friendly basis at multiple levels of interchange. In the late 1980s the Spanish took steps to reduce U.S. military presence in Spain, and some of the old resentments are still present. But these have ameliorated over time, and one could say that the relations are now good with every likelihood of getting better.

Latin America Because of the common ties of history, language, and culture going back to the colonial era, Spain likes to think that it has a special relationship with Latin America.[8] Spain has tried in Latin America to contrast its values once again of humanism, spiritualism, and organicism with the supposed crassness, materialism, and pragmatism—to say nothing of interventionism—of the United States.

For a long time in the nineteenth and twentieth centuries Spain lacked the concrete capacity to back up any of these hortatory claims with real activities and programs. Furthermore Spain's activities in preaching to the Latin Americans about what they should or should not do and what their beliefs and ideology should be were resented by the Latin Americans, who didn't see the need to take directions from the still-hated mother country.

Franco elaborated a philosophy of *Hispanismo,* which he tried feebly to export to Latin America. It was based on Franco's own notions of authority, Catholicism, discipline, organicism, and corporatism—all themes that had considerable resonance in Latin America. But Spain still lacked the resources to back up the pronouncements with realistic programs. Later, as Spain went through its transition to democracy, it tried to offer that as a model for Latin America to follow.

Spain is now wealthier than before and, hence, has programs of trade, investment, cultural exchange, and so on with Latin America that it earlier lacked. And there are, after all, cultural, linguistic, and even political affinities between the two areas that are strong and that all but guarantee a lasting "special relationship." However, Spain still lacks the institutional and economic base to have a strong presence in Latin America and certainly will not supplant the

United States in the region in the near future. Furthermore, as Spain has become more closely integrated into Europe, its interests in Latin America have faded. Spain would still like to serve as a bridge between Latin America and the EEC, but Latin America tends to feel it doesn't need a bridge to anywhere and it often resents Spain's efforts to treat it still as a colonial possession.

Portugal

For a considerable period after the 1974 revolution, Portugal was preoccupied with its internal political situation. With the exception of freeing its African colonies from colonialism and establishing relations with the Communist countries, Portugal did not pay serious, sustained, or high-level attention to foreign affairs. The revolution, the street demonstrations, the rapid political shifts, the birth of democracy—these domestic happenings are what mainly concerned the Portuguese after April 25, 1974, not foreign policy. Only after the revolution had run its course and the country returned to normalcy did Portugal begin seriously to reconstruct its foreign policy.

Africa During the 1960s and early 1970s, Portugal had been fighting three colonial wars at the same time on the African continent. These campaigns had eventually hurt the economy, drained morale, and become politically unpopular. Hence, in the midst of the most conflictive phases of the 1974 revolution, Portugal moved quickly to grant independence to its colonies. The manner in which this was carried out, however, and the results that were produced proved to be very controversial.

General Spínola, whose 1974 book *Portugal and the Future*[9] had helped launch the revolution in Portugal, had proposed stopping the wars, achieving a peaceful resolution, and granting independence to the colonies. But he wanted to maintain good relations with the colonies and to link them together with Portugal and possibly Brazil through a grand, Portuguese-speaking, Lusitanian confederation of nations that would resemble the British Commonwealth. However, this was rejected by the radical and more impatient members of the Armed Forces Movement (MFA) who were, at this time, strongly influenced by the Portuguese Communist party (PCP).

In Guinea-Bissau, after brief negotiations and a cease-fire, Portugal granted independence to its former colony and turned power over to the Marxist-Leninist African Party for the Independence of Guinea and Cabo Verde (*Partido Africano da Independência de Guiné e Cabo Verde*—PAIGC). In the much larger territory of Mozambique, Portugal turned over the reins of government to the Front for the Liberation of Mozambique (*Frente de Libertação de Mocambique*—FRELIMO), another Marxist-Leninist guerrilla group. And in Angola, Portugal's most valuable African colony, power was given to the similarly Marxist-Leninist Popular Movement for the Liberation of Angola (*Movimento Popular de Libertação de Angola*—MPLA) which, among the three factions fighting for independence, was the only one allied with the Soviet Union.

The haste with which independence was granted and the simple turning over of power to the very Marxist-Leninist elements Portugal had long been fighting, without any further guarantees, proved to be very controversial. For one thing, it left stranded hundreds of thousands of Portuguese settlers, many of whom had lived in the colonies for generations. They lost their homes, lands, positions, everything; most of them, embittered, found their way back to Portugal where, for a long time, they added to the unemployment problems and lived for many years in squalid conditions. Second, it left the African colonies stranded because they lacked the teachers, educators, managers, and so on to make a successful transition to independence. Plagued by continuing civil wars and violence, political conditions and living standards in these newly independent states continued to deteriorate. Third, there were alternatives besides turning power over to the Soviet-allied Marxist-Leninist groups that Portugal might have pursued that would not have produced such disastrous outcomes, but domestic forces in Portugal ruled out the following of a more patient and moderate strategy.

For many years Portugal's relations with its former colonies remained strained; they resented Portuguese colonialism and at the same time felt the mother country had not only exploited them but then later on had abandoned them and left them in the lurch. However, after 15 years relations began to normalize. Trade was resumed, Portuguese educators and technicians were welcomed back, and new ties among the Portuguese-speaking nations (but not on such a grandiose basis as envisioned in Spínola's Lusitanian federation) began to be forged. Portugal served as a useful intermediary in discussions of the conflicts in Southern Africa as well as interlocutor among the contending forces in Angola and Mozambique. Hence, although Portugal will no longer play a large role in southern Africa, it will play some role.

Europe Portugal's relations with Europe are now closer than they have ever been. This includes relations with individual countries as well as with the EC.

Because of geographic distance and location at the farthest point on the Iberian Peninsula, as well as its African and Latin American interests, Portugal had long been isolated from Europe—politically, economically, psychologically—even more so than Spain. But now Portugal is integrally a part of Europe; its trade and political connections mean that it is definitively a European country and no longer can claim that it has a South Atlantic vocation.

Portugal is very worried, however, even more so than Spain, that it may not be able to compete in a Europe without tariff walls. A good part of Portuguese business, banking, and industry is not sufficiently efficient to compete in Europe without protection. Many Portuguese firms will undoubtedly go under as Portugal is fully integrated economically into Europe, but the government is counting on the benefits of integration outweighing the losses.

Spain Portugal's relations with Spain are normal and decent but always wary, strained. Portugal likes to say that neither a good marriage nor a good wind ever comes from Spain. This is because Portugal is so small, weak, and poor and Spain is so much larger, far stronger, and twice as prosperous. Portugal understands that Spain still considers Portugal as its "lost province"; and although no one thinks Spain will attempt to seize Portugal militarily, the Portuguese do worry that the stronger Spanish state and economy may weaken and gradually absorb them. Spain and Portugal have good relations and there are increased commercial and other ties between the two countries, but a main tenet of Portuguese foreign policy has always been to maintain an alliance system that will isolate Spain and give Portugal important support in time of trouble.

France One of those countries that Portugal seeks to use to balance Spain's power is France. Portugal is close to France culturally and follows French intellectual trends; the French newspaper *Le Monde* is often displayed on Portuguese coffee tables, and until recently French (now it is English) was the second language of educated Portuguese. Portugal has sent a large number of its unemployed workers to France; at the same time, in Lisbon French schools and French cultural missions are very active. But along with these ties, Portugal has long wanted a strong French presence on the other side of the Pyrenees as a way of checking Spain.

Great Britain Portugal's ties with Great Britain are also historic, and date back to a treaty of alliance signed in 1373, making it the longest alliance in the Western world. Britain sees Portugal as its point of access on the European continent when other avenues are closed (as during World War II); Portugal sees Britain as its protector, first against Spain and second against France, which occupied Portugal under Napoleon. In addition, Portugal has long admired British democracy, its strong currency and banking, and its historic empire. In turn, British capital has invested heavily in the Portuguese wine and port industry, and many British pensioners find that, because of the lower cost of living, they can retire in Portugal more comfortably than in their own country.

Germany Portugal has not had a lot of contact historically with Germany, although the two were strong rivals for a long time in southern Africa. But in the 1960s and early 1970s West Germany began to develop a vigorous diplomatic and commercial presence in Portugal as it did in Spain; next to France, West Germany became the second largest recipient of Portuguese emigration. During the mid-1970s revolution, German parties, foundations, and the embassy were very active in assisting Portuguese democratic forces (especially the Socialists) against the Communists. The German connections remain chiefly diplomatic and commercial, although with Germany's unification and interest in Eastern Europe its ties to Portugal may be reduced.

The European Community Portugal is now definitively a European country, although still with lingering doubts about that fact. Portugal is a member of NATO and, since 1986, a member of the European Economic Community (EEC). But more than that, now that it is a Western, parliamentary democracy, Portugal is also more

European politically and psychologically. The old issues of whether Portugal would be First, Second, or Third World; Socialist or Capitalist; European or South Atlanticist are no longer issues. Portugal still worries at times whether its identity will be lost in the broader European community, and whether its industries and commerce will be able to withstand the shock of European competition. Since it joined the EEC in 1986 Portugal has, in fact, prospered, but the real test will come in the later 1990s.

Communist Countries Immediately after the revolution of 1974, Portugal abandoned its historic anti-Communist posture for one that favored enhanced relations with the Communist countries. Within weeks during the summer of 1974 diplomatic relations were established with the Soviet Union, Yugoslavia, Hungary, Romania, Czechoslovakia, Bulgaria, and the German Democratic Republic (East Germany). This was followed by a series of bilateral pacts increasing trade and commercial, political, and cultural ties with the Eastern bloc. The Soviet national airline Aeroflot began using Lisbon as a stopover and refueling station between Moscow and Havana, and the Soviet diplomatic presence in Lisbon increased to the size of the U.S. mission. These changes were pushed not just by the PCP but also by the MFA and by many noncommunist Portuguese who wanted their country to diversify its political and economic ties.

But this diplomatic opening to the Communist countries soon began to fade. As long as the Portuguese Communist Party showed signs of successfully seizing power through 1975, the Communist countries were seriously involved in Portugal; but when the PCP failed in its bid and more moderate Portuguese forces prevailed, the Communist countries quickly lost interest. They failed to deliver on the assistance programs promised earlier and began to reduce their embassy staffs. The tourism, trade, and credits that once seemed to be imminently forthcoming from Eastern Europe and the Soviets dried up, particularly as Portugal gravitated from a Socialist to center-right governments in the 1980s. The dramatic changes in Eastern Europe and the Soviet Union in the late 1980s away from communism and toward democracy accelerated this process—or else led to a renewing of ties on the basis of their democratic commonalities. By the beginning of the 1990s the Soviet Union's and other Communist countries' diplomatic and other presence in Portugal had been greatly reduced.

United States The United States has long considered itself a friend and ally of Portugal; the feeling is, generally, mutual. These sentiments have been reinforced by the increasingly large number of Portuguese immigrants (mainly from the Azores) to the United States and the growing economic and political importance of this Portuguese community.

During both World Wars I and II, the United States, as well as Britain, were granted the right to use naval and air bases in the Azores Islands. During the Cold War, U.S. interests in Portugal were mainly strategic and military: The United States wanted continued use of the Portuguese bases and, in return, assisted Portugal through the Marshall Plan and in the form of economic and military assistance. Relations were strained in the 1960s because the United States took an anticolonial stand with regard to Portuguese Africa and imposed an arms embargo; in retaliation, Portugal refused for a time to renew the bases agreement.

The United States was not worried initially by the Portuguese revolution of 1974, assuming that Spínola, the military, and the historically conservative Portuguese people would keep things in hand. But as the revolution lurched to the Left and it appeared possible the Communists might take over, the United States became worried and launched a campaign to prevent that from happening. The U.S. embassy in Lisbon, then under Frank Carlucci, began vigorous diplomatic activity; the United States used its assistance program to aid the democratic groups, and along with NATO allies the United States provided assistance to the Socialist party and Socialist trade unions as the best alternative to a Communist takeover. The United States also sought to rally the moderate elements within the MFA and in Portugal generally. The campaign paid off as Portugal gradually returned to the democratic fold.

During the late 1970s the U.S. assistance, presence, and involvement remained high. A new, larger embassy was built on the outskirts of Lisbon to replace the cramped quarters in the city's center. But as Portugal settled down in the 1980s and the Communist threat receded, the embassy's size and assistance program were greatly reduced. The bases remained an issue of some friction sometimes, but basically the United States now maintained more or less "normal" relations with a "normal" country. Portugal's ascension into the EEC meant that the country, henceforth, was more a European than an American "project," and the new affluence and firmer establishment of democratic institutions implied that the United States had less to worry about diplomatically. The United States also welcomed Portuguese intermediation in negotiations over the future of southern Africa.

Other Countries and Areas Portugal still retains a special interest in its former colony, Brazil. The Portuguese sometimes look down on Brazilians as "people from the tropics"; the Brazilians have their own jokes about the Portuguese. The relations are shaped by the fact that the former colony is much larger and more powerful economically than its former mother country. Hence, Brazilian investment in Portugal in recent decades has been considerably greater than Portuguese investment in Brazil. Brazilian *novelas* (soap operas) also dominate Portuguese television, leading to additional, nationalistic resentments. But mainly the relations are good and normal, and any "special" relationship is now largely historic, cultural, and nostalgic rather than a reflection of more concrete interests.

Portugal has also sought to maintain good relations with the North African and Middle Eastern countries, in part because of geography and in part because of Portugal's oil needs. Portugal produces no petroleum of its own and is almost entirely dependent on imported oil. Its "tilt" toward the Islamic countries has sometimes produced strains, particularly when the Middle East is in turmoil and when the United States wishes to use the bases in the Azores in pursuit of its own Middle Eastern policies.

Like Spain, Portugal is a member of the United Nations (UN) and the Organization for Economic Cooperation and Development (OECD).

A SUMMING UP

Spain and Portugal have made some remarkable strides economically and socially as well as politically. Long poor and isolated from the modern industrial world, and trapped by a mercantilist policy that retarded development, Spain and Portugal lagged way behind the rest of Europe. But since the late 1950s both countries have taken off economically. Their economic takeoffs have enabled them to carry out beneficial social programs that they could not afford earlier. Their economic growth and the modernization of Iberian society to which the economic development gave rise seem additionally to have provided a firmer basis for Spanish and Portuguese democracy. Being members of the EC should help the Iberian nations not only to continue their economic growth but to further consolidate their democracies as well. In this connection—and it is a theme to which we return in the conclusion—it bears repeating that Spain is still twice as affluent as Portugal and with a far more powerful and solid economic base.

In foreign affairs, both Spain and Portugal have broken out of their historic shells of isolation and inferiority. Greater affluence has enabled both countries to pursue a more activist foreign policy than they had followed in decades, even centuries. At the same time, their entry into Europe and the quite solid establishment of democracy in both countries mean that they can now be treated by others as "normal" countries. They are no longer pariah states as they were under Franco and Salazar, nor does the outside world have to worry anymore that in the wake of Franco's death and the toppling of the Salazar/Caetano regime the Communists will seize power. As both countries have settled down and resolved some of their historic internal problems, they have been able to carry out a more "normal" and vigorous foreign policy, and in turn, have increasingly been treated by others as "normal" nations.

NOTES

1. Charles W. Anderson, *The Political Economy of Modern Spain: Policy-Making in an Authoritarian System* (Madison, Wis.: University of Wisconsin Press, 1970).
2. Victor Pérez-Díaz, "The Emergence of Democratic Spain and the 'Invention' of a Democratic Tradition," Presentation made at Harvard University, Center for European Studies, February 27, 1991.
3. An excellent survey is John Hooper, *The Spaniards: A Portrait of the New Spain* (London: Penguin, 1987).

4. For the details see Howard J. Wiarda, *Corporatism and Development: The Portuguese Experience* (Amherst, Mass.: University of Massachusetts Press, 1977).
5. The best studies are by Eric Baklanoff, *The Economic Transformation of Spain and Portugal* (New York: Praeger, 1978).
6. The image is from historian Barbara Tuchman, *The Proud Tower: A Portrait of the World before the War, 1890–1914* (New York: Macmillan, 1966).
7. An excellent summary of Spain's foreign policy, whose analysis is incorporated in this chapter, is Congressional Reference Service, *Spain: A Country Study* (Washington, D.C.: Government Printing Office, 1991).
8. Howard J. Wiarda (ed.), *The Iberian–Latin American Connection: Implications for U.S. Policy* (Boulder, Colo.: Westview Press, 1986).
9. António de Spínola, *Portugal e o Futuro* (Lisbon: Arcadiá, 1974).

Chapter 10

Conclusion

The weight of tradition, of history, and of the past has long hung heavily over Iberia. Isolated, withdrawn, cut off from the main modernizing currents of Western Europe, Spain and Portugal remained locked into the structures of the sixteenth century. They failed to experience the Renaissance, the Enlightenment, the Protestant Reformation, the scientific revolution ushered in with Galileo and Newton, the movement toward representative government of Locke and others, and the capitalistic revolution leading to industrialism—all the major transformations that we associate with the making of the modern world. Instead, Iberia continued as closed, Catholic, traditionalist, mercantilist, absolutist, and authoritarian—all the traits associated with the "Hapsburgian Model." A shorthand way to describe this is to say that Spain and Portugal remained essentially feudal, medieval, and premodern.

It should not be surprising that Spain and Portugal would be established on this basis in the fifteenth and sixteenth centuries; those were, after all, the prevailing institutions of the time. What is remarkable is that they persisted so long. They lasted through the seventeenth and eighteenth centuries of Spanish and Portuguese decline, in partially attenuated form in the nineteenth century, and in updated form on into the Franco and Salazar regimes. Some of these traditional traits and institutions are still present in Spain and Portugal today.

In the late eighteenth century liberalism began to arise in Iberia, helping to produce in the nineteenth century the phenomenon of the "two Spains" and the "two Portugals"—two "nations," two "societies," wholly separate and apart, existing within the same national boundaries. It also produced almost continuous conflict and civil war between these two conceptions, which were not just ideological rivals but had their reflections in distinct sectors of Spanish and Portuguese society as well. Traditionalism was strong in the Church, the army, the landed class, and the countryside; liberalism was strong in the emerging middle class, among commercial interests, with the intellectuals, and in the cities. Between these two conceptions there could be no compromise in Spain and Portugal; they were always at each other's throats. Therefore, from the Spanish and Portuguese points of view, liberalism and republicanism, as exemplified by the Portuguese republic of 1910–26 and the Spanish republic of 1931–36, seemed not to work; they produced chiefly chaos, disintegration, excess, libertinage, crisis, and ultimately, revolution or bloody civil war. Liberalism, they reasoned, may work for Great Britain or the United States, but for Spain and Portugal something else was needed.

But if in the modern age traditionalism was no longer viable, liberalism didn't work, and socialism was unacceptable, what else was left? That is the question Franco and Salazar sought to answer. On the one hand, but only to a certain extent, both these long-term authoritarians tried to remain true to the historic faith in traditionalism, Catholicism, and an ordered society. On the other, they recognized that Spain and Portugal needed to modernize, needed at a minimum to update their historic institutions. To Franco and Salazar, corporatism seemed for a time to provide the answer, a way out of their dilemma, a "third way." Corporatism seemed to be a means by which they could both retain their traditional authoritarianism and ordered structures while at the same time, in a modern sense, organize both labor and capital for integral national development. In other words, Franco and Salazar were traditionalists in some senses, seeking to preserve historic institutions and the sociopolitical status quo; but they were modernizers in other senses, unleashing powerful economic and modernizing forces that ultimately, they could not control.[1]

Unfortunately for Spain and Portugal, corporatism did not work very well either. Franco ignored or abandoned it first and moved to a system of greater political pragmatism and economic liberalism that stimulated vast social and political changes, which, over the long run, had the effect of undermining his regime. Portugal's corporatist system, which had earlier been largely shunted aside, was overthrown in revolution in 1974. There had been advantages to the corporative systems of Franco and Salazar: centralized decision making, a disciplined and orderly society, preservation of historic national values. But the disadvantages—absence of participation, no popular choice, dictatorship, absence of civil liberties and freedom, secret police, censorship, isolation from Europe, dependence on one man, no democracy—came to greatly outweigh the advantages. Almost all Spaniards and Portuguese eventually recognized this, so when the end finally came for these two regimes in the mid-1970s, few lamented their passing.

Now Spain and Portugal have embarked on a democratic course. The transition to democracy made in both countries has been bold, impressive, and inspiring. Overcoming major structural and institutional obstacles as well as the uncertainty of beginning a new course, Spain and Portugal have made significant strides toward democracy. But given the sad and pathetic prior history of republicanism and liberalism in Iberia, we must naturally ask how firmly established are these new democracies? Will they last? How much has really changed? How firm is democracy's base, and what does that base consist of? Will Spain and Portugal revert in the future to some new form of authoritarianism? Are the recent changes permanent or merely cyclical, bound to lead later on to impatience and disillusionment with democracy and to new calls for the discipline and order of a military regime? That cyclical process, after all, has been the history of Spain and Portugal in the nineteenth and twentieth centuries.

In fact the changes in Iberia since the mid-1970s (actually since 1960, thus encompassing the last decade and a half of the Franco and Salazar/Caetano regimes) have been little short of phenomenal. Literacy has risen dramatically, the pace of urbanization has quickened, and vast social changes leading to modernization are under way. The middle class is far larger and more secure, the trade unions are better organized and are recognized as legitimate political participants, and business and industry are well established. Spain and Portugal have joined NATO and the EC; their webs of international connections are far stronger than before, and the traditional isolation has broken down. Economic growth has been over the long term close to "miraculous"; affluence has increased and spread, some of it has even trickled down; and Spain and Portugal have been caught up in the world culture of consumerism, pragmatism, materialism, secularism, and changed morality. The changes in both countries are so great as to render them all but unrecognizable from 30 years ago. The changes also provide a much firmer social and institutional base for democracy than was true the previous times these two countries tried republicanism.

Although democracy is clearly being consolidated, pockets of resistance to it remain. These include elements within the Church, the army, the Guardia, and the economic elites. Many Spanish and Portuguese peasants are not enamored of democracy; the countryside is still more traditional than the cities. Nor have the police, the bureaucracy, and the judiciary changed greatly since democracy was established; and in times of political or economic troubles the new middle class could conceivably feel threatened and consider an alternative solution.

But note that we spoke of "elements" within these groups, not the entire institution or social sector. It is clear that in Spain and Portugal today those historic institutions that constitute the traditional triumvirate of power—Church, army, oligarchy—have also undergone vast changes, have accepted democracy for the most part, and are no longer automatically or necessarily hostile to it. Note also that we spoke of "pockets" of resistance, no longer fully half of a society or a culture of resistance. In Spain and Portugal not only have new groups and social forces risen up and been incorporated into the system, but the old groups have changed fundamentally as well.

In some of this author's earlier writings, he cautioned newly democratic Spain and Portugal to be careful not to go too far, not to antagonize the "other Spain" or the "other Portugal" or to try to rule entirely without it. In the past, that has been a formula for conflict, disaster, and civil war; and in the 1970s such cautions were probably appropriate. But by the 1990s conditions in both countries have changed sufficiently that the earlier warnings can probably be withdrawn. There is no longer a "second Spain" or a "second Portugal" (conservative, traditionalist, antidemocratic) capable of mobilizing sufficient support to overthrow democracy. The split that goes back to the eighteenth century, under the impact of vast economic development and massive sociopolitical modernization, has largely been erased. There are divisions in Spain and Portugal but no longer of that older type capable of tearing these countries apart. The historic division in the Spanish and Portuguese soul that dominated so much of the nineteenth and early twentieth century history has been mended—or, if not mended, then ameliorated, erased, or patched over so that it is no longer as troublesome. Spain and Portugal may still divide over newer class and political issues, but the older ruptures no longer seem dangerous or so disruptive.

We are now in a position to begin answering the questions posed earlier that have always been so difficult for Spain and Portugal. In terms of the historic conflict between traditionalism and modernity, for example, it now appears that modernity has finally triumphed, definitively so. It is no longer an even battle between these two, as it was in the 1920s and 1930s; rather, the social, cultural, and economic changes since then have tilted the balance away from traditionalism to modernity. It took some 30 years, but the developmental accomplishments have been major.

In terms of the conflict between the democratic and the authoritarian traditions that have long vied for power in Spain and Portugal on almost equal terms, it now appears that we have an answer to that issue too. Democracy has triumphed. Eight-five percent of all Spaniards and Portuguese favor democracy over any other system. Almost no one stands for or favors authoritarianism anymore. Authoritarianism has been discredited and largely routed. There are still *pockets* of authoritarianism in Spain and Portugal but no longer a whole culture of authoritarianism, a whole way of life encompassing vast sectors of the population. At the same time, although democracy has triumphed, the institutions of democracy—political parties, interest groups and pluralism, parliament—are not as firmly established and legitimated as we would like. Nevertheless, in overall terms democracy has been strongly established, and a strong democratic political culture has come into existence.

A third question is whether Spain and Portugal are now closer to the First World of modern, industrial, capitalistic nations or to the Third World of poor, underdeveloped ones. The answer is again clear, and it is not necessarily the answer that would have been given 25 or 30 years ago. Iberia is now First World: modern, industrial, capitalistic. A few short decades ago, mired in poverty and backwardness, Spain and Portugal might have been closer to the Third World—and sometimes, as in the Portuguese revolution of 1974, the ideology and feeling of belonging to the Third World came out publicly. But with the economic, social, and political progress of recent years, Spain and Portugal have become First World—and, again, definitively so.

In the past, the answers that outside scholars provided to the question of whether Iberia was First versus Third World, developed versus underdeveloped, often depended on their research perspectives and backgrounds. Scholars who studied Spain and Portugal after studying Latin America, particularly those who studied the Franco and Salazar regimes, found such striking parallels and affinities that they often interpreted Iberia through Latin American eyes, saw Spain and Portugal as only slightly more developed nations than those they had studied in Latin America, and tended to consider them together as part of a common Iberic-Latin cultural and sociopolitical area. Spain and Portugal as well as Latin America, in this view, were part of the Third World.[2] In contrast, those who studied Spain and Portugal after first working in Europe or from a European perspective tended to see Iberia as a part of the First World—a less developed part, to be sure, but still European and not Third World. This latter interpretation, it should be said, is how most Spaniards and Portuguese preferred to see themselves, especially toward the end of the Franco and Salazar regimes—as "European" and not "Latin American."

In actuality, these differing views and interpretations reflected the fact that for a long time Spain and Portugal were located, on a variety of indices, between the First and Third Worlds. Spain is now classified as an "industrial market" economy by the World Bank, but it falls at the lowest rung in that category and even today its per capita income is only one-third of that of such wealthier European nations as Sweden, Norway, and Switzerland. Portugal is at the uppermost reaches of the "developing nations" category, although its recent economic spurt may well have vaulted it over the barrier into the "developed nation" category. In short, our ambivalence about how to classify and interpret Spain and Portugal reflected the real-life facts that the two countries themselves were uncertain about their preferences and destinies and that the developmental indices used cast them as "transitional" or "in between."

At this stage the option of First World versus Third World in Iberia is no longer open. By all the objective economic criteria Spain has made it into the First World and Portugal nearly so. In addition, and even predating their joining the EEC, Spain's and

Portugal's trade and commerce were so heavily oriented toward Europe that realistically, by the 1960s, they no longer had the luxury of choosing which bloc they wished to be associated with. They were already by that time European and First World whether they wished to be or not. Now, of course, these economic ties have been strongly reinforced by cultural (European), political (Western democracies), and strategic (NATO) ties. It is likely at this stage that these ties are unbreakable and irreversible.

The changes in both countries in the last 15 to 20 years have been enormous. These include impressive economic development, vast social modernization, and political democratization. However, in concentrating on these developmental parallels between the two Iberian nations, we should not neglect the considerable differences that still exist between them. Spain has a per capita income *twice* that of Portugal and a gross national production eight times as large. Literacy is higher in Spain and, by all indices, social modernization has proceeded farther. In addition, Spain's social, political, and economic institutions are considerably more developed than Portugal's.

Hence, it should not surprise us that Spanish democracy also seems firmer than the Portuguese, on a more solid base, and better consolidated. Democracy in Spain, therefore, seems to be firmly in place, quite well entrenched, and with only small pockets of opposition. Portugal's democracy is also solid, particularly after the political stability and economic boom of the late 1980s, but its institutional and social base is still weaker than Spain's and therefore could, conceivably, be upset. At present that seems unlikely to happen, and I am not suggesting that such a democratic reversal is being predicted let alone that it would be desirable. In fact such a democratic reversal *in either country* would be a disaster—for the country affected, first of all; for Europe, which now has a big stake in Iberia's success; and for the United States, which has also strongly supported Spain's and Portugal's democratization. Looking at the two countries comparatively, however, Spain's future appears to be assuredly democratic; Portugal will *most likely* remain in the democratic camp, but its position is still a little more uncertain.

The accomplishments of Spain and Portugal in the economic sphere in the last 30 years and in the political sphere during the last 20 are little short of miraculous. They are all the more remarkable for having received so little worldwide attention. Spain has moved from an underdeveloped to an advanced industrial economy; Portugal is just about to, or may have already crossed the threshold into the developed category. Politically, both countries have successfully moved from authoritarianism to democracy. These are most impressive accomplishments, and they deserve far more attention than they have so far received. These are not easy tasks, and the number of countries that have successfully made these transitions is very small. The changes in Iberia rank right up there with the transformations underway in the Soviet Union, the throwing off of communism in Eastern Europe, and the reunification of Germany as among the most significant events of the late twentieth century.

Although Spain and Portugal have indeed been transformed and in all areas of the national life, the continuities must be borne in mind as well. Even with all the changes toward a European system, Spain and Portugal remain in many ways distinctive. They approach and approximate the European political model, but they are not there yet; more than that, they retain—and are likely to continue to retain—particularly Iberian features and ways of doing things that are uniquely their own, products of their own histories and sociocultural traditions. They are no longer "different" in the way Franco and Salazar used to emphasize for their own political purposes, but they still often retain their own cultures, societal norms and institutions, and even political forms.

Spanish and Portuguese democracy, for example, still seems closer to the organic, unified view of Rousseau than to the Anglo-American conception of Locke. On another dimension, Spain and Portugal have jettisoned the authoritarian-corporatist institutions of their old dictatorships, but they still are organized, in part, on a corporative as well as a democratic basis. They are no longer corporative in an old-fashioned, quasi-medieval sense but in a modern or "neocorporative" sense in which both labor and employers are integrated into the state (such as through the "social pacts" the government worked out with the unions and business) in an effort to achieve harmonious national development.[3] There is room for further studies of how Spain and Portugal have gone not just from authoritarianism to democracy but from an older form of authoritarian-corporatism to a new and more advanced, more open form.

Intriguing also is the notion advanced in Chapter 8 of a contract state. This concept refers to the compacts ("fundamental" or "organic" laws) worked out between the state and the armed forces, the state and organized labor, the state and the autonomous regions, the state and the Catholic church, and so forth. What is so fascinating about these arrangements is that they have roots deep in the Iberian past and correspond to the historic Iberian understanding of representative government and democracy. That is, when the state and its component social and corporate units are in harmony, are governed by mutually satisfactory compacts, and the rights and responsibilities of each are spelled out in law—this has historically been defined in Iberia as "democracy."

Spain, particularly, and Portugal, in a less explicit way, have resurrected this ancient system of Iberian "democracy" while at the same time creating all the institutions (parliament, parties, elections, and so on) of a Western and European form of democracy, and managing to blend and reconcile the two. In other words, Spain has both an imported form of democracy that it has taken from Western Europe and one with home-grown or indigenous roots, both of which seem to be working rather well. Again, further study of these institutions and practices is required. But if it is true that Spain has successfully blended "outside" and "inside" forms of democracy, then that is not only a great accomplishment; it also has enormous implications for the field of comparative politics and for other nations of the world. Many of these nations, especially in the Third World, have also been trying—most often unsuccessfully—to achieve the same blend, to take what is best from the Western tradition (democracy) and fuse it with native, indigenous forms and ways of doing things. If Spain and Portugal can manage such a fusion successfully, then they will have provided not only a remarkable case of development and democratization, but they will perhaps also have formed a model that other nations may wish to imitate.[4]

NOTES

1. The details are provided in Howard J. Wiarda, *Corporatism and Development: The Portuguese Experience* (Amherst, Mass.: University of Massachusetts, 1977).
2. See Kalman H. Silvert's analysis of what he calls the "Mediterranean Ethos," in "The Costs of Anti-Nationalism: Argentina," in Silvert (ed.),

Expectant Peoples: Nationalism and Development (New York: Vintage, 1967); also Laurence S. Graham, "Latin America: Illusion or Reality? A Case for a New Analytic Framework for the Region," in Howard J. Wiarda (ed.), *Politics and Social Change in Latin America: The Distinct Tradition* (Amherst, Mass.: University of Massachusetts, 1983; revised edition, Boulder, Colo.: Westview Press, 1992); and Wiarda, "Toward a Framework for the Study of Political Change in the Iberic-Latin Tradition: The Corporative Model," *World Politics*, XXV (January 1973): 206–35.
3. Martin O. Heisler, *Politics in Europe: The Corporatist Polity Model* (New York: McKay, 1974); Suzanne Berger (ed.), *Organizing Interests in Western Europe: Pluralism, Corporatism, and the Transformation of Politics* (New York: Cambridge University Press, 1981).
4. For some broader comments on the Third World's quest for a model incorporating the best of Western and indigenous practices see A. H. Somjee, *Parallels and Actuals of Political Development* (London: Macmillan, 1986); and Howard J. Wiarda, *Ethnocentrism in Foreign Policy: Can We Understand the Third World?* (Washington, D.C.: American Enterprise Institute for Public Policy Research, 1985).

Suggested Readings

Abel, Christopher, and Nissa Torrents (eds.), *Spain: Conditional Democracy*, London: Croom Helm, 1984.

Aceves, Joseph, *Social Change in a Spanish Village*, Cambridge, Mass.: Schenkman, 1971.

Anderson, Charles W., *The Political Economy of Modern Spain: Policy-Making in an Authoritarian System*, Madison, Wis.: University of Wisconsin Press, 1970.

Arrango, E. Ramón, *The Spanish Political System: Franco's Legacy*, Boulder, Colo.: Westview Press, 1978.

Arrighi, Giouahni (ed.), *Semiperipheral Development: The Politics of Southern Europe in the Twentieth Century*, Beverly Hills, Calif.: Sage, 1985.

Baklanoff, Eric, *The Economic Transformation of Spain and Portugal*, New York: Praeger, 1978.

Bender, Gerald J., *Angola under the Portuguese: The Myth and the Reality*, Berkeley, Calif.: University of California Press, 1978.

Bermeo, Nancy, *The Revolution within the Revolution: Workers' Control in Rural Portugal*, Princeton, N.J.: Princeton University Press, 1986.

Bonime-Blanc, Andrea, *Spain's Transition to Democracy: The Politics of Constitution-Making*, Boulder, Colo.: Westview Press, 1987.

Brennan, Gerald, *The Spanish Labyrinth: An Account of the Social and Political Background of the Spanish Civil War*, Cambridge, England: Cambridge University Press, 1971.

Brettell, Caroline B., *Men Who Migrate, Women Who Wait: Population and History in a Portuguese Parish*, Princeton, N.J.: Princeton University Press, 1986.

Bruce, Neil, *Portugal: The Last Empire*, New York: Wiley, 1975.

Bruneau, Thomas C., and Alex Macleod, *Politics in Contemporary Portugal*, Boulder, Colo.: Lynne Rienner, 1986.

———, Victor, M. P. da Rosa, and Alex Macleod (eds.), *Portugal in Development: Emigration, Industrialization, the European Community*, Ottawa, Canada: University of Ottawa Press, 1984.

Carr, Raymond, *Spain, 1808–1939*, Oxford, England: Clarendon Press, 1966.

——— and Juan Pablo Fusi, *Spain: From Dictatorship to Democracy*, London: Allen and Unwin, 1979.

Clark, Robert P., *The Basques*, Reno, Nev.: University of Nevada Press, 1980.

——— and Michael H. Haltzel (eds.), *Spain in the 1980s: The Democratic Transition and a New International Role*, Cambridge, Mass.: A Wilson Center Book, Ballinger Publishing, 1987.

Cortada, James W. (ed.), *Spain in the Twentieth Century World*, Westport, Conn.: Greenwood, 1980.

Cottrell, Alvin J., and James D. Theberge (eds.), *The Western Mediterranean: Its Politics, Economic, and Strategic Importance*, New York: Praeger, 1974.

Crow, John A., *Spain: The Root and the Flower*, Berkeley, Calif.: University of California Press, 1985.

Cutileiro, José, *A Portuguese Rural Society*, Oxford, England: Clarendon, 1971.

Eaton, Samuel D., *The Forces of Freedom in Spain*, Stanford, Calif.: Hoover Institution Press, 1981.

Gallagher, Thomas, *Portugal: A Twentieth Century Interpretation*, Manchester, England: Manchester University Press, 1983.

Gellner, Ernest, and John Waterbury (eds.), *Patrons and Clients in Mediterranean Societies*, London: Duckworth, 1977.

Graham, Lawrence S., and Douglas L. Wheeler (eds.), *In Search of Modern Portugal: The Revolution and Its Consequences*, Madison, Wis.: University of Wisconsin Press, 1983.

——— and Harry Makler (eds.), *Contemporary Portugal: The Revolution and Its Antecedents*, Austin, Tex.: University of Texas Press, 1979.

Gunther, Richard, *Politics and Culture in Spain*, Ann Arbor, Mich.: Institute for Social Research, University of Michigan, 1988.

———, *Public Policy in a No-Party State: Spanish Planning and Budgeting in the Twilight of the Franquist Era*, Berkeley, Calif.: University of California Press, 1980.

———, Giacomo Sani, and Goldie Shabad, *Spain after Franco: The Making of a Competitive Party System*, Berkeley, Calif.: University of California Press, 1986.

Herr, Richard, *An Historical Essay on Modern Spain*, Berkeley, Calif.: University of California Press, 1971.

Hooper, John, *The Spaniards: A Portrait of the New Spain*, London: Penguin, 1987.

Jackson, Gabriel, *The Spanish Republic and the Civil War, 1931–1939*, Princeton, N.J.: Princeton University Press, 1965.

Kohler, Beate, *Political Forces in Spain, Greece, and Portugal*, London: Butterworth, 1982.

Lancaster, Thomas, D., *Political Stability and Democratic Change: Energy in Spain's Transition*, University Park, Penn.: Pennsylvania State University Press, 1989.

——— and Gary Prevost (eds.), *Politics and Change in Spain*, New York: Praeger, 1985.

Linz, Juan, "An Authoritarian Regime: Spain," in E. Allardt and Stein Rokkan (eds.), *Mass Politics*, New York: The Free Press, 1970.

———, "A Century of Politics and Interests in Spain," in Suzanne Berger (ed.), *Organizing Interests in Western Europe*, New York: Cambridge University Press, 1981.

Malefakis, Edward, *Agrarian Reform and Peasant Revolution in Spain: Origins of the Civil War*, New Haven, Conn.: Yale University Press, 1970.

Maravall, José, *The Transition to Democracy in Spain*, London: Croom Helm, 1982.

Marias, Julián, *Understanding Spain*, Ann Arbor, Mich.: University of Michigan Press, 1990.

Matthews, Herbert L., *The Yoke and the Arrows: A Report on Spain*, New York: Braziller, 1961.

Maxwell, Kenneth (ed.), *Portugal in the 1980s*, New York: Greenwood Press, 1986.

Medhurst, Kenneth N., (ed.), *Government in Spain*, Oxford, England: Pergamon Press, 1973.

Michener, James A., *Iberia: Spanish Travels and Reflections*, New York: Random House, 1968.

Mujal-Leon, Eusebio, *Communism and Political Change in Spain*, Bloomington, Ind.: Indiana University Press, 1981.

Opello, Walter C., Jr., *Portugal's Political Development: A Comparative Approach*, Boulder, Colo.: Westview Press, 1985.

Payne, Stanley, *Falange*, Stanford, Calif.: Stanford University Press, 1961.

———, *Franco's Spain*, New York: Crowell, 1967.

———, *A History of Spain and Portugal*, 2 vols., Madison, Wis.: University of Wisconsin Press, 1973.

———, *Politics and the Military in Modern Spain*, Stanford, Calif.: Stanford University Press, 1967.

———, *Spanish Catholicism: An Historical Overview*, Madison, Wis.: University of Wisconsin Press, 1984.

———, *The Spanish Revolution*, New York: Norton, 1970.

Pike, Frederick, B., *Hispanismo, 1898–1936: Spanish Conservatives and Liberals and Their Relations with Spanish America*, Notre Dame, Ind.: Notre Dame University Press, 1971.

Pollack, Benny, *The Paradox of Spanish Foreign Policy*, New York: St. Martin's Press, 1987.

Pourch, Douglas, *The Portuguese Armed Forces and the Revolution*, London: Croom Helm, 1977.

Pridham, Geoffrey (ed.), *The New Mediterranean Democracies: Regime Transition in Spain, Greece, and Portugal*, London: Frank Cass, 1984.

Robinson, Richard, *Contemporary Portugal*, London: Allen and Unwin, 1979.

Schmitter, Philippe, *Corporatism and Public Policy in Authoritarian Portugal*, Beverly Hills, Calif.: Sage, 1975.

Solsten, Eric (ed.), *Portugal: A Country Study*, Washington, D.C.: Library of Congress, Government Printing Office, 1992.

——— and Sandra W. Meditz (eds.), *Spain: A Country Study*, Washington, D.C.: Library of Congress, Government Printing Office, 1990.

Stuart, Douglas T. (ed.), *Politics and Security in the Southern Region of the Atlantic Alliance*, Baltimore, Md.: Johns Hopkins University Press, 1988.

Trythall, J. W. D., *Franco: A Biography*, London: Rupert Hart-Davis, 1970.

Vicens Vives, Jaime, *Approaches to the History of Spain*, Berkeley, Calif.: University of California Press, 1970.

Welles, Benjamin, *Spain: The Gentle Anarchy*, New York: Praeger, 1965.

Wheeler, Douglas L., *Republican Portugal: A Political History, 1920–1926*, Madison, Wis.: University of Wisconsin Press, 1978.

Wiarda, Howard J., *Corporatism and Development: The Portuguese Experience*, Amherst, Mass.: University of Massachusetts Press, 1977.

———, *From Corporatism to Neo-Syndicatism: The State, Organized Labor, and the Changing Industrial Relations Systems of Southern

Europe, Cambridge, Mass.: Harvard University, Center for European Studies, Monograph #4, 1981.

——— , *Transcending Corporatism? The Portuguese Corporative System and the Revolution of 1974*, Columbia, S.C.: University of South Carolina, Institute of International Studies, 1976.

——— and Iêda S. Wiarda, *The Transition to Democracy in Spain and Portugal*, Washington, D.C.: University Press of America, 1989.

——— (ed.), *The Iberian–Latin American Connection: Implications for U.S. Policy*, Boulder, Colo.: Westview Press, 1986.

Williams, Allan (ed.), *Southern Europe Transformed: Political and Economic Change in Greece, Italy, Portugal, and Spain*, London: Harper & Row, 1984.

Index

Abortion, 133
Absolutism, 28, 33, 34
Africa, 1, 68, 71, 219, 232
Agriculture, 19, 40
Alentejo, 173
Alfonso X (the Wise), 28
Alfonso XIII, 36, 38
Aliança Democrática (AD), 76, 169
Aliança Nacional Popular (ANP), 160
Alianza Popular (AP), 82, 168
Amaral, Diogo Freitas do, 169
Amiguismo, 114
Amnesty, 81
Anarchism, 36, 39, 157
Andalusia, 204
Angola, 69, 71, 233
Anti-Americanism, 230
Antidemocratic elements, 7
Aquinas, St. Thomas, 96
Aragon, 17, 26, 27, 29, 184
Arías Navarro, Carlos, 80, 81, 199
Aristotle, 27, 48
Armed forces, 78, 130–132, 142, 177, 186, 194, 200. *See also* Army; Military
Armed Forces Movement (MFA), 74, 165, 178, 179, 192, 200, 232
Army, 30, 37, 39, 40, 45, 57, 105, 117, 129, 139, 151, 244. *See also* Armed Forces; Military
Assembly of the Republic, 196
Associations, 125, 126
Asturias, 26

Augustine, St., 96
Autarky, 63, 209
Authoritarian/corporatist, 5, 248
Authoritarianism, 2, 4, 6, 10, 21, 31, 42, 43, 53, 55–60, 87–88, 92, 94–96, 106–110, 142, 157, 181
Authoritarians, 8
Autonomy, 83
Averroës, 24
Azores, 3, 171, 205, 218, 237

Balearic Islands, 205
Balsemão, Francisco Pinto, 76, 169
Banks, 140
Barcelona, 137, 173
Basques, 3, 20, 118, 172, 173, 193, 203
Bourbon Monarchy, 34, 105, 156
Bragança Monarchy, 4, 36, 170
Brazil, 238
Bureaucracy, 30, 33, 59, 88, 140, 150, 151, 202, 244
Bureaucratic state, 152, 200
Business, 101, 111, 117, 136, 144, 146, 152, 186, 243

Cabinet, 196, 199
Caciquismo, 114, 130, 135
Caetano, Marcello, 1, 43, 49, 68, 71, 72, 78, 89, 160
Calvo-Sotelo, Leopoldo, 83, 84, 199, 225
Canary Islands, 3, 205
Capitalism, 47

Carillo, Santiago, 164
Carlist wars, 36, 105, 156
Carlucci, Frank, 237
Carrero Blanco, Luis, 68, 80
Carthaginians, 20
Casas do Povo, 50
Casas dos pescadores, 50
Castile, 17, 29, 184
Castro, Américo, 24
Catalonia, 172, 184, 203
Catholic social teachings, 45, 47
Catholicism, 4, 25, 31, 45, 88, 92, 93–94, 113, 133, 194. *See also* Roman Catholic Church
Caudillos, 36, 135
Celts, 20
Censorship, 58, 66, 73
Centrism, 115
Centro Democrático y Social, 167, 173
Ceuta, 227
Charles I (V), 30
Christian-Democrats (movement, party), 52, 60, 62, 75, 124, 125, 144, 148, 161
Christianity, 22
Cities, 25, 29
Civil service, 150
Civil society, 187
Civil war, 39
Clans, 98, 126, 151
Class structure, 21, 33, 65, 96–98, 108, 124
Clergy, 27
Cold War, 229
Common Market, 220
Communist countries, 236
Communist party, 163, 165, 173, 232, 236
Communists, 39, 60, 61, 62, 74, 75, 81, 107, 124, 125, 147, 157, 161, 177, 191
Comparative politics, 6
Confederación Española de Organizaciones Empresariales (CEOE), 146
Cofederación Sindical de Comisiones Obreras, 147
Congress of Deputies, 199
Conservatism, 105, 117

Constituent Assembly, 191
Constitution of 1812, 35
Constitution of 1931, 38, 185
Constitution of 1976 (Portugal), 191
Constitution of 1977, 82, 193
Consumerism, 114
Contract state, 151–153, 206, 248
Corporations, 26, 27, 28, 48
Corporations ministry, 52
Corporatism, 2, 21, 41, 42, 43, 47–54, 56, 67, 68, 83, 101–104, 121, 148, 152, 176, 190, 218, 242
Corregidores, 29
Cortes, 27, 29, 82, 193, 199, 200
Council of Government, 205
Council of Ministers, 196, 199
Council of State, 49, 53, 192, 200
Council of the Revolution, 192
Counter Reformation, 93
Covadonga, 24
Cuartelazo, 179
Cunhal, Alvaro, 165

Dante, 96
Dark Ages, 23
Decline, 32
Democracy, 4, 5, 6, 9, 10, 11, 12, 28, 65, 71, 76, 81, 113, 116–118, 142, 144, 180, 245, 247, 249
Democratic party, 157
Development, 10, 11, 12, 13
Descontento, 179
Dictatorship, 54
"Different," 5, 13, 67
Divine right monarchy, 97
Divorce, 133, 144
Domestic policy, 208, 209
Don Carlos, 156
Don Juan, 80
Dual power structure, 180

Eanes, Ramalho, 76, 170, 192, 195
Eastern Europe, 7, 229
Economic determinism, 91
Economic elites, 244
Economic growth, 64, 123, 210, 214, 239, 243, 247
Economic policy, 214, 218

Economy, 3, 6, 40, 44, 63, 75, 210
Education, 112, 123, 216
Elections, 58, 75, 159, 173
Elites, 65, 96, 117, 129, 134–136, 139, 145, 151
El Salvador, 226
Emigration, 111
Empires, 32, 41, 217
England, 31
Enlightenment, 4, 35, 105, 241
Eurocommunist, 164
Europe, 3, 5, 6, 12, 67, 79, 116, 234, 246
European Economic Community (EEC), 3, 6, 77, 123, 215, 220, 224, 235
Euskadiko Ezkerra, 172
Expresso, 168
Extremadura, 26

Factions, 156
Falangist, 52, 53, 57, 137, 158
Falta de civilización, 37, 136
Families, 56, 101
Family system, 88, 98, 115, 126, 151
Fascism, 45, 51, 53, 60, 171, 223
Fascist Italy, 39
Ferdinand of Aragon, 29, 135, 184
Feudalism, 25
First World, 12, 245
Foreign ministry, 85
Foreign policy, 3, 208, 221
Fraga, Manuel, 82, 168
France, 226, 234
Franco, Francisco, 1, 2, 7, 40, 41, 42, 43–69, 78, 80, 107, 157, 186
French occupation, 222
French Revolution, 35
Frente de Libertação de Moçambique (FRELIMO), 233
Fueros (foros), 28, 95, 156, 204, 206

Galicia, 26, 46, 172, 203, 204
Geertz, Clifford, 91
Gender, 88, 115
General Cortes, 200
Generations, 66
Geography, 17

Germany, 227, 235
Gibraltar, 227, 228
Golpe de estado, 179
González, Felipe, 81, 84, 85, 128, 145, 166, 199, 214, 225, 226
Government, 182
Goya, Francisco, 35
Great Britain, 228, 235
Greeks, 20
Gross national product, 122
Group rights, 183
Grupos, 99, 189, 200
Guardia, 57, 130, 244
Guerrillas, 71
Guilds, 50
Guinea-Bissau, 69, 71, 233

Hapsburgian model, 4, 29, 41, 42, 109, 170, 185, 187, 189, 210, 241
Hapsburg monarch, 4, 31, 34
Harri Batasuna, 172
Hierarchy, 96
Hispanismo, 231
History, weight of, 16
Holy Roman Empire, 30
Housing, 216

Iberian Pact, 227
Iglesias, José, 179
Imperial tradition, 21
Individualism, 25
Industrialization, 8, 64, 67, 110, 211, 217, 241
Inquisition, 25, 36, 93
Intereses, 120, 153
Integralists, 60
Interest groups, 125, 142, 151, 176, 187
Intermediary organizations, 149
International Monetary Fund (IMF), 219
Intersindical, 147, 161, 164
Invertebrated society, 41
Isabella, La Católica, 29, 135, 184
Isabella II, 156
Islamic influence, 23, 93, 133
Isolation, 8, 17
Italy, 125

Jesuits, 36, 134
Jews, 29, 33, 93, 223
João II, 28
Juan Carlos, 68, 80, 81, 198
Judiciary, 244

King, 177, 196

Labor, 40, 101, 146–148, 152, 206
Labor statute, 50, 190
Land, 32
Latin America, 13, 30, 231, 246
Leadership, 175
Left, 39, 162, 228
León, 26, 27, 184
Liberalism, 10, 35, 36, 38, 41, 51, 62, 68, 105, 107, 108, 117, 151, 156, 241
Limited pluralism, 55
Linz, Juan, 55
Lipset, S. M., 11
Lisbon, 4
Literacy, 112, 243
Lumpenproletariat, 111
Lusitania, 17, 26, 232

Machismo, 25
Madeira, 3, 171, 205
Madrid, 4, 173
Maimonides, 24
Marxism, 84, 106, 107, 124, 162, 163, 164, 233
Materialism, 114
Mediterranean Sea, 3
Melilla, 227
Mercantilism, 31, 190, 209, 218
Mesta, 27, 184
Middle class, 35, 37, 46, 47, 65, 67, 98, 105, 111, 136, 141, 149, 151, 213, 217, 243
Middle East, 229, 238
Militarism 24, 25, 36
Military, 72, 83, 88, 101, 120, 126, 152, 184. *See also* Armed forces; Army
Military orders, 27, 28, 29, 130, 184, 185
Military regime, 45, 55
Militias, 38, 47

Ministry of syndicates, 53, 54
Modernization, 11, 12, 35
Molina, 96
Monarchists, 157, 170
Monarchy, 32, 33, 36, 37, 38, 68, 78, 83, 135, 196
Moncloa Pact, 82
Moorish occupation, 4, 23
Moors, 29, 33
Moran, Fernando, 85
Morocco, 228
Movimento Popular de Libertação de Angola (MPLA), 233
Mozambique, 69, 71, 233
Mussolini, Benito, 45

Napoleon, 35
National Movement, 53, 57, 81
NATO (North Atlantic Treaty Organization), 3, 131, 143, 224
Navarre, 26
Nazi Germany, 39
Neocorporatism, 118, 148, 248
Netherlands, 31
Nicaragua, 226
Nobility, 35, 97, 105, 129, 135, 144, 185
North Africa, 19, 47

Oligarchy, 37, 126, 135
Opposition, 60, 161
Opus Dei, 56, 64, 134, 140, 186
Organicist, 9, 48, 101–104, 153, 183, 206, 249
Organization for Economic Cooperation and Development, 238
Ortega y Gasset, José, 41

Pacte Democràtic per Catalunya, 172
Palestine Liberation Organization (PLO), 229
Parliament, 50, 196, 199
Participation, 28, 86
Partido Africano da Independência de Guiné e Cabo Verde (PAIGC), 233
Partido Comunista Española (PCE), 82, 147, 164
Partido Militar, 178
Partido Nacionalista Vasco, 172

Partido Socialista Obrero Española (PSOE), 82, 84, 147, 166, 214, 225
Party of Democratic Renovation, 170
Party spectrum, 162
Party system, 155
Patrimonialism, 100–101, 114
Patronage, 9, 56, 126, 150, 159, 176
Peasants, 141, 148–149, 151
Peoples, 19
Perón, Juan, 117
Personalistic parties, 170
Philip II, 30
Phoenicians, 20
Pluralism, 59, 121, 138, 142, 149, 151
Political change, 67
Political culture, 16, 66, 86–87, 90–119, 144
Political institutions, 40
Political parties, 62, 73, 81, 125, 155, 175, 187, 206
Political Reform Act, 82
Police, 88
Pombal, 34, 156
Popular Democratic Movement (MPD), 163
Popular front, 39
Popular sovereignty, 28
Population, 122, 123
Portugal, emergence of, 26
President, 192, 194–195
Preto, Rolão, 60
Prime minister, 195, 198
Primo de Rivera, General, 38
Pronunciamiento, 179
Propaganda, 109
Protestantism, 133
Protestant Reformation, 4, 30, 32, 241
Public opinion, 187
Public sector, 202
Pye, Lucian, 66
Pyrenees Mountains, 1, 18, 221

Reconquest, 24–26, 184
Reforma, 77, 81
Regional issue, 41, 152, 171, 177, 194, 203, 206
Remittances, 213
Renaissance, 4

Representation, 28
Repression, 55–60, 106–110
Republic, 37, 38, 44, 47, 105, 107, 185
Republican Guard, 190
Republicans, 157
Resources, 19
Retornados, 77
Revolución, 179
Revolution, in Portugal, 2, 71, 74
Right, 38, 60, 171
Rights, 95
River system, 18
Roman Catholic Church, 25, 34, 37, 38, 40, 47, 55, 56, 58, 88, 93–94, 101, 105, 113, 117, 120, 126, 129, 132–134, 140, 144, 151, 152, 184, 186, 206, 244. *See also* Catholicism
Roman influence, 16, 20–22
Rostow, W. W., 11, 136
Rotativismo, 37, 74
Rousseauian democracy, 9, 10, 35, 118, 248
Ruptura, 77, 81

Sá Carneiro, Francisco, 76, 168, 196
Salazar, Antonio, 1, 2, 7, 41, 42, 43–69, 107, 157, 186, 218
Santa Hermandad, 29
Schein, Edgar, 91
Scholasticism, 31
Schools, 108
Secret police, 57, 68, 73, 190
Senate, 199
Self-government, 22
Seneca, 127
Seville, 128, 173
Siglo de Oro, 30
Silva, Anibal Cavaco, 77, 169, 196
Sindicatos, 50, 51, 53
Sinecures, 33
Soares, Mario, 76, 166, 195, 196, 219
Social basis of politics, 124–126
Social change, 44, 63, 65, 67, 110–112, 136–138, 213, 243
Social Democratic party (PSD), 76, 77, 168, 173, 220
Social democrats, 60, 61, 62, 75, 124, 161, 173, 203

Socialist International (SI), 85, 226
Socialist party, 173
Socialists, 38, 39, 60, 74, 75, 76, 81, 125, 126, 147, 157, 161, 164, 165, 173, 177, 191, 193, 214, 219, 237
Socialization, 108, 109
Social pacts, 78, 214
Social peace, 108
Social problem, 40, 216
Social programs, 52, 64, 189, 211, 213, 239
Social welfare, 214, 219
Society, 27, 28, 78, 182, 184, 185
Socioeconomic change, 87, 121
Soto, 96
Southern Europe, 7
Soviet Union, 39, 71, 183, 229, 236
"Spanish miracle," 64, 212
Spanish model, 8, 13
Spínola, Antonio de, 73, 74, 75, 232
State, 27, 28, 59, 150, 152, 177, 182, 189
State–society relations, 48, 120, 182, 205
Statist regime, 9
Strait of Gibralter, 23, 25
Strikes, 68
Strong government, 9
Students, 141, 149
Study groups, 62
Suárez, 96
Suárez, Adolfo, 81, 83, 145, 164, 167, 173, 199
"Success democrats," 7, 118

Talleyrand, 2
Tartesians, 20
Technocrats, 64
Tensions, 65
Territory, 19
Third World, 2, 250
Thomistic, 9, 27, 35, 48, 96
Tocqueville, Alexis de, 36, 151

Topography, 17
Totalitarianism, 10
Tourism, 66, 111, 213
Towns, 27, 28, 101
Trade unions, 50, 51, 56, 62, 65, 68, 126, 137, 141, 151, 217, 243
Traditional institutions, 11, 12, 35, 107, 117, 138, 156, 241
Transitions to democracy, 3, 44, 66, 70–89, 182, 243
Two Portugals, 35, 104–106, 156
Two Spains, 35, 39, 104–106, 156, 173

Underground, 62, 161
Unemployment, 219, 220
Ungovernability, 106
União Geral dos Trabalhadores (UGT), 147
União Nacional, 57, 73, 158
Unión del Centro Democrático (UCD), 82, 167, 173, 193
Unión General de Trabajadores (UGT), 147
Unions, 186, 215
United Nations, 238
United States, 41, 75, 183, 222, 230, 237–238
Universities, 28, 101, 206
University of Coimbra, 44

Valencia, 26
Vatican, 133
Violence, 38
Visigoths, 22
Vitoria, 96

Welfare, 216
Western tradition, 2
Women, 24, 115
Workers' commissions, 54, 62
Working class, 37, 67, 111, 213
World War II, 51